Matthew

THE CROSSWAY CLASSIC COMMENTARIES

Matthew

EXPOSITORY THOUGHTS ON THE GOSPELS

by

J. C. Ryle

Series Editors

Alister McGrath and J. I. Packer

CROSSWAY BOOKS • WHEATON, ILLINOIS
A DIVISION OF GOOD NEWS PUBLISHERS

Matthew.

Copyright © 1993 by Watermark.

Published by Crossway Books
    A division of Good News Publishers
    1300 Crescent Street
    Wheaton, Illinois 60187.

Art Direction: Mark Schramm

First printing, 1993

Printed in the United States of America

Library of Congress Cataloging-in-Publication Data
Ryle, J. C. (John Charles), 1816-1900
    Matthew / J. C. Ryle.
        p.   cm. — (Expository thoughts on the Gospels)   (Crossway classic commentaries : v. 1)
    Originally published: New York : R. Carter, 1860.
    1. Bible. N.T. Matthew—Commentaries.   I. Bible. N.T. Matthew. English. Authorized. 1993.   II. Title.   III. Series.   IV. Series: Ryle, J. C. (John Charles), 1816-1900. Expository thoughts on the Gospels.
BS2575.3.R955 1993   226.2'07—dc20   92-47006
ISBN 0-89107-726-X

01		00		99		98		97		96		95		94		93
15	14	13	12	11	10	9	8	7	6	5	4	3	2	1

Contents

Chapter 6

Chapter 7

Chapter 8

Chapter 9

Chapter 10

Chapter 11

Series Preface

The purpose of the Crossway Classic Commentaries is to make some of the most valuable commentaries on the books of the Bible, by some of the greatest Bible teachers and theologians in the last five hundred years, available to a new generation. These books will help today's readers learn truth, wisdom, and devotion from such authors as J. C. Ryle, Martin Luther, John Calvin, J. B. Lightfoot, John Owen, Charles Spurgeon, Charles Hodge, and Matthew Henry.

We do not apologize for the age of some of the items chosen. In the realm of practical exposition promoting godliness, the old is often better than the new. Spiritual vision and authority, based on an accurate handling of the biblical text, are the qualities that have been primarily sought in deciding what to include.

So far as is possible, everything is tailored to the needs and enrichment of thoughtful readers — lay Christians, students, and those in the ministry. The originals, some of which were written at a high technical level, have been abridged as needed, simplified stylistically, and unburdened of foreign words. However, the intention of this series is never to change any thoughts of the original authors, but to faithfully convey them in an understandable fashion.

The publishers are grateful to Dr. Alister A. McGrath of Wycliffe Hall, Oxford, Dr. J. I. Packer of Regent College, Vancouver, and Watermark of Norfolk, England, for the work of selecting and editing that now brings this project to fruition.

Introduction

The Right Reverend John Charles Ryle, D.D., "the best man in the Church of England" according to his great Baptist peer, C. H. Spurgeon, was Bishop of Liverpool from 1880 to 1900. Liverpool was a new diocese, and Ryle, a senior evangelical leader of large mind, firm principles, deep spirituality, and great gifts as a communicator, gave it an evangelical stamp that is not yet completely eroded. Prior to his appointment he had become one of the most noted evangelical writers of his day. His tracts ("Home Truths") sold by tens of thousands, as did Spurgeon's weekly printed sermons; his books *Knots Untied*, *Old Paths*, *Holiness*, and *Practical Religion*, along with his popular historical studies of the leaders of the English Reformation and of the Evangelical Revival, became steady sellers; and the seven-volume series of *Expository Thoughts on the Gospels* was already in its fifteenth edition by 1883. Of all nineteenth-century Anglican evangelicals, Ryle has unquestionably exercised the most widespread and sustained influence.

Spurgeon's *Commenting and Commentaries*, written primarily for the guidance of preachers with limited education and resources, contains a catalog of 1,437 Bible commentaries, with all of which he was himself familiar. Of Ryle's *Expository Thoughts* he wrote: "We prize these volumes. They are diffuse, but not more so than family reading requires. Mr. Ryle had evidently studied all previous writers upon the Gospels, and has given forth his individual utterance of considerable value."

The volume on Matthew, reproduced here, was the first in Ryle's series. He wrote it while he was vicar of Helmingham, Suffolk, and it was published in 1856 — "for family and private use," as the original title page says. Though written in popular sermon style, in units that would take about ten minutes to read aloud, it has learning behind it. Ryle's list of the forty-five commentaries he had consulted (see his Preface) covers all the serious scholarly work on interpreting Matthew that had been done up to his time. The age of the modern "critical" commentary, concentrating on the immediate historical and situational background of the text and the writer's linguistic nuances to the virtual exclusion of all else, had not dawned when Ryle wrote. The commentaries he studied were more concerned with the abiding message of the text as a guide to godliness, and that was his concern too. In a taut, energetic, pithy, down-to-earth, drumbeat style he enforces each passage's practical lessons. What makes this exposition *classic*? Just the fact that he does this particular job at least as well as, perhaps better than, and certainly more forcefully than anyone else before or since.

The image most people have of Victorian writing is of long-winded, heavy-footed, sluggish, sententious sentimentalism, and they approach Victorian writers with suspicion. Victorian though he is, Ryle, however, does not fit this mold. He is terse and lively, like John Bunyan and William Tyndale; his sentences are short, punchy, man-to-man affairs; his rhetoric consists not of piled-up periods, verbose and wearisome, but of quick, sharp hammer-blows that nail truth to the conscience and break the rocks of self-righteousness and self-sufficiency in fallen human hearts. Massive wisdom about God and life, piercing clarity about sin and error, solid rootage in the realities of redemption, and a consistent, adoring Christ-centeredness make Ryle's expositions edifying and satisfying to the spiritually hungry in this or any age. Ryle is *classic*! Taste and see.

J. I. PACKER

Preface

by
J. C. Ryle

In sending forth the first volume of a new expository work on the Gospels, I feel it necessary, in order to prevent misapprehension, to offer some explanation of the character and design of the work.

These *Expository Thoughts* are not a learned critical commentary. I do not profess to expound every verse of the Gospel, to grapple with every difficulty, to attempt the solution of every hard text, and to examine every disputed reading or translation.

The *Expository Thoughts* are not a continuous and homiletic exposition, containing practical remarks on every verse, like the commentaries of Brentius and Gualter.

The plan I have adopted in drawing up the *Expository Thoughts* is as follows: I have divided the sacred text into sections or passages, averaging about twelve verses in each. I have then supplied a continuous series of short, plain "expositions" of each of these passages. In each exposition I have generally begun by stating as briefly as possible the main scope and purpose of the passage under consideration. I have then selected two, three, or four prominent points in the passage, singled them out from the rest, dwelt exclusively on them, and endeavored to enforce them plainly and vigorously on the reader's attention. The points selected will be found to be sometimes doctrinal, and sometimes practical. The only rule in selection has been to seize on the really leading points of the passage.

In style and composition I frankly avow that I have studied, as far as possible, to be plain and pointed, and to choose what an old divine calls "picked and packed" words. I have tried to place myself in the position of someone who is reading aloud to others, and must arrest their attention if he can. I have said to myself in writing each exposition, "I am addressing a mixed company, and I have but a short time." Keeping this in view, I have constantly left unsaid many things that might have been said, and have endeavored to dwell chiefly on the things needful to salvation. I have deliberately passed over many subjects of secondary importance, in order to say something that might strike and stick in consciences. I have felt that a few points, well remembered and fastened down, are better than a quantity of truth lying loosely, and thinly scattered over the mind.

A few footnotes, explaining difficult passages, have occasionally been added to the exposition. I have thought it good to add these notes for the information of readers who may feel a wish to know what can be said about the "deep things" of Scripture, and may have no commentary of their own. [These are included in square brackets in the text of this edition. – Ed.]

I cannot, of course, expect that the opinions expressed in these expositions, whether about doctrine, practice or prophecy, will be satisfactory and acceptable to everyone. I can only say, I have spoken out freely, and kept back nothing that seemed to me true. I have set down nothing but what I conscientiously believe to be the real meaning of the inspired writer, and the mind of the Spirit. I have always held that truth is most likely to be reached when men on all sides conceal nothing, but tell out all their minds. Right or wrong, I have endeavored to tell out my own mind. It is my firm conviction that I have said nothing in these expositions which is not in perfect harmony with the Thirty-Nine Articles of my own Church, and does not agree in the main with all the Protestant Confessions of Faith. The words of an old divine will explain the kind of theology to which I ever desire to adhere and conform: "I know no true religion but Christianity; no true Christianity but the doctrine of Christ; of his divine person (Colossians 1:15), of his divine office (1 Timothy 2:5), of his divine righteousness (Jeremiah 23:6), and of his divine Spirit, which all that are his receive (Romans 8:9). I know no true ministers of Christ but such as make it their business, in their calling, to commend Jesus Christ, in his saving fullness of grace and glory, to the faith and love of men. I know no true Christian but one united to Christ by faith, and abiding in him by faith and love, to the glorifying of the name of Jesus Christ, in the beauties of Gospel holiness. Ministers and Christians of this spirit have for many years been my brethren and companions, and I hope ever shall be, withersoever the hand of the Lord may lead me." [Traill's Preface to *Throne of Grace*.]

I am deeply aware of the many imperfections and defects of the volume which is now sent forth. No one perhaps will see them more clearly than I do myself. At the same time I think it only fair to say that no exposition in this volume has been composed without deliberate reflection, and laborious examination of other men's opinions. There are very few passages handled in these expositions concerning which I have not at least *looked* at the views of the following writers: Chrysostom, Augustine, Theophylact, Euthymius, Calvin, Brentius, Bucer, Musculus, Gualter, Beza, Bullinger, Pellican, Ferus, Calovius, Cocceius, Baxter, Poole, Hammond, Lightfoot, Hall, Du Veil, Piscator, Paraeus, Jansenius, Leigh, Ness, Mayer, Trapp, Henry, Whitby, Gill, Doddridge, Burkitt, Quesnel, Bengel, Scott, A. Clark, Pearce, Adams, Watson, Olshausen, Alford, Barnes, Stier. I can truly say, that I have spent hours, days and weeks in examining the opinions of these writers, and that when I differ from them it is not because I do not know their views.

Commentaries and expositions of Scripture are so numerous in the present day that I feel it necessary to say something about the type of reader whom I have specially had in view in publishing these *Expository Thoughts*.

In the first place, I indulge the hope that the work may be found *suitable for use at family prayers*. The supply of works adapted for this purpose has never yet been equal to the demand.

In the next place, I cannot help hoping that the work may prove *an aid to those who visit the sick and the poor*. The number of persons who visit hospitals, sick-rooms and cottages with an earnest desire to do spiritual good is now very great. There is reason to believe that books suitable for reading on such occasions are much wanted.

Last, but not least, I trust that the work may not be found unprofitable *for private reading, as a companion to the Gospels*. There are not a few whose callings and engagements make it impossible for them to read large commentaries and expositions of God's Word. I have thought that they may find it helpful to their memories to have a few leading points set before their minds in connection with what they read.

I now send forth the volume with an earnest prayer that it may tend to the promotion of pure and undefiled religion, help to extend the knowledge of Christ, and be a humble instrument in aid of the glorious work of converting and edifying immortal souls.

J. C. RYLE

Matthew
Chapter 1

The genealogy of Christ *(1:1–17)*

These verses begin the New Testament. Let us always read them with serious and solemn feelings. The book before us contains not "the word of men, but . . . the word of God" (1 Thessalonians 2:13). Every verse in it was written by the inspiration of the Holy Spirit.

Let us thank God daily for giving us the Scriptures. The poorest Englishman who understands his Bible knows more about religion than the wisest philosophers of Greece and Rome.

Let us never forget the deep responsibility which possession of the Bible places on us. We shall be judged on the last day according to our light. From everyone who has been given much, much will be demanded.

Let us read the Bible reverently and diligently, with an honest determination to believe and practice all we find in it. It is no light matter how we use this book. Above all, let us never read the Bible without praying for the teaching of the Holy Spirit. He alone can apply truth to our hearts and make us profit from what we read.

The New Testament begins with the history of the life, death and resurrection of our Lord Jesus Christ. No part of the Bible is so important as this, and no part is so full and complete. Four distinct Gospels tell us the story of Christ's actions and his death. Four times we read the precious account of his works and words. How thankful we ought to be for this! To know Christ is life eternal. To believe in Christ is to have peace with God. To follow Christ is to be a true Christian. To be with Christ will be heaven itself. We can never hear too much about the Lord Jesus Christ.

The Gospel of St. Matthew begins with a long list of names. Sixteen verses are taken up with tracing a pedigree from Abraham to David, and from David to the family in which Jesus was born. Let no one think that these verses are useless. Nothing is useless in creation. The least mosses, and the smallest insects, serve some good end. Nothing is useless in the Bible. Every word of it is inspired. The chapters and verses which seem at first sight unprofitable, are all given for some good reason. The person who looks carefully at these sixteen verses will not fail to see in them useful lessons.

1. God always keeps his word

First, we learn from this list of names that God always keeps his word. He had promised that "all peoples on earth will be blessed through you" (Genesis 12:3). He had promised to raise up a Saviour from the family of David (Isaiah 11:1). These sixteen verses prove that Jesus was the Son of David and the Son of Abraham, and that God's promise was fulfilled. Thoughtless and ungodly people should remember this lesson, and be afraid. Whatever they may think, God will keep his word. If they do not repent they will surely perish. True Christians should remember this lesson, and take comfort. Their Father in heaven will be true to all his promises. He has said that he will save all believers in Christ. If he has said it, he will certainly do it. "God is not a man, that he should lie" (Numbers 23:19). "He will remain faithful, for he cannot disown himself" (2 Timothy 2:13).

2. The sinfulness and corruption of human nature

Second, we learn from this list of names the sinfulness and corruption of human nature. It is instructive to observe how many godly parents in this list had wicked and ungodly sons. The names of Rehoboam, Jehoram, Amon and Jeconiah should teach us humbling lessons. They all had pious fathers. But they were all wicked men. Grace does not run in families. It needs something more than good examples and good advice to make us children of God. Those who are born again are not born "of natural descent, nor of human decision or a husband's will, but born of God" (John 1:13). Praying parents should pray night and day that their children may be born of the Spirit.

3. Jesus Christ's mercy and compassion

Third, we learn from this list of names how great is the mercy and compassion of our Lord Jesus Christ. Let us think how polluted and unclean human nature is, and then think how he humbled himself to be born of a woman, and made "in human likeness" (Philippians 2:7). Some of the names we read in this list remind us of shameful and sad histories. Some of the names are of people never mentioned elsewhere in the Bible. But at the end comes the name of the Lord Jesus Christ. Though he is the eternal God, he humbled himself to become man, in order to provide salvation for sinners. "Though he was rich, yet for your sakes he became poor" (2 Corinthians 8:9).

We should always read this list with thankful hearts. We see here that no human being can be beyond the reach of Christ's sympathy and compassion. Our sins may have been as black and great as those of any whom St. Matthew names. But they cannot shut us out of heaven, if we repent and believe the Gospel. If the Lord Jesus was not ashamed to be born of a woman whose pedigree contained such names as those we have read today, we need not think that he will be ashamed to call us his brothers and sisters, and to give us eternal life.

The incarnation and name of Christ (1:18–25)

These verses begin by telling us two great truths. They tell us how the Lord Jesus Christ took our nature upon him, and became man. They tell us also that his birth was miraculous. His mother Mary was a virgin.

These are very mysterious subjects. We cannot fathom these depths. They are truths which are beyond our understanding. Let us not attempt to explain things which are above our feeble reason. Let us be content to believe with reverence, and let us not speculate about matters which we cannot understand. It is enough for us to know that with him who made the world nothing is impossible. We may safely rest in the words of the Apostles' Creed: "Jesus Christ was conceived by the Holy Spirit, and born of the Virgin Mary."

1. Joseph

First, let us observe the conduct of Joseph described in these verses. It is a beautiful example of godly wisdom and tender consideration for others. He saw the "appearance of evil" in the one who was to be his wife. But he did nothing rashly. He waited patiently to have the line of duty made clear. In all probability he laid the matter before God in prayer. "The one who trusts will never be dismayed" (Isaiah 28:16).

The patience of Joseph was graciously rewarded. He received a direct message from God on the subject of his anxiety, and was at once relieved from all his fears. How good it is to wait upon God! Who has ever cast his cares upon God in sincere prayer, and found him to fail? "In all your ways acknowledge him, and he will make your paths straight" (Proverbs 3:6).

2. The two names given to our Lord

Second, let us observe in these verses the two names given to our Lord. One is "Jesus," the other "Emmanuel." One describes his office, the other his nature. Both are deeply interesting.

The name Jesus means "Saviour." It is the same name as "Joshua" in the Old Testament. It is given to our Lord because "he saves his people from their sins." This is his special office. He saves them from the guilt of sin, by washing them in his own atoning blood. He saves them from the dominion of sin, by putting in their hearts the sanctifying Spirit. He saves them from the presence of sin, when he takes them out of this world to rest with him. He will save them from all the consequences of sin, when he gives them a glorious body at the last day. Blessed and holy are Christ's people! From sorrow, cross and conflict they are not saved; but they are "saved from sin" for evermore. They are cleansed from guilt by Christ's blood. They are made fit for heaven by Christ's Spirit. This is salvation! The person who clings to sin is not yet saved.

"Jesus" is a very encouraging name to heavy-laden sinners. He who is King of kings and Lord of lords might lawfully have taken some more high-sounding title. But he did not do so. The rulers of this world have often called themselves Great, Conqueror, Bold, Magnificent, and the like. The Son of God was content to call himself "Saviour." The souls who desire salvation may draw close to the Father with boldness, and have access with confidence through Christ. It is his office and his delight to show mercy. "God did not send his Son into the world to condemn the world, but to save the world through him" (John 3:17).

Jesus is a name which is especially sweet and precious to believers. It has often done them good when the favor of kings and princes would have been disregarded. It has given them what money cannot buy, an inner peace. It has eased their weary consciences, and given rest to their heavy hearts. The Song of Songs speaks of the experience of many, when it says, "Your name is like perfume poured out" (Song of Songs 1:3). Happy is the person who trusts not merely in vague notions of God's mercy and goodness, but in "Jesus."

The name "Emmanuel" is seldom found in the Bible, but it is scarcely less interesting than the name "Jesus." It is the name which is given to our Lord from his nature as God-man, as "God revealed in the body." It means "God with us."

Let us take care that we clearly understand that there was a union of two natures, the divine and human, in the person of our Lord Jesus Christ. It is a point of the deepest importance. We should settle it firmly in our minds that our Saviour is perfect man as well as perfect God, and perfect God as well as perfect man. If we once lose sight of this great foundation truth, we may run into fearful heresies. The name Emmanuel takes in the whole mystery. Jesus is "God with us." He had a nature like our own in all things, except for sin. But though Jesus was "with us" in human flesh and blood, he was at the same time truly God.

We shall often find as we read the Gospels that our Saviour could be weary and hungry and thirsty. He could weep and groan and feel pain like one of us. In all this we see *the man* Christ Jesus. We see the nature he took on him, when he was born of the Virgin Mary. But we shall also find in the same Gospels that our Saviour knew men's hearts and thoughts. He had power over demons. He could work the mightiest miracles with a word. He was ministered to by angels. He allowed a disciple to call him "my God." He said, "Before Abraham was born, I am!" (John 8:58) and "I and the Father are one" (John 10:30). In all this we see *the eternal God*. We see him "who is God over all, forever praised!" (Romans 9:5).

If we want to have a strong foundation for our faith and hope, we must keep constantly in view our Saviour's *divinity*. He in whose blood we are invited to trust is the Almighty God. All power is in heaven and earth. No one can snatch us out of his hand. If we are true believers in Jesus, our heart need not be troubled or afraid.

If we want to have sweet comfort in suffering and trial, we must keep constantly in view our Saviour's *humanity*. He is the man Christ Jesus, who lay in the arms of the Virgin Mary as a little infant, and knows the heart of a man. He can sympathize with our weaknesses. He has himself experienced Satan's temptations. He has endured hunger. He has shed tears. He has felt pain. We may trust him unreservedly with our sorrows. He will not despise us. We may pour out our hearts before him in prayer boldly, and keep nothing back. He can sympathize with his people.

Let these thoughts sink down into our minds. Let us bless God for the encouraging truths which the first chapter of the New Testament contains. It tells us of one who "saves his people from their sins." But this is not all. It tells us that this Saviour is "Emmanuel," God himself, and yet God with us, God revealed in a human body like our own. This is glad tidings. This is indeed good news. Let us feed on these truths in our hearts by faith with thanksgiving.

Matthew
Chapter 2

The wise men from the East *(2:1–12)*

It is not known who these wise men were. Their names and dwelling-place are both kept back from us. We are only told that they came "from the east." Whether they were Babylonians or Arabs we cannot say. Whether they learned to expect Christ from the ten tribes who went into captivity, or from the prophecies of Daniel, we do not know. It matters little who they were. The point which concerns us most is the important lesson which their story gives us.

1. True servants in unexpected places
These verses show us that there may be true servants of God in places where we should not expect to find them. The Lord Jesus has many "hidden ones," like these wise men. Their story on earth may be as little known as that of Melchizedek, Jethro and Job. But their names are in the book of life, and they will be found with Christ on the day of his appearing. It is well to remember this. We must not look round the earth and say hastily, "All is barren." The grace of God is not tied to places and families. The Holy Spirit can lead souls to Christ without the help of any outward means. Men may be born in dark places of the earth, like these wise men, and yet like them be made "wise for salvation." There are some travelling to heaven at this moment, of whom the Church and the world know nothing. They flourish in secret places like the "lily among thorns," and seem to "waste their sweetness on the desert air." But Christ loves them, and they love Christ.

2. Those who give Christ most honor

Second, these verses show that it is not always those who have most religious privileges who give Christ most honor. We might have thought that the scribes and Pharisees would have been the first to hasten to Bethlehem, on the slightest rumor that the Saviour was born. But it was not so. A few unknown strangers from a distant land were the first, except for the shepherds mentioned by St. Luke, to rejoice at his birth. "He came to that which was his own, but his own did not receive him" (John 1:11). What a mournful picture this is of human nature! How often the same kind of thing may be seen among ourselves! How often the very people who live nearest to the means of grace are those who neglect them most! There is only too much truth in the old proverb, "The nearer the church the farther from God." Familiarity with sacred things has an awful tendency to make men despise them. There are many who, from residence and convenience, ought to be first and foremost in the worship of God, and yet are always last. There are many who might well be expected to be last, who are always first.

3. Head knowledge without heart knowledge

Third, these verses show us that there may be knowledge of Scripture in the head, while there is no grace in the heart. We are told that King Herod sent to inquire of the priests and elders "where the Christ was to be born" (verse 4). We are told that they gave him a quick answer, and showed an accurate acquaintance with the letter of Scripture. But they never went to Bethlehem to seek the coming Saviour. They would not believe in him when he ministered among them. Their heads were better than their hearts. Let us beware of resting satisfied with head knowledge. It is an excellent thing when rightly used. But a person may have much of it, and still perish everlastingly. What is the state of our hearts? This is the great question. A little grace is better than many gifts. Gifts alone save no one; but grace leads on to glory.

4. Spiritual diligence

Fourth, these verses show us a splendid example of spiritual diligence. What trouble it must have cost these wise men to travel from their homes to the house where Jesus was born! How many weary miles they must have journeyed! The fatigues of an Eastern traveler are far greater than we can at all understand. The time that such a journey would occupy must have been very great. The dangers to be encountered were neither few nor small. But none of these things moved them. They had set their hearts on seeing him "who has been born king of the Jews" (verse 2), and they never rested till they saw him. They prove to us the truth of the old saying, "Where there is a will there is a way."

It would be well for all professing Christians if they were more ready to follow the example of these good men. Where is our self-denial? What pains do we take about means of grace? What diligence do we show about following Christ? What does our religion cost us? These are serious questions. They deserve serious consideration. The truly "wise," it may be feared, are very few.

5. Faith

Fifth, these verses show us a striking example of faith. These wise men believed in Christ when they had never seen him; but that was not all. They believed in him when the scribes and Pharisees were unbelieving; but that again was not all. They believed in him when they saw him as a little infant on Mary's knees, and worshiped him as a King. This was the crowning point of their faith. They saw no miracles to convince them. They heard no teaching to persuade them. They saw no signs of divinity and greatness to overawe them. They saw nothing but a new-born infant, helpless and weak, and needing a mother's care like any of us. And yet when they saw that infant, they believed that they saw the divine Saviour of the world! "They bowed down and worshiped him" (verse 11).

We read of no greater faith than this in the whole volume of the Bible. It is a faith that deserves to be placed side by side with that of the penitent thief. The thief saw someone dying the death of a criminal, and yet prayed to him, and "called him Lord." The wise men saw a new-born baby on the lap of a poor woman, and yet worshiped him, and confessed that he was Christ. Blessed indeed are those who can believe in this way!

This is the kind of faith that God delights to honor. We see the proof of that to this very day. Wherever the Bible is read the conduct of these wise men is known, and told as a memorial to them. Let us walk in the steps of their faith. Let us not be ashamed to believe in Jesus and confess him, though all around us remain indifferent and unbelieving. Have we not a thousand times more evidence than the wise men had, to make us believe that Jesus is the Christ? Beyond doubt we have. Yet where is our faith?

The flight into Egypt, and subsequent home in Nazareth (2:13–23)

1. Rulers are seldom friendly to God's cause

Let us observe in this passage how true it is that the rulers of this world are seldom friendly to the cause of God. The Lord Jesus comes down from heaven to save sinners, and at once we are told that Herod the king seeks to kill him (verse 13).

Greatness and riches are a perilous possession for the soul. Those who seek to have them do not know what they seek. They lead people into many temptations. They are likely to fill the heart with pride, and to chain the affections down to things below. "Not many were influential; not many were of noble birth" (1 Corinthians 1:26). "How hard it is for the rich to enter the kingdom of God!" (Mark 10:23).

Do we envy the rich and great? Does our heart sometimes say, "Oh, that I had their place, and rank, and wealth?" Let us beware of giving way to such feelings. The very wealth which we admire may be gradually sinking its possessors down into hell. A little more money might be our ruin. Like Herod, we might run into every excess of wickedness and cruelty. "Watch out! Be on your guard against all kinds of greed" (Luke 12:15). "Be content with what you have" (Hebrews 13:5).

Do we think that Christ's cause depends on the power and patronage of princes? We are mistaken. They have seldom done much to advance true religion; they have far more frequently been the enemies of the truth. "Do not put your trust in princes" (Psalm 146:3). There are many people like Herod. Those who are like Josiah and Edward VI of England are few.

2. A man of sorrows

Second, let us observe how the Lord Jesus was "a man of sorrows," even from his infancy. Trouble awaits him as soon as he enters into the world. His life is in danger from Herod's hatred. His mother and Joseph are obliged to take him away by night, and "escape to Egypt" (verse 13). It was only a type of all his experience upon earth. The waves of humiliation began to beat over him even when he was at his mother's breast.

The Lord Jesus is just the Savior that the suffering and sorrowful need. He knows well what we mean when we tell him in prayer about our troubles. He can sympathize with us when we cry to him under cruel persecution. Let us keep nothing back from him. Let us make him our close friend. Let us pour out our hearts before him. He has had great experience of affliction.

3. Kings are mortal

Third, let us observe how death can remove the kings of this world like other people. The rulers of millions have no power to hold on to life when the hour of their departure comes. The murderer of helpless infants must himself die. Joseph and Mary hear the news that Herod is dead and at once they return in safety to their own land.

True Christians should never be greatly moved by persecution. Their enemies may be strong, and they may be weak; but still they ought not to be afraid. They should remember that "the mirth of the wicked is brief" (Job 20:5). What has become of the Pharaohs, Neros and Diocletians who at one time fiercely persecuted the people of God? Where is the enmity of Charles IX of France, and bloody Mary of England? They did their utmost to cast the truth down to the ground. But the truth rose again from the earth, and still lives; and they are dead and moldering in the grave. Let not the heart of any believer fail. Death is a mighty leveler, and can take any mountain out of the way of Christ's church. "The Lord lives" for ever. His enemies are only human. The truth will always prevail.

4. An obscure place

Fourth, let us observe what a lesson in humility is taught us by the place where the Son of God lived when he was on earth. He lived with his mother and Joseph "in a town called Nazareth" (verse 23). Nazareth was a small town in Galilee. It was an obscure place, not mentioned once in the Old Testament. Hebron, Shiloh, Gibeon, Ramah and Bethel were far more important places. But the Lord Jesus passed by them all, and chose Nazareth. This was humility!

In Nazareth the Lord Jesus lived thirty years. It was there he grew up from infancy to childhood, and from childhood to boyhood, and from boyhood to youth, and from youth to manhood. We know little of the manner in which those thirty years were spent. That he was obedient to Mary and Joseph we are expressly told (Luke 2:51). That he worked in the carpenter's shop with Joseph is highly probable. We only know that almost five-sixths of the time that the Saviour of the world was on earth was passed among the poor of this world and in complete obscurity. Truly this was humility!

Let us learn wisdom from our Saviour's example. We are most of us far too ready to "seek great things" in this world: let us "seek them not" (Jeremiah 45:5). To have a place and a title and a position in society is not nearly so important as people think. It is a great sin to be covetous and worldly and proud: but it is no sin to be poor. It matters not so much what money we have, and where we live, as what we are in the sight of God. Where are we going when we die? Shall we live forever in heaven? These are the main things which should concern us.

Above all, let us daily strive to copy our Saviour's humility. Pride is the oldest and commonest of sins; humility is the rarest and most beautiful of graces. For humility let us labor; for humility let us pray. Our knowledge may be scanty, our faith may be weak, our strength may be small; but if we are disciples of him who "dwelt at Nazareth," let us at any rate be humble.

Matthew
Chapter 3

The ministry of John the Baptist *(3:1–12)*

These verses describe the ministry of John the Baptist, the forerunner of our Lord Jesus Christ: it is a ministry that deserves close attention. Few preachers ever produced such effects as John the Baptist: "People went out to him from Jerusalem and all Judea and the whole region of the Jordan" (verse 5). No one ever received such praise from the great head of the church: Jesus called him "a lamp that burned and gave light" (John 5:35); the great bishop of souls himself declared that "among those born of women there has not risen anyone greater than John the Baptist" (Matthew 11:11). Let us then study the leading features of his ministry.

1. Sin and repentance
John the Baptist spoke plainly about sin. He taught the absolute necessity of repentance (verse 2) before anyone can be saved; he preached that repentance must be proved by its "fruit" (verse 8); he warned his hearers not to rest on outward privileges, or outward union with the church.

This is just the teaching that we all need. We are naturally dead, and blind, and asleep in spiritual things; we are ready to content ourselves with a mere formal religion, and to flatter ourselves that if we go to church we shall be saved: we need to be told that, unless we "repent . . . and turn to God" (Acts 3:19), we shall all perish.

2. The Lord Jesus Christ
John spoke plainly about our Lord Jesus Christ. He taught people that

one "more powerful" than himself was coming among them (verse 11). He was nothing more than a servant: the coming one was the King. He himself could only baptize with water: the coming one could "baptize . . . with the Holy Spirit" (verse 11), would take away sins, and would one day judge the world.

This again is the very teaching that human nature requires. We need to be sent direct to Christ: we are all ready to stop short of this; we want to rest in our union with the church, our regular use of the sacraments, and our diligent attendance on an established ministry. We need to be told the absolute necessity of union with Christ himself by faith. He is the appointed fountain of mercy, grace, life, and peace. We must each have personal dealings with him about our souls. What do we know about the Lord Jesus? What have we got from him? These are the questions on which our salvation hinges.

3. The Holy Spirit

John the Baptist spoke plainly about the Holy Spirit. He preached that there was such a thing as the baptism of the Holy Spirit. He taught that it was the special work of the Lord Jesus to give people this baptism.

This again is a teaching which we greatly require. We need to be told that forgiveness of sin is not the only thing necessary for salvation. There is another thing, and that is the baptizing of our hearts by the Holy Spirit. There must not only be the work of Christ *for* us but the work of the Holy Spirit *in* us; there must not only be a title to heaven purchased for us by the blood of Christ, but a readiness for heaven wrought in us by the Spirit of Christ. Let us never rest till we know by experience something of the baptism of the Spirit. Baptism in water is a great privilege, but let us see to it that we are also baptized in the Holy Spirit.

3. The danger of unbelief

John the Baptist spoke plainly about the awful danger of the impenitent and unbelieving. He told his hearers that "wrath" was coming (verse 7); he preached about "unquenchable fire" (verse 12), in which the "chaff" would one day be burned.

This again is a teaching which is deeply important. We need to be warned severely that it is no light matter whether we repent or not; we need to be reminded that there is a hell as well as a heaven, and an everlasting punishment for the wicked as well as everlasting life for the godly. We are fearfully apt to forget this. We talk about the love and mercy of God, and we do not remember sufficiently his justice and holiness. Let us be very careful on this point. It is no real kindness to keep back the terrors of the Lord. It is good for us all to be taught that it is possible to be lost forever, and that all unconverted people are hanging over the brink of the pit.

5. The safety of believers

Lastly, John the Baptist spoke plainly about the safety of true believers. He taught that there was "a barn" for all who are Christ's "wheat" (verse 12), and that they would be gathered together there on the day he appears.

This again is a teaching which human nature greatly requires. The best of believers need much encouragement. They are still in the body; they live in a wicked world; they are often tempted by the devil. They ought to be often reminded that Jesus will never leave them or forsake them (Hebrews 13:5). He will guide them safely through this life, and at length give them eternal glory. They will be hidden on the day of wrath; they will be as safe as Noah was in the ark.

Let these things sink down deeply into our hearts. We live in a day of much false teaching. Let us never forget the leading features of a faithful ministry. Happy would it have been for the church of Christ if all its ministers had been more like John the Baptist!

The baptism of Christ (3:13–17)

We have here the account of our Lord Jesus Christ's baptism. This was his first step when he entered on his ministry. When the Jewish priests took up their office they were washed with water (Exodus 29:4), and when our great High Priest begins the great work he came into the world to accomplish he is publicly baptized.

1. The honor of baptism

First, we should notice in these verses the honor placed on the sacrament of baptism. An ordinance which the Lord Jesus himself took part in is not to be thought of lightly. An ordinance to which the great head of the church submitted should always be held in honor in the eyes of professing Christians.

There are few subjects in religion over which greater mistakes have occurred than baptism. There are few which require so much fencing and guarding. Let us arm our minds with two general cautions.

Let us beware, on the one hand, that we do not attach a superstitious importance to the water of baptism. We must not expect that water to act as a charm. We must not suppose that all baptized people, as a matter of course, receive the grace of God at the moment that they are baptized. To say that all who come to baptism receive the same benefit, and that it does not matter a jot whether they come with faith and prayer or in utter indifference – to say such things appears to contradict the plainest lessons of Scripture.

Let us beware, on the other hand, that we do not dishonor the sacrament of baptism. It is dishonored when it is hastily passed over as a mere form, or thrust out of sight and never publicly noticed in the congregation. A sacrament ordained by Christ himself should not be treated in this way. The admission of every new member into the visible church, whether young or grown up, is an event which ought to excite a keen interest in a Christian congregation. It is an event that ought to call forth the fervent prayers of all praying people. The more deeply we are convinced that baptism and grace are not inseparably tied together, the more we ought to feel bound to join in prayer for a blessing whenever anyone is baptized.

2. The solemnity of Jesus' baptism

Second, we should notice in these verses the particularly solemn circumstances which occurred at the baptism of our Lord Jesus Christ. Such a baptism will never happen again as long as the world stands.

We are told about the presence of all three persons of the blessed Trinity. God the Son, revealed in the body, is baptized; God the Spirit descends like a dove, and rests upon him; God the Father speaks from heaven with a voice. In a word, we have the presence of Father, Son and Holy Spirit revealed. We may regard this as a public announcement that the work of Christ was the result of the eternal wills of all three persons of the blessed Trinity. It was the whole Trinity which, at the beginning of the creation, said, "Let us make man" (Genesis 1:26); it was the whole Trinity again which, at the beginning of the Gospel, seemed to say, "Let us save man."

We are told of "a voice from heaven" at our Lord's baptism; "heaven was opened," and words were heard (verses 16–17). This was a most significant miracle. We read of no voice from heaven before this, except at the giving of the law on Sinai. Both occasions were of particular importance. It therefore seemed good to our Father in heaven to mark both with particular honor. At the introduction both of the Law and Gospel he himself spoke. "God spoke all these words" (Exodus 20:1).

How striking and deeply instructive are the Father's words: "This is my Son, whom I love" (verse 17). He declares, in these words, that Jesus is the divine Saviour, sealed and appointed from all eternity to carry out the work of redemption. He proclaims that he accepts him as the mediator between God and man. He publishes to the world that he is satisfied with him as the propitiation, the substitute, the ransom-payer for the lost family of Adam, and the head of a redeemed people. In him he sees his holy "law great and glorious" (Isaiah 42:21). Through him he can "be just and the one who justifies those who have faith in Jesus" (Romans 3:26).

Let us carefully ponder these words. They are full of rich food for thought; they are full of peace, joy, comfort, and consolation for all who have fled for refuge to the Lord Jesus Christ and committed their souls to him for salvation. Such people may rejoice in the thought that, though in themselves sinful, yet in God's sight they are counted righteous. The Father regards them as members of his beloved Son. He sees in them no blemish, and for his Son's sake is "well pleased" (verse 17; see also Ephesians 1:6).

Matthew
Chapter 4

The temptation of Christ *(4:1–11)*

The first event in our Lord's ministry which St. Matthew records after his baptism is his temptation. This is a deep and mysterious subject. There are many things about these temptations which we cannot explain; but in them there are plain practical lessons, which we do well to learn.

1. A real and powerful enemy
First, let us learn what a real and powerful enemy we have in the devil. He is not afraid to assault even the Lord Jesus himself. Three times he attacks God's own Son: our Saviour was "tempted by the devil" (verse 1).

It was the devil who brought sin into the world at the beginning. He vexed Job, deceived David, and caused Peter to fall heavily; the Bible calls him a "murderer" and a "liar" (John 8:44) and a "roaring lion" (1 Peter 5:8). His enmity to our souls neither slumbers nor sleeps. For nearly 6,000 years he has been doing the same work, ruining men and women and drawing them to hell. His cunning and subtlety pass human understanding, and he often "masquerades as an angel of light" (2 Corinthians 11:14).

Let us keep alert and pray daily against his schemes. There is no enemy worse than an enemy who is never seen and never dies, who is near us wherever we live, and goes with us wherever we go. Not least, we must beware of that habit of foolish talking and jesting about the devil which is unhappily so common. Let us remember that if we want to be saved we must not only crucify the flesh and overcome the world, but also "resist the devil" (James 4:7).

18

2. No strange thing

Second, let us learn that we must not think temptation a strange thing. "No servant is greater than his master" (John 13:16). If Satan came to Christ, he will also come to Christians.

It would be good for believers if they would remember this. They are too apt to forget it. They often find evil thoughts arising in their minds, which they can truly say they hate. Doubts, questions, and sinful thoughts are suggested to them, against which their whole inner being revolts; but let not these things destroy their peace and rob them of their comfort. Let them remember there is a devil, and so not be surprised to find him near them. To be tempted is in itself no sin: it is the yielding to temptation, and the giving it a place in our hearts, which we must fear.

3. The chief weapon

Third, let us learn that the chief weapon we ought to use in resisting Satan is the Bible. Three times the great enemy offered temptations to our Lord. Three times his offer was refused with a text of Scripture as the reason: "It is written . . ." (verses 6, 7 and 10).

Here is one among many reasons why we ought to be diligent readers of our Bibles: the Word is the "sword of the Spirit" (Ephesians 6:17); we shall never fight a good fight if we do not use it as our principal weapon. The Word is the "lamp" for our feet (Psalm 119:105); we shall never keep the King's highway to heaven if we do not journey by its light. It may well be feared that there is not enough Bible-reading among us. It is not sufficient to have the book; we must actually read it, and pray over it ourselves. It will do us no good if it only lies still in our houses. We must be actually familiar with its contents, and have its texts stored in our memories and minds. Knowledge of the Bible never comes by intuition; it can only be got by hard, regular, daily, attentive, wakeful reading. Do we grudge the time and trouble this will cost us? If we do we are not yet fit for the kingdom of God.

4. A sympathizing Saviour

Fourth, let us learn what a sympathizing Saviour the Lord Jesus Christ is. "Because he himself suffered when he was tempted, he is able to help those who are being tempted" (Hebrews 2:18).

The sympathy of Jesus is a truth which ought to be especially dear to believers. They will find in it a mine of strong consolation. They should never forget that they have a mighty Friend in heaven, who feels for them in all their temptations and can enter into all their spiritual anxieties. Are they ever tempted by Satan to distrust God's care and goodness? So was Jesus. Are they ever tempted to presume on God's mercy, and to run into danger without warrant? So also was Jesus. Are they ever tempted to commit a private sin for the sake of some great apparent advantage? So also was Jesus. Are they ever tempted to listen to some misapplication of Scripture, as an excuse for doing wrong? So also was Jesus. He is just the Saviour that tempted people require. Let them flee to him for help, and spread before him all their troubles. They will find his ear always ready to hear, and his heart always ready to feel. He can understand their sorrows.

May we all know the value of a sympathizing Saviour by experience! There is nothing to be compared to it in this cold and deceitful world. Those who seek their happiness in this life only, and despise the religion of the Bible, have no idea what true comfort they are missing.

The beginning of Christ's ministry, and the calling of the first disciples (4:12-25)

We have in these verses the beginning of our Lord's ministry among mankind. He enters on his labors among a dark and ignorant people; he chooses men to be his companions and disciples. He confirms his ministry by miracles which rouse the attention of "all Syria" (verse 24), and draw multitudes to hear him.

1. The way Jesus began his work
First, let us notice the way in which our Lord commenced his mighty work. He "began to preach" (verse 17).

There is no job so honorable as that of the preacher. There is no work so important to human souls. It is a job which the Son of God was not ashamed to do. It is a job to which he appointed his twelve apostles. It is a job to which St. Paul in his old age specially directs Timothy's attention – he charges him with almost his last breath to "preach the Word"

(2 Timothy 4:2). It is the principal means God has always chosen to use to convert and edify souls. The brightest days of the church have been those when preaching has been honored; the darkest days of the church have been those when it has been treated as something unimportant. Let us honor the sacraments and public prayers of the church, and reverently use them; but let us beware that we do not place them above preaching.

2. Jesus' first doctrine

Second, let us notice the first doctrine which the Lord Jesus proclaimed to the world. He "began to preach, 'Repent'" (verse 17).

The necessity of repentance is one of the great foundation stones which lie at the very bottom of Christianity. It is a truth which needs to be pressed on all mankind without exception. High or low, rich or poor, all have sinned, and are guilty before God; and all must repent and turn to God if they want to be saved. It is a truth which does not receive the attention it deserves. True repentance is no light matter: it is a thorough change of heart about sin, a change showing itself in godly sorrow for sin – in heart-felt confession of sin – in a complete breaking off from sinful habits, and a lasting hatred of all sin. Such repentance is the inseparable companion of saving faith in Christ. Let us prize the doctrine highly. No Christian teaching can be called sound if it does not constantly bring us to "turn to God in repentance and have faith in our Lord Jesus" (Acts 20:21).

3. The humblest class

Third, let us notice the class of men whom the Lord Jesus chose to be his disciples. They were of the poorest and humblest rank in life. Peter, Andrew, James and John were all "fishermen" (verse 18).

The religion of our Lord Jesus Christ was not intended only for the rich and learned. It was intended for all the world, and the majority of all the world will always be the poor. Poverty and ignorance of books excluded thousands from the notice of the boastful philosophers of the heathen world; they exclude no one from the highest place in the service of Christ. Is a man humble? Does he feel his sins? Is he willing to hear Christ's voice and follow him? If so, he may be the poorest of the poor, but he will be found as high as any in the kingdom of heaven.

Intellect, money and rank are worth nothing without grace.

The religion of Christ must have been from heaven, or it could never have prospered and spread over the earth as it has done. It is vain for unbelievers to attempt to answer this argument; it cannot be answered. A religion which did not flatter the rich, the great, and the learned – a religion which offered no license to the bodily inclinations of the human heart – a religion whose first teachers were poor fishermen, without wealth, rank or power – such a religion could never have turned the world upside down, if it had not been of God. Look at the Roman emperors and the heathen priests with their splendid temples on the one side! Look at the few unlearned working men with the Gospel on the other! Were there ever two parties so unequally matched? Yet the weak proved strong, and the strong proved weak. Heathenism fell, and Christianity took its place. Christianity must have been of God.

4. The character of the miracles

Fourth, let us notice the general character of the miracles by which our Lord confirmed his mission. Here we are told about them in general; later we shall find many of them described individually. What is their character? They were miracles of mercy and kindness. Our Lord "went around doing good" (Acts 10:38).

These miracles are meant to teach us our Lord's power. He could heal sick people with a touch, and cast out devils with a word; he is "able to save completely those who come to God through him" (Hebrews 7:25). He is almighty.

These miracles are meant to be signs of our Lord's skill as a spiritual physician. No physical disease was incurable by him; he has the power to cure every ailment of our souls. There is no broken heart that he cannot heal; there is no wounded conscience that he cannot cure. Fallen, crushed, bruised, plague-stricken as we all are by sin, Jesus by his blood and Spirit can make us whole. Only let us ask him.

Not least, these miracles are intended to show us Christ's heart. He is a most compassionate Saviour. He rejected no one who came to him; he refused no one, however loathsome and diseased. He had an ear to hear all, and a hand to help all, and a heart to feel for all. There is no kindness like his. His compassions never fail.

May we all remember that the Lord Jesus is "the same yesterday and today and forever" (Hebrews 13:8). High in heaven at God's right hand, he is not in the least altered. He is just as able to save, just as willing to receive, just as ready to help, as he was 1900 years ago. Would we have spread out our needs before him then? Let us do so now. He can heal "every disease and sickness" (verse 23).

Matthew
Chapter 5

The Beatitudes *(5:1–12)*

The three chapters which begin with these verses deserve the special attention of all readers of the Bible. They contain what is commonly called the Sermon on the Mount.

Every word of the Lord Jesus ought to be most precious to professing Christians. It is the voice of the chief Shepherd; it is the charge of the great Bishop and head of the church; it is the Master speaking; it is the word of the one who spoke in a way no one else ever spoke (John 7:46), and we shall all be judged by him on the last day.

Do we want to know what kind of people Christians ought to be? Do we want to know the character at which Christians ought to aim? Do we want to know the outer way of life and inner habit of mind which suit a follower of Christ? Then let us often study the Sermon on the Mount. Let us often ponder each sentence, and test ourselves by it. Not least, let us often consider which people are called "blessed" at the beginning of the Sermon. Those the great High Priest blesses are blessed indeed!

1. The poor in spirit

The Lord Jesus calls "blessed" those who are poor in spirit (verse 3). He means the humble, and lowly-minded, and self-abased; he means those who are deeply convinced of their own sinfulness in God's sight: these are people who are not "wise in their own eyes and clever in their own sight" (Isaiah 5:21). They are not "rich" and have not "acquired wealth"; they do not fancy they "do not need a thing"; they regard themselves as "wretched, pitiful, poor, blind and naked" (Revelation

3:17). Blessed are all such! Humility is the very first letter in the alphabet of Christianity. We must begin low, if we want to build high.

2. Those who mourn

The Lord Jesus calls "blessed" those who mourn (verse 4). He means those who sorrow for sin, and grieve daily over their own shortcomings. These people are more concerned about sin than about anything on earth: the remembrance of it is grievous to them; the burden of it is intolerable. Blessed are all such! "The sacrifices of God are a broken spirit" and a contrite heart (Psalm 51:17). One day they will weep no more: "they will be comforted."

3. The meek

The Lord Jesus calls "blessed" those who are meek (verse 5). He means those who are of a patient and contented spirit. They are willing to put up with little honor here below; they can bear injuries without resentment; they are not ready to take offense. Like Lazarus in the parable, they are content to wait for their good things (Luke 16:20). Blessed are all such! They are never losers in the long run. One day they will "reign on the earth" (Revelation 5:10).

4. Those who hunger and thirst for righteousness

The Lord Jesus calls "blessed" those who hunger and thirst for righteousness (verse 6). He means those who desire above all things to be entirely conformed to the mind of God. They long not so much to be rich, or wealthy, or learned, as to be holy. Blessed are all such! They will have enough one day. They will awake and will be satisfied with seeing God's likeness (Psalm 17:15).

5. The merciful

The Lord Jesus calls "blessed" those who are merciful (verse 7). He means those who are full of compassion towards others. They pity all who are suffering either from sin or sorrow, and long to make their sufferings less; they are "always doing good" (Acts 9:36). Blessed are all such! Both in this life and in that which is to come they will reap a rich reward.

6. The pure in heart

The Lord Jesus calls "blessed" those who are pure in heart (verse 8). He means those who do not aim merely at outward correctness, but at inner holiness. They are not satisfied with a mere external show of religion: they strive to have a conscience always without offense, and they seek to serve God with the spirit and the inner being. Blessed are all such! The heart is the person. "Man looks at the outward appearance, but the LORD looks at the heart" (1 Samuel 16:7). The most spiritually-minded will have most communion with God.

7. The peacemakers

The Lord Jesus call "blessed" those who are peacemakers (verse 9). He means those who use all their influence to promote peace and love on earth, in private and in public, at home and abroad. He means those who strive to make all people love one another, by teaching the Gospel which says, "Love is the fulfillment of the law" (Romans 13:10). Blessed are all such! They are doing the very work which the Son of God began when he came to earth the first time, and which he will finish when he returns the second time.

8. Those who are persecuted for righteousness' sake

Lastly, the Lord Jesus calls "blessed" those who are persecuted for righteousness' sake (verse 10). He means those who are laughed at, mocked, despised and badly treated because they endeavor to live as true Christians. Blessed are all such! They drink of the same cup which their Master drank. They are now confessing him before men, and he will confess them before his Father and the angels on the last day. Great is their reward (verse 12).

These are the eight foundation stones which the Lord lays down at the beginning of the Sermon on the Mount. Eight great testing truths are placed before us. May we mark well each one of them, and learn wisdom.

Let us learn how the principles of Christ are entirely contrary to the principles of the world. It is vain to deny it: they are almost diametrically opposed. The very characters which the Lord Jesus praises the world despises; the very pride, and thoughtlessness, and high tempers, and worldliness, and selfishness, and formality, and unlovingness, which abound everywhere, the Lord Jesus condemns.

Let us learn how the teaching of Christ is sadly different from the practice of many professing Christians. Where shall we find men and women among those who go to churches and chapels, who are striving to live up to the pattern we have read of today? There is too much reason to fear that many baptized people are utterly ignorant of what the New Testament commands.

Above all, let us learn how holy and spiritually minded all believers should be. They should never aim at any standard lower than that of the Sermon on the Mount. Christianity is eminently a practical religion: sound doctrine is its root and foundation, but holy living should always be its fruit; and if we want to know what holy living is, let us often think about who Jesus calls "blessed."

Christian character in the world; Christ's teaching and the Old Testament (5:13–20)

1. Christian character in the world

First, these verses teach us the character which true Christians must support and maintain in the world.

The Lord Jesus tells us that true Christians are to be in the world *like "salt."* "You are the salt of the earth" (verse 13). Now salt has a peculiar taste of its own, utterly unlike anything else. When mingled with other substances it preserves them from corruption; it imparts part of its taste to everything it is mixed with. It is useful so long as it preserves its flavor, but no longer. Are we true Christians? Then let us see here our job and our duties!

The Lord Jesus tells us that true Christians are to be in the world *like light.* "You are the light of the world" (verse 14). Now it is the property of light to be utterly distinct from darkness. The least spark in a dark room can be seen at once. Of all things created, light is the most useful: it fertilizes; it guides; it cheers. It was the first thing called into being (Genesis 1:3). Without it the world would be a gloomy blank. Are we true Christians? Then think again about our position and its responsibility!

Surely, if words mean anything, we are meant to learn from these two metaphors that there must be something marked, distinct and special about our character if we are true Christians. It will never do to idle through life, thinking and living like others, if we mean to be owned by Christ as his people. Have we grace? Then it must be *seen*. Have we the Spirit? Then there must be *fruit*. Have we any saving religion? Then there must be a difference of habits, tastes and turn of mind, between us and those who think only of the world. It is perfectly clear that true Christianity is something more than being baptized and going to church. "Salt" and "light" evidently imply something *special* both in heart and life, in faith and practice. We must dare to be unusual and unlike the world if we mean to be saved.

2. Christ's teaching and the Old Testament

Second, these verses teach us the relation between Christ's teaching and that of the Old Testament.

This is a point of great importance, and one about which great errors prevail. Our Lord clears up the point in one striking sentence. He says: "Do not think that I have come to abolish the Law or the Prophets; I have not come to abolish them but to fulfill them" (verse 17). These are remarkable words. They were deeply important when Jesus said them, because they satisfied the natural anxiety of the Jews on the point; they will be deeply important as long as the world stands, as a testimony that the religion of the Old and New Testaments is one harmonious whole.

The Lord Jesus came to fulfill the predictions of the prophets, who had long foretold that a Saviour would one day appear. He came to fulfill the ceremonial law by becoming the great sacrifice for sin, to which all the Mosaic offerings had always pointed. He came to fulfill the moral law, by perfect obedience to it, which we could never have achieved; and by paying the penalty for our breach of it with his atoning blood, which we could never have paid. In all these ways he exalted the law of God, and made its importance more evident even than it had been before. In a word, "it pleased the LORD for the sake of his righteousness to make his law great and glorious" (Isaiah 42:21).

There are deep lessons of wisdom to be learned from these words of our Lord about "the Law and the Prophets." Let us consider them well, and lay them up in our hearts.

1. Despising the Old Testament

First, let us beware of despising the Old Testament, for whatever reason. Let us never listen to those who tell us to throw it aside as an obsolete, antiquated, useless book. The religion of the Old Testament is the germ of Christianity. The Old Testament is the Gospel in the bud; the New Testament is the Gospel in full flower. The Old Testament is the Gospel in the blade; the New Testament is the Gospel in full ear. The saints in the Old Testament saw many things through a glass darkly; but they all looked by faith to the same Saviour, and were led by the same Spirit as ourselves. These are no light matters. Much unfaithfulness begins with an ignorant contempt of the Old Testament.

2. The Ten Commandments

Second, let us beware of despising the law of the Ten Commandments. Let us not suppose for a moment that it is set aside by the Gospel, or that Christians have nothing to do with it. The coming of Christ did not alter the position of the Ten Commandments one hair's breadth. If anything, it exalted and raised their authority (Romans 3:31). The law of the Ten Commandments is God's eternal measure of right and wrong. By it we get our knowledge of sin; by it the Spirit shows people their need of Christ, and drives them to him. Christ refers his people to it as their rule and guide for holy living. In its right place it is just as important as "the glorious Gospel." It cannot save us: we canot be justified by it; but never, never let us despise it. It is a symptom of an ignorant ministry, and an unhealthy state of religion, when the law is reckoned unimportant. The true Christian delights in God's law (Romans 7:22).

3. The standard of personal holiness

Third, let us beware of supposing that the Gospel has lowered the standard of personal holiness, and that the Christian is not intended to be as strict and careful about his daily life as the Jew. This is an immense mistake, but one that is unhappily very common. So far from this being the case, the sanctification of the New Testament saint ought to exceed that of the person who has nothing but the Old Testament for a guide. The more light we have, the more we ought to love God: the more clearly we see our own complete and full forgiveness in Christ, the more heartily ought we to work for his glory. We know what it cost to redeem us far better than the Old Testament saints did. We have read what happened in Gethsemane and on Calvary, and they only saw it dimly and indistinctly as a thing yet to come. May we never forget our obligations! The Christian who is content with a low standard of personal holiness has got much to learn.

The spirituality of the law (5:21–37)

These verses deserve the closest attention of all readers of the Bible. A right understanding of the doctrines they contain lies at the very root of Christianity. The Lord Jesus here explains more fully the meaning of his words, "I have not come to abolish them but to fulfill them" (verse 17). He teaches us that his Gospel makes much of the Law, and exalts its authority: he shows us that the Law, as expounded by him, was a far more spiritual and heart-searching rule than most of the Jews supposed; and he proves this by selecting three commandments out of the ten as examples of what he means.

"Do not murder"
He expounds the sixth commandment. Many thought that they kept this part of God's law so long as they did not commit actual murder. The Lord Jesus shows that its requirements go much further than this. It condemns all angry and passionate language, and especially when used without a cause. Let us mark this well. We may be perfectly innocent of taking life, and yet be guilty of breaking the sixth commandment!

"Do not commit adultery"
He expounds the seventh commandment. Many supposed that they kept this part of God's law if they did not actually commit adultery. The Lord Jesus teaches that we may break it in our thoughts, hearts and imaginations, even when our outward conduct is moral and correct. The God with whom we have to do looks far beyond actions. With him even a glance of the eye may be a sin!

"Do not break your oath"
He expounds the third commandment. Many fancied that they kept this part of God's law so long as they did not swear falsely, and performed their oaths. The Lord Jesus forbids all vain and light swearing altogether. All swearing by created things, even when God's name is not mentioned – all calling upon God to witness, except on the most solemn occasions – is a great sin.

Now all this is very instructive. It ought to raise very serious reflections in our minds: it calls us loudly to use great searching of heart. And what does it teach?

1. God's holiness
It teaches us the exceeding holiness of God. He is a most pure and perfect Being, who sees faults and imperfections where our eyes often see none. He reads our inner motives; he notes our words and thoughts, as well as our actions: "You desire truth in the inner parts" (Psalm 51:6). It would be good if people would consider this part of God's character more than they do! There would be no room for pride, self-righteousness and indifference if people only saw God "as he is" (1 John 3:2).

2. Human ignorance
It teaches us the exceeding ignorance of human beings in spiritual things. I fear there are thousands and tens of thousands of professing Christians who know no more of the requirements of God's law than the most ignorant Jews. They know the letter of the Ten Commandments well enough; they fancy, like the young ruler, "all these I have kept" (Matthew 19:20). They never dream that it is possible to break the sixth and seventh commandments if they do not break them by outward acts or deeds. And so they live on satisfied with themselves, and quite content with their little bit of religion. Happy indeed are those who really understand God's law!

3. Our need of Christ's atonement
It teaches us our great need of the Lord Jesus Christ's atoning blood to save us. What man or woman on earth can ever stand before such a God as this, and plead "not guilty"? Who is there that has ever grown to

years of discretion, and not broken the commandments thousands of times? "There is no one righteous, not even one" (Romans 3:10). Without a powerful mediator we should every one be condemned on judgment day. Ignorance of the real meaning of the law is one plain reason why so many do not value the Gospel, and content themselves with a little formal Christianity. They do not see the strictness and holiness of God's Ten Commandments; if they did, they would never rest till they were safe in Christ.

4. Avoiding sin

Fourth, this passage teaches us the great importance of avoiding all occasions of sin. If we really desire to be holy, we must watch our ways and keep our tongues from sin (Psalm 39:1). We must be ready to make up quarrels and disagreements, in case they gradually lead on to greater evils. "Starting a quarrel is like breaching a dam" (Proverbs 17:14). We must labor to crucify our flesh and put the parts of our bodies to death, to make any sacrifice and endure any bodily inconvenience rather than sin. We must bridle our lips and hourly exercise strictness over our words. Let men call us pedantic, if they wish, for doing so; let them say, if they please, that we are "too particular." We need not be moved. We are merely doing as our Lord Jesus Christ tells us, and if this is the case we have no cause to be ashamed.

The Christian law of love (5:38–48)

We have here our Lord Jesus Christ's rules for our conduct towards one another. If you want to know how you ought to feel and act towards other people, you should often study these verses. They deserve to be written in letters of gold. They have called forth praise even from the enemies of Christianity. Let us mark well what they contain.

1. Forgiveness

The Lord Jesus forbids everything like an unforgiving and revengeful spirit. "I tell you, Do not resist an evil person" (verse 39). A readiness

to resent injuries, a quickness in taking offense, a quarrelsome and con-
tentious disposition, a keenness in asserting our rights – all are contrary
to the mind of Christ. The world may see no harm in these habits of
mind, but they do not suit the character of the Christian. Our Master
says, "Do not resist an evil person."

2. Universal love

The Lord Jesus enjoins on us a spirit of universal love and charity. "I
tell you: Love your enemies" (verse 44). We ought to put away all
malice: we ought to return good for evil, and blessing for cursing.
Moreover we are not to love in word only, but in deed; we are to deny
ourselves, and take trouble, in order to be kind and courteous: if anyone "forces you to go one mile, go with him two miles" (verse 41). We
are to put up with much and bear much, rather than hurt another, or
give offense. In all things we are to be unselfish. Our thought must
never be, "How do others behave to me?" but "What would Christ
have me do?"

A standard of conduct like this may seem, at first sight, extravagantly
high. But we must never content ourselves with aiming at one lower.
We must observe the two weighty arguments which our Lord uses to
back up this part of his instruction. They deserve serious attention.

1. Children of God

For one thing, if we do not aim at the spirit and temper which are here
recommended, we are not yet children of God. What does our "Father
in heaven" do? He is kind to all: he sends rain on the righteous and the
unrighteous alike; he causes "his sun" to shine on all without distinction (verse 45). A child should be like his father: but where is our likeness to our Father in heaven if we cannot show mercy and kindness to
everybody? Where is the evidence that we are new creatures if we have
no love? It is altogether lacking. We must yet be "born again" (John
3:7).

2. Of the world

For another thing, if we do not aim at the spirit here recommended, we
are obviously still of the world. "What are you doing more than

others?" is our Lord's solemn question (verse 47). Even those who have no religion can love those who love them (verse 46). They can do good and show kindness when affection or interest moves them. But a Christian ought to be influenced by higher principles than these. Do we flinch from the test? Do we find it impossible to do good to our enemies? If that is the case we may be sure we have yet to be converted. As yet we have not "received . . . the Spirit who is from God" (1 Corinthians 2:12).

There is much in all this which calls loudly for solemn reflection. There are few passages of Scripture so calculated to raise in our minds humbling thoughts. We have here a lovely picture of Christians as they ought to be. We cannot look at it without painful feelings: we must all admit that it differs widely from Christians as they are. Let us carry away from it two general lessons.

1. Recommending Christianity
First, if the spirit of these ten verses were more continually remembered by true believers, they would recommend Christianity to the world far more than they do. We must not allow ourselves to suppose that the least words in this passage are trifling and of small moment: they are not so. Attention to the spirit of this passage makes our religion beautiful. Neglect of the things which it contains deforms our religion. Unfailing courtesy, kindness, tenderness and consideration for others are some of the greatest ornaments to the character of a child of God. The world can understand these things if it cannot understand doctrine. There is no religion in rudeness, roughness, bluntness, and incivility. The perfection of practical Christianity consists in attending to the little duties of holiness as well as to the great.

2. A happier world
Second, if the spirit of these ten verses had more dominion and power in the world, how much happier the world would be than it is. Quarreling, strife, selfishness and unkindness cause half the miseries by which mankind is visited! Who can fail to see that nothing would tend to increase happiness so much as the spread of the Christian love here recommended by our Lord? Let us remember this. Those who fancy

that true religion has any tendency to make people unhappy are greatly mistaken. It is the absence of it that does this, not its presence. True religion has exactly the opposite effect. It tends to promote peace, charity, kindness and goodwill among people. The more people are brought under the teaching of the Holy Spirit, the more they will love one another, and the more happy they will be.

Matthew
Chapter 6

Ostentation in almsgiving and prayer *(6:1–8)*

In this part of the Sermon on the Mount the Lord Jesus gives us instruction on two subjects: one is that of giving alms; the other is that of prayer. Both were subjects to which the Jews attached great importance; both in themselves deserve the serious attention of all professing Christians.

Almsgiving
Let us observe that our Lord takes it for granted that all who call themselves his disciples will give alms. He assumes as a matter of course that they will think it a solemn duty to give, according to their means, to relieve the needs of others. The only question he deals with is the manner in which the duty should be done. This is a weighty lesson: it condemns the selfish stinginess of many in the matter of giving money. How many are "rich towards themselves," but poor towards God! How many never give a cent to do good to the bodies and souls of men! And have such persons any right to be called Christians in their present state of mind? It may well be doubted. A giving Saviour should have giving disciples.

Prayer
Our Lord also takes it for granted that all who call themselves his disciples will pray. He assumes this as a matter of course: he only gives directions as to the best way of praying. This is another lesson which deserves to be continually remembered: it teaches plainly that prayerless people are not genuine Christians. It is not enough to join in the

prayers of the congregation on Sundays, or attend the prayers of a family on week days: there must be private prayer also. Without this we may be outward members of Christ's church, but we are not living members of Christ.

But what are the rules laid down for our guidance about almsgiving and praying? They are few and simple; but they contain much for thought.

Ostentation

In giving, everything like ostentation is to be abhorred and avoided. "When you give to the needy, do not announce it with trumpets" (verse 2). We are not to give as if we wished everybody to see how liberal and charitable we are, and desire the praise of other people. We are to shun everything like display: we are to give quietly, and make as little noise as possible about our charitable donations; we are to aim at the spirit of the proverbial saying, "Do not let your left hand know what your right hand is doing" (verse 3).

Alone with God

In praying, the principal object to be sought is to be alone with God. "When you pray, go into your room" (verse 6). We should endeavor to find some place where no mortal eye sees us, and where we can pour out our hearts with the feeling that no one is looking at us but God. This is a rule which many find very difficult to follow; the poor man and the servant often find it almost impossible to be really alone; but it is a rule which we must make great efforts to obey. Necessity, in such cases, is often the mother of invention. When people really want to find some place where they can be in secret with their God, they will generally find a way.

A heart-searching God

In all our duties, whether giving or praying, the great thing to be kept in mind is that we have to do with a heart-seaching and all-knowing God. "Your Father . . . sees what is done in secret" (verse 6). Everything like formality, affectation, or mere bodily service, is abominable and worthless in God's sight. He takes no account of the quantity of money we give, or the quantity of words we use: the one thing at which his all-seeing eye looks is the nature of our motives and the state of our hearts.

May we all remember these things. Here lies a rock on which many are continually getting spiritually shipwrecked. They flatter themselves that all must be right with their souls if they only perform a certain amount of "religious duties." They forget that God does not regard the quantity, but the quality of our service. His favor is not to be bought, as many seem to suppose, by the formal repetition of a number of words, or by the self-righteous payment of a sum of money to a charity. Where are our hearts? Are we doing everything, whether we give or pray, "as if you were serving the Lord, not men" (Ephesians 6:7)? Do we realize the eye of God? Do we simply and solely desire to please him who "sees what is done in secret," and by whom "deeds are weighed" (1 Samuel 2:3)? Are we sincere? These are the sort of questions we should often ask our souls.

The Lord's Prayer and the duty of forgiveness (6:9–15)

These verses are few in number, and are soon read, but they are of immense importance. They contain that wonderful pattern of prayer with which the Lord Jesus has supplied his people, commonly called the Lord's Prayer.

Perhaps no part of Scripture is so well known as this. Its words are familiar wherever Christianity is found. Thousands – tens of thousands – who have never seen a Bible or heard the pure Gospel are acquainted with the "Our Father," or "Paternoster." It would be happy for the world if this prayer was as well known in the spirit as it is in the letter.

No part of Scripture is so full and so simple at the same time as this. It is the first prayer which we learn when we are little children: here is its simplicity. It contains the germ of everything which the most advanced saint can desire: here is its fullness. The more we ponder every word it contains, the more we shall feel this prayer is of God.

The Lord's Prayer consists of ten parts or sentences. There is one declaration of the Being to whom we pray; there are three prayers respecting his name, his kingdom and his will; there are four prayers respecting our daily needs, our sins or weakness, and our dangers; there is one profession of our feeling towards others; there is one concluding ascription of praise.

In all these parts we are taught to say "we" and "our." We are to remember others as well as ourselves.

On each of these parts a volume might be written. We must content ourselves at present with taking up sentence after sentence, and marking out the lessons which each sentence contains.

"Our Father in heaven"

The first sentence declares who we are to pray to: "Our Father in heaven" (verse 9). We are not to pray to saints and angels, but to the everlasting Father, the Father of spirits, the Lord of heaven and earth. We call him Father in the lowest sense, as our Creator: as St. Paul told the Athenians, "in him we live and move and have our being . . . We are his offspring" (Acts 17:28). We call him Father in the highest sense, as the Father of our Lord Jesus Christ, reconciling us to himself through the death of his Son (Colossians 1:20–22). We profess what the Old Testament saints only saw dimly and afar off – we profess to be his children by faith in Christ, and to have "the Spirit of sonship. And by him we cry, 'Abba, Father'" (Romans 8:15). This, we must never forget, is the sonship that we must desire if we want to be saved. Without faith in Christ's blood and union with him, it is useless to talk of trusting in the "Fatherhood" of God.

"Hallowed be your name"

The second sentence is a request concerning God's name: "Hallowed be your name" (verse 9). By the "name" of God we mean all those attributes through which he is revealed to us – his power, wisdom, holiness, justice, mercy and truth. By asking that they may be "hallowed," we mean that they may be made known and glorified. The glory of God is the first thing that God's children should desire. It is the object of one of our Lord's own prayers: "Father, glorify your name!" (John 12:28). It is the purpose for which the world was created; it is the end for which the saints are called and converted: it is the chief thing we should seek – "that in all things God may be praised" (1 Peter 4:11).

"Your kingdom come"

The third sentence is a request concerning God's kingdom: "your kingdom come" (verse 10). By his kingdom we mean, first, the kingdom of grace which God sets up and maintains in the hearts of all living members of Christ by his Spirit and Word. But we mean chiefly the kingdom of glory which one day will be set up when Jesus comes the second time, and "they will all know me, from the least of them to the greatest" (Hebrews 8:11). This is the time when sin, sorrow and Satan will be driven out of the world. It is the time when the Jews will be converted, and the full number of the Gentiles will come in (Romans 11:25), and a time that is to be desired more than anything. It therefore fills a foremost place in the Lord's Prayer. What we ask is expressed in the words of the Burial Service: "that it may please God to hasten his kingdom."

"Your will be done on earth as it is in heaven"

The fourth sentence is a request concerning God's will. "Your will be done on earth as it is in heaven" (verse 10). We here pray that God's laws may be obeyed by men as perfectly, readily and unceasingly as they are by angels in heaven. We ask that those who do not obey his laws now may be taught to obey them, and that those who do obey them may obey them better. Our truest happiness is perfect submission to God's will, and it is the purest love to pray that all mankind may know it, obey it and submit to it.

"Give us today our daily bread"

The fifth sentence is a request concerning our own daily needs: "Give us today our daily bread" (verse 11). We are here taught to acknowledge our entire dependence on God for the supply of our daily necessities. As Israel required daily manna, so we require daily "bread." We confess that we are poor, weak creatures in need, and beseech our Maker to take care of us. We ask for "bread" as the simplest of our wants, and in that word we include all that our bodies require.

"Forgive us our debts"

The sixth sentence is a request concerning our sins: "Forgive us our debts" (verse 12). We confess that we are sinners, and need daily grants of pardon and forgiveness. This part of the Lord's Prayer deserves especially to be remembered. It condemns all self-righteousness and self-justifying. We are instructed here to keep up a continual habit of confession at the throne of grace, and a continual habit of seeking mercy and remission. Let this never be forgotten. We need daily to wash our feet (John 13:10).

"As we also have forgiven our debtors"

The seventh sentence is a claim about our own feelings towards others: we ask our Father to "forgive us our debts, as we also have forgiven our debtors" (verse 12). This is the only statement in the whole prayer, and the only part on which our Lord comments and dwells when he has concluded the prayer. Its object is to remind us that we must not expect our prayers for forgiveness to be heard if we pray with malice and spite in our hearts towards others. To pray in such a frame of mind is mere formality and hypocrisy. It is even worse than hypocrisy: it is as much as saying, "Do not forgive me at all." Our prayers are nothing without love. We must not expect to be forgiven if we cannot forgive.

"Lead us not into temptation"

The eighth sentence is a request concerning our weakness: "Lead us not into temptation" (verse 13). It teaches us that we are liable at all times to be led astray and to fall. It instructs us to confess our infirmity and beseech God to hold us up, and not allow us to run into sin. We ask him, who orders all things in heaven and earth, to restrain us from going into that which would injure our souls, and never to let us be tempted beyond what we can bear (1 Corinthians 10:13).

"Deliver us from the evil one"

The ninth sentence is a request concerning our dangers: "Deliver us from the evil one" (verse 13), or simply "Deliver us from evil" [KJV, and NIV footnote, ed. note]. We are here taught to ask God to deliver us from the evil that is in the world, the evil that is within our own hearts, and not least from the evil one, the devil. We confess that, so long as we are in the body, we are constantly seeing, hearing and feeling the presence of evil. It is about us, and within us, and around us on every side. We entreat him who alone can preserve us, to be continually delivering us from its power (John 17:15).

"For yours is the kingdom and the power and the glory"

The last sentence is an ascription of praise: "Yours is the kingdom and the power and the glory" (verse 13 [KJV, and NIV footnote, ed. note]). We declare in these words our belief that the kingdoms of this world are the rightful property of our Father; that to him alone belongs all "power"; and that he alone deserves to receive all "glory." And we conclude by offering to him our hearts, giving him all honor and praise, and rejoicing that he is King of kings, and Lord of lords.

And now let us examine ourselves and see whether we really desire to have the things which we are taught to ask for in the Lord's Prayer. Thousands, it may be feared, repeat these words daily as a form, but never consider what they are saying. They care nothing for the "glory," the "kingdom," or the "will" of God: they have no sense of dependence, sinfulness, weakness, or danger; they have no love or charity towards their enemies. And yet they repeat the Lord's Prayer! These things ought not to be so. May we resolve that, by God's help, our hearts shall always go together with our lips! Happy is the person who can really call God "Father" through Jesus Christ the Saviour, and can therefore say a heartfelt "Amen" to all that the Lord's Prayer contains.

Fasting, worldliness and singleness of purpose (6:16–24)

Fasting

Fasting, or occasional abstinence from food in order to bring the body into subjection to the spirit, is a practice frequently mentioned in the Bible, generally in connection with prayer. David fasted when his child was sick (2 Samuel 12:16); Daniel fasted when he sought special light from God (Daniel 9:3); Paul and Barnabas fasted when they appointed elders (Acts 14:23); Esther fasted before going in to Ahasuerus (Esther 4:16). It is a subject about which we find no direct command in the New Testament. It seems to be left to everyone's discretion, whether he will fast or not. In this absence of direct command we may see great wisdom. Many a poor man never has enough to eat, and it would be an insult to tell him to fast: many sick people can hardly be kept well with the closest attention to diet, and could not fast without bringing on illness. It is a matter in which each person must be persuaded in their own mind, and not rashly condemn others who do not agree. One thing only must never be forgotten: those who fast should do it quietly, secretly and without ostentation. Let them not "show men they are fasting." Let them not fast to man, but to God.

Worldliness

Worldliness is one of the greatest dangers that beset the human soul. It is no wonder that we find our Lord speaking strongly about it: it is an insidious, specious, plausible enemy; it seems so innocent to pay close attention to our business! It seems so harmless to seek our happiness in this world, so long as we keep clear of open sins! Yet here is a rock on which many are shipwrecked for all eternity. They "store up . . . treasures on earth," and forget to "store up . . . treasures in heaven" (verses 19–20). May we all remember this! Where are our hearts? What do we love best? Are our chief affections on things on earth, or things in heaven? Life or death depends on the answer we can give to these questions. If our treasure is earthly, our hearts will be earthly too. "For where your treasure is, there your heart will be also" (verse 21).

Singleness of purpose

Singleness of purpose is one great secret of spiritual prosperity. If our eyes do not see clearly we cannot walk without stumbling and falling. If we attempt to work for two different masters, we are sure to give satisfaction to neither. It is just the same with respect to our souls. We cannot serve Christ and the world at the same time: it is vain to attempt it. The thing cannot be done: the ark and Dagon will never stand together (see 1 Samuel 5). God must be king over our hearts: his law, his will, his precepts must receive our first attention; then, and not till then, everything in our inner being will fall into its right place. Unless our hearts are set in order like this, everything will be in confusion. "Your whole body will be full of darkness" (verse 23).

Cheerfulness

Let us learn from our Lord's instructions about fasting the great importance of cheerfulness in our religion. Those words, "put oil on your head and wash your face" (verse 17) are full of deep meaning. They should teach us to aim at letting men see that Christianity makes us happy. Never let us forget that there is no religion in looking melancholy and gloomy. Are we dissatisfied with Christ's wages and Christ's service? Surely not! Then let us not look as if we were.

Keeping alert

Let us learn from our Lord's caution about worldliness how we need to watch and pray against an earthly spirit. What are the vast majority of professing Christians round us doing? They are storing up treasures on earth: there can be no mistake about it. Their tastes, their ways, their habits, tell a fearful tale. They are not storing up treasure in heaven. Let us beware that we do not sink into hell by paying excessive attention to lawful things. Open transgression of God's law slays its thousands, but worldliness its tens of thousands.

The secret of failure

What is the true secret of the failures which so many Christians seem to make in their religion? There are failures in all quarters. There are thousands in our churches uncomfortable, ill at ease, and dissatisfied with themselves; and they hardly know why. The reason is revealed here: they are trying to keep in with both sides. They are endeavoring to please God and please human beings, to serve Christ and serve the world at the same time. Let us not commit this mistake. Let us be committed, thorough-going, uncompromising followers of Christ. Let our motto be that of Paul: "One thing I do" (Philippians 3:13). Then we shall be happy Christians: we shall feel the sun shining on our faces; heart, head, and conscience will all be full of light. Commitment is the secret of happiness in religion. Be committed to Christ and "your whole body will be full of light."

Caring too much for this world *(6:25–34)*

These verses are a striking example of the combined wisdom and compassion of our Lord Jesus Christ's teaching. He knows people's hearts: he knows that we are always ready to counter warnings against worldliness by the argument that we cannot help being anxious about the things of this life. "Have we not our families to provide for? Must not our bodily needs be met? How can we possibly get through life if we think first of our souls?" The Lord Jesus foresaw such thoughts and provided an answer.

An anxious spirit

He forbids us to keep up an anxious spirit about the things of this world. Four times over he says, "Do not worry" (verses 25, 28, 31 and 34). About life, about food, about clothing, about tomorrow, "do not worry." Do not be over-careful, over-anxious. Prudent provision for the future is right; wearing, corroding, self-tormenting anxiety is wrong.

God's providential care

He reminds us of the providential care that God continually takes of everything that he has created. Has he given us "life" (verse 25)? Then he will surely not let us lack anything necessary for its maintenance. Has he given us a "body" (verse 25)? Then he will surely not let us die for lack of clothing. He calls us into being and will doubtless find meat to feed us.

Over-anxiety

He points out the uselessness of over-anxiety. Our life is certainly in God's hand; all the care in the world will not make us continue a minute beyond the time which God has appointed. We cannot add one hour to our lives; we shall not die till our work is done.

The birds of the air

He sends us to the birds of the air for instruction. They make no provision for the future: "they do not sow or reap or store away in barns" (verse 26); they do not store food for the future. They literally live from day to day on what they can pick up by using the instinct God has put in them. They ought to teach us that no one doing their duty in the position to which God has called him, will ever be allowed to come to poverty.

The flowers of the field

He tells us to look at the flowers of the field. Year after year they are decked with the brightest colors, without the slightest labor or exertion on their part: "they do not labor or spin" (verse 28). God, by his almighty power, clothes them with beauty every season. The same God is the Father of all believers. Why should they doubt that he is able to provide them with clothing, just as he cares for the "lilies of the field"? Anyone who thinks about perishable flowers will surely not neglect the bodies in which immortal souls dwell.

Worry unworthy of a Christian

He suggests to us that over-carefulness about the things of this world is most unworthy of a Christian. One great feature of paganism is living for the present. Let the pagan be anxious if he wants to; he knows nothing of a Father in heaven. But let the Christian, who has clearer light and knowledge, give proof of it by his faith and contentment. When we are bereaved of those we love, we are not to "grieve like the rest of men, who have no hope" (1 Thessalonians 4:13). When we are tried by anxieties about this life, we are not to be over-careful, as if we had no God, and no Christ.

A gracious promise

He offers us a gracious promise as a remedy against an anxious spirit. He assures us that if we "seek first" and foremost to have a place in the kingdom of grace and glory, everything that we really want in this world will be given to us "as well" as our heavenly inheritance (verse 33). "In all things God works for the good of those who love him" (Romans 8:28). "No good thing does he withhold from those whose walk is blameless" (Psalm 84:11).

Maxim

Last of all, he seals up all his instruction on this subject by laying down one of the wisest maxims. "Tomorrow will worry about itself. Each day has enough trouble of its own" (verse 34). We are not to carry cares before they come: we are to attend to today's business, and leave tomorrow's anxieties till tomorrow dawns. We may die before tomorrow: we know not what may happen tomorrow; we may only be sure of this one thing, that if tomorrow brings a cross, he who sends it can and will send grace to bear it.

In all this passage there is a treasury of golden lessons. Let us seek to use them in our daily life: let us not only read them, but turn them to practical account; let us watch and pray against an anxious and over-careful spirit. It deeply concerns our happiness to do so. Half our miseries are caused by fancying things that we think are coming upon us: half the things that we expect to come upon us never come at all. Where is our faith? Where is our confidence in our Saviour's words? We may well be ashamed of ourselves when we read these verses and then look into our hearts. We may be sure that David's words are true: "I was young and now I am old, yet I have never seen the righteous forsaken or their children begging bread" (Psalm 37:25).

Matthew
Chapter 7

Censoriousness forbidden (7:1–5)

This is one of those passages of Scripture which we must be careful not to strain beyond its proper meaning. It is frequently abused and misapplied by the enemies of true religion. It is possible to press the words of the Bible so far that they yield not medicine, but poison.

When our Lord says, "Do not judge" (verse 1), he does not mean that it is wrong, under any circumstances, to pass an unfavorable judgment on the conduct and opinions of others. We ought to have decided opinions: we are to "test everything" (1 Thessalonians 5:21); we are to "test the spirits" (1 John 4:1). Nor does he mean that it is wrong to reprove the sins and faults of others until we are perfect and faultless ourselves. Such an interpretation would contradict other parts of Scripture. It would make it impossible to condemn error and false doctrine; it would debar anyone from attempting the office of a minister or a judge. The earth would fall "into the hands of the wicked" (Job 9:24). Heresy would flourish; wrong-doing would abound.

What our Lord means to condemn is a censorious and fault-finding spirit. A readiness to blame others for trifling offenses or matters of indifference, a habit of passing rash and hasty judgments, a disposition to magnify the errors and infirmities of our neighbors and make the worst of them – this is what our Lord forbids. It was common among the Pharisees. It has always been common from their day down to the present time. We must watch against it. We should "believe all things" and "hope all things" about others, and be very slow to find fault. This is Christian love (see 1 Corinthians 13:7, KJV).

Discretion in who we talk to about religion *(7:6)*

This verse teaches us the importance of exercising discretion over the people we speak to about religion. Everything is beautiful in its place and season. Our zeal is to be tempered by a prudent consideration of times, places and persons. "Do not rebuke a mocker," says Solomon, "or he will hate you" (Proverbs 9:8). It is not everybody to whom it is wise to open our minds on spiritual matters. There are many who, from violent tempers or openly profligate habits, are utterly incapable of valuing the things of the Gospel. They will even fly into a passion and run into greater excesses of sin if we try to do good to their souls. To name the name of Christ to such people is truly to "throw your pearls to pigs." It does not do them good, but harm: it rouses all their corruption and makes them angry. In short, they are like the Jews at Corinth (Acts 18:6), or like Nabal, about whom it is written that he was "such a wicked man that no one can talk to him" (1 Samuel 25:17).

The lesson before us is one which is particularly difficult to use properly. The right application of it needs great wisdom. We are most of us far more likely to err on the side of over-caution than of over-zeal: we are generally far more disposed to remember the "time to be silent" than the "time to speak" (Ecclesiastes 3:7). It is a lesson, however, which ought to stir up a spirit of self-inquiry in all our hearts. Do we ourselves never check our friends from giving us good advice, by being morose and irritable? Have we never obliged others to hold their peace and say nothing, by being proud and contemptuous of their advice? Have we never turned against our kind advisers, and silenced them by our violence and passion? We may well fear that we have often erred in this matter.

The duty of prayer *(7:7–11)*

These verses teach us the duty of prayer, and the rich encouragements there are to pray. There is a beautiful connection between this lesson and that which goes before it. If we want to know when to be silent, and when to speak, when to bring forward holy things and produce our "pearls," we must pray. This is a subject to which the Lord Jesus evidently attaches great importance: the language that he uses is a plain proof of this. He employs three different words to express the idea of prayer: "ask," "seek" and "knock" (verses 7–8). He holds out the broadest, fullest promise to those who pray: "Everyone who asks receives" (verse 8). He illustrates God's readiness to hear our prayers by an argument drawn from the well-known practice of parents on earth. "Evil" and selfish as they are by nature, they do not neglect the bodily needs of their children. So how much more will a God of love and mercy attend to the cries of those who are his children by grace!

Let us take special notice of these words of our Lord about prayer. Few of his sayings, perhaps, are so well known and so often repeated as this. The poorest and most unlearned can generally tell us that "if we do not seek we shall not find." But what is the good of knowing it, if we do not use it? Knowledge which is not improved and well employed will only increase our condemnation on the last day.

Do we know anything of this asking, seeking and knocking? Why should we not? There is nothing so simple and plain as praying if we really have a will to pray. Sadly, there is nothing which we are so slow to do: we will use many of the forms of religion, attend many ordinances, do many things that are right, before we will do this; and yet without this no soul can be saved!

Do we ever really pray? If not, we shall be without excuse before God at the last day, unless we repent. We shall not be condemned for not doing what we could not have done, or not knowing what we could not have known; but we shall find that one main reason why we are lost is that we never asked to be saved.

Do we indeed pray? Then let us pray on, and not faint. It is not lost labor; it is not useless. It will bear fruit after many days. Those words have never yet failed: "Everyone who asks receives."

Concluding lessons (7:12–20)

In this part of the Sermon on the Mount our Lord begins to draw his discourse to a conclusion. The lessons he here forces on our notice are broad, general and full of the deepest wisdom. Let us mark them in succession.

1. The rule of duty towards others

First, he lays down a general principle for our guidance in all doubtful questions between people. "Do to others what you would have them do to you" (verse 12). We are not to deal with others as others deal with us: this is mere selfishness and heathenism. We are to deal with others as we would like others to deal with us – this is real Christianity.

This is a golden rule indeed! It does not merely forbid all petty malice and revenge, all cheating and overreaching: it does much more. It settles a hundred difficult points which, in a world like this, are continually arising between people. It prevents the necessity of laying down endless little rules for our conduct in specific cases. It sweeps the whole debatable ground with one mighty principle. It shows us a balance and measure by which everyone may see at once what is his duty. Is there something we would not like our neighbor to do to us? Then let us always remember that this is the thing we ought not to do to him. Is there a thing we would like him to do to us? Then this is the very thing we ought to do to him. How many intricate questions would be decided at once if this rule were honestly used!

2. The two gates

Second, our Lord gives us a general caution against the path many people travel in religion (verses 13–14). It is not enough to think as others think, and do as others do. It must not satisfy us to follow the fashion, and swim with the stream of those among whom we live. He tells us that the way that leads to everlasting life is "narrow," and "only a few" travel in it. He tells us that the way that leads to everlasting destruction is "broad," and full of travelers: "many enter through it."

These are fearful truths! They ought to raise great searchings of heart in the minds of all who hear them. "Which way am I going? By what road am I traveling?" In one or other of the two ways here described, every one of us may be found. May God give us an honest, self-inquiring spirit, and show us what we are!

We may well tremble and be afraid if our religion is that of the multitude. If we can say no more than this, that "we go where others go, and worship where others worship, and hope we shall do as well as others at last," we are literally pronouncing our own condemnation. What is this but being in the "broad way"? What is this but being in the road whose end is "destruction"? Our religion at present is not saving religion.

We have no reason to be discouraged and cast down if the religion we profess is not popular and few agree with us. We must remember the words of our Lord Jesus Christ in this passage: "small is the gate." Repentance, faith in Christ and holiness of life have never been fashionable. The true flock of Christ has always been small. We must not mind if we are thought singular and peculiar and bigoted and narrow-minded. This is "the narrow road." Surely it is better to enter into life eternal with a few, than to go to "destruction" with a great company.

3. Warning against false prophets

Third, the Lord Jesus gives us a general warning against false teachers in the church. We are to "watch out for false prophets" (verse 15). The connection between this passage and the preceding one is striking. Do we want to keep clear of this "broad road"? We must beware of false prophets. They will arise: they began in the days of the apostles; even then the seeds of error were sown. They have appeared continually ever since. We must be prepared for them, and be on our guard.

This is a warning which is much needed. There are thousands who seem ready to believe anything in religion if they hear it from an ordained minister. They forget that clergymen may err as much as laymen: they are not infallible. Their teaching must be weighed in the balance of holy Scripture: they are to be followed and believed so long as their doctrine agrees with the Bible, but not a minute longer. We are to try them "by their fruit" (verse 16). Sound doctrine and holy living are the marks of true prophets. Let us remember this. Our minister's mistakes will not excuse our own. "If a blind man leads a blind man, both will fall into a pit" (Matthew 15:14).

What is the best safeguard against false teaching? Beyond all doubt the regular study of the Word of God, with prayer for the teaching of the Holy Spirit. The Bible was given to be a lamp to our feet and a light for our path (Psalm 119:105). The man who reads it aright will never be allowed greatly to err. It is neglect of the Bible which makes so many a prey to the first false teacher whom they hear. They would have us believe that "they are not learned, and do not claim to have definite opinions." The plain truth is that they are lazy and idle about reading the Bible, and do not like the trouble of thinking for themselves. Nothing supplies false prophets with followers so much as spiritual sloth under a cloak of humility.

May we all bear in mind our Lord's warning! The world, the devil and the flesh are not the only dangers in the way of the Christian; there is still another one, and that is the "false prophet" – the wolf in sheep's clothing. Happy is he who prays over his Bible and knows the difference between truth and error in religion! There is a difference, and we are meant to know it, and to use our knowledge.

Profession without practice (7:21–29)

The Lord Jesus winds up the Sermon on the Mount by a passage of heart-piercing application. He turns from false prophets to false professors, from unsound teachers to unsound hearers. Here is a word for all. May we have grace to apply it to our own hearts!

1. The uselessness of mere outward profession

The first lesson here is the uselessness of a mere outward profession of Christianity. Not everyone who says "Lord, Lord," will enter the kingdom of heaven (verse 21). Not all those who profess and call themselves Christians will be saved.

Let us take notice of this. It requires far more than most people seem to think necessary to save a soul. We may be baptized in the name of Christ, and boast confidently of our ecclesiastical privileges; we may possess head knowledge, and be quite satisfied with our own state; we may even be preachers, and teachers of others, and "perform many miracles" in connection with our church, but all this time are we practically doing the will of our Father in heaven? Do we truly repent, truly believe in Christ, and live holy and humble lives? If not, in spite of all our privileges and profession of faith, we shall miss heaven at last, and be forever cast away. We shall hear those awful words, "I never knew you. Away from me, you evildoers!" (verse 23).

The day of judgment will reveal strange things. The hopes of many who were thought great Christians while they lived will be utterly confounded. The rottenness of their religion will be exposed and put to shame before the whole world. It will then be proved that to be saved means something more than "making a profession." We must make a "practice" of our Christianity as well as a "profession." Let us often think of that great day: let us often "judge ourselves, that we be not judged" and condemned by the Lord. Whatever else we are, let us aim at being real, true and sincere.

2. The two builders

The second lesson here is a striking picture of two classes of Christian hearers: those who hear and do nothing, and those who hear and do as well as hear. They are both placed before us and their stories followed to their respective ends.

The person who hears Christian teaching and practices it is like "a wise man who built his house on the rock" (verse 24). He does not content himself with listening to exhortations to repent, believe in Christ and live a holy life. He actually repents; he actually believes. He actually ceases to do evil, learns to do good, abhors what is sinful, and clings to that which is good. He is a doer as well as a hearer (James 1:22).

And what is the result? In the time of trial his religion does not fail him; the floods of sickness, sorrow, poverty, disappointments, bereavements beat upon him in vain. His soul stands unmoved; his faith does not give way; his Christian comforts do not utterly forsake him. His religion may have cost him trouble in the past; his foundation may have been obtained with much labor and many tears: to discover his own interest in Christ may have required many a day of earnest seeking and many an hour of wrestling in prayer. But his labor has not been thrown away as he now reaps a rich reward. The religion that can stand trial is the true religion.

The person who hears Christian teaching and never gets beyond hearing is like "a foolish man who built his house on sand" (verse 26). He satisfies himself with listening and approving, but he goes no further. He flatters himself, perhaps, that all is right with his soul because he has feelings, convictions and desires of a spiritual kind. In these he rests. He never really breaks off from sin and casts aside the spirit of the world; he never really holds on to Christ; he never really takes up the cross. He is a hearer of truth, but nothing more.

And what is the end of this person's religion? It breaks down entirely under the first flood of tribulation. It fails him completely, like a summer-dried fountain, when his need is the sorest. It leaves its possessor high and dry, like a wreck on a sand-bank, a scandal to the church, a by-word to the unbeliever and a misery to himself. Most true is that what costs little is worth little! A religion which costs us nothing, and consists in nothing but hearing sermons, will always prove at last to be a useless thing.

So ends the Sermon on the Mount. Such a sermon never was preached before; such a sermon perhaps has never been preached since. Let us see that it has a lasting influence on our own souls. It is addressed to us as well as to those who first heard it; we are the ones who will have to give account of its heart-searching lessons. It is no light matter what we think of them. The word that Jesus has spoken, "that very word . . . will condemn" us "at the last day" (John 12:48).

Matthew
Chapter 8

Miraculous healings *(8:1–15)*

The eighth chapter of St. Matthew's Gospel is full of our Lord's miracles: no less than five are specially recorded. There is beautiful fitness in this. It was fitting that the greatest sermon ever preached should be immediately followed by mighty proofs that the preacher was the Son of God. Those who heard the Sermon on the Mount would be obliged to confess that as "no one ever spoke the way this man does" (John 7:46), so also no one did such works.

The verses contain three great miracles: a leper is healed with a touch, a paralytic is made well by a word, a woman sick with a fever is restored in a moment to health and strength. On the face of these three miracles we may read three striking lessons. Let us examine them and lay them to heart.

1. Christ's great power
First, let us learn how great is the power of our Lord Jesus Christ. Leprosy was the most fearful disease by which man's body could be afflicted. The person who had it was like a dead person while he was still alive; it was a complaint regarded by physicians as incurable (see 2 Kings 5:7). Yet Jesus says, "'Be clean!' Immediately he was cured of his leprosy" (verse 3).

To heal a person of paralysis without even seeing him, by only speaking a word, is to do what our minds cannot even conceive: yet Jesus commands, and at once it is done (verses 6, 8 and 14). To give a woman prostrate with a fever, not merely relief, but strength to do work in an instant, would baffle the skill of all the physicians on earth:

56

yet Jesus "touched" Peter's wife's mother and "she got up and began to wait on him" (verse 15). These are the doings of one who is almighty. There is no escape from the conclusion. This was "the finger of God" (Exodus 8:19).

We see here a broad foundation for the faith of a Christian. We are told in the Gospel to come to Jesus, to believe in Jesus, to live the life of faith in Jesus; we are encouraged to lean on him, to cast all our care on him, to rest all the weight of our souls on him. We may do so without fear: he can bear all; he is a strong rock: he is almighty. It was a fine saying of an old saint, "My faith can sleep sound on no other pillow than Christ's omnipotence." He can give life to the dead; he can give power to the weak; he "increases the power of the weak" (Isaiah 40:29). Let us trust him and not be afraid. The world is full of snares; our hearts are weak. But with Jesus nothing is impossible.

2. Christ's compassion

Second, let us learn the mercifulness and compassion of our Lord Jesus Christ. The circumstances of the three cases we are now considering were all different. He heard the leper's pitiful cry, "Lord, if you are willing, you can make me clean" (verse 2). He was told of the centurion's servant, but he never saw him. He saw Peter's wife's mother, "lying in bed with a fever" (verse 14), and we are not told that he spoke a word. Yet in each case the heart of the Lord Jesus was one and the same. In each case he was quick to show mercy, and ready to heal. Each poor sufferer was tenderly pitied, and each effectively relieved.

We see here another strong foundation for our faith. Our great High Priest is very gracious. He is able to sympathize with our weaknesses (Hebrews 4:15); he is never tired of doing us good. He knows that we are a weak and feeble people in the midst of a weary and troubled world. He is as ready to bear with us and help us, as he was 1900 years ago. It is as true of him now as it was then that he "does not despise men" (Job 36:5). No heart can feel for us so much as the heart of Christ.

3. The precious grace of faith

Third, let us learn what a precious thing is the grace of faith. We know little about the centurion described in these verses; his name, his nation, his past history are all hidden from us. But one thing we do know, and that is that he believed. "Lord," he says, "I do not deserve to have you come under my roof. But just say the word, and my servant will be healed" (verse 8). He believed, let us remember, when teachers of the law and Pharisees were unbelievers; he believed, though a Gentile born, when Israel was blinded. Our Lord pronounced upon him the commendation which has been read all over the world from that time to this: "I have not found anyone in Israel with such great faith" (verse 10).

Let us hold firmly on to this lesson. It deserves to be remembered. To believe Christ's power and willingness to help, and to make practical use of our belief, is a rare and precious gift: let us always be thankful if we have it. To be willing to come to Jesus as helpless, lost sinners and commit our souls into his hands is a mighty privilege; let us always bless God if this willingness is ours, for it is his gift. Such faith is better than all other gifts and knowledge in the world. Many a poor converted heathen, who knows nothing but that he is sick of sin, and trusts in Jesus, will sit down in heaven while many learned scholars are rejected for evermore. Blessed indeed are they that believe!

What do we each know of this faith? This is the great question. Our learning may be small, but do we believe? Our opportunities of giving and working for Christ's cause may be few, but do we believe? We may neither be able to preach, nor write, nor argue for the Gospel, but do we believe? May we never rest till we can answer this inquiry! Faith in Christ appears a small and simple thing to the children of this world. They see in it nothing great or grand. But faith in Christ is most precious in God's sight and, like most precious things, is rare. By it true Christians live; by it they stand; by it they overcome the world. Without this faith no one can be saved.

Christ's wisdom in dealing with followers *(8:16–22)*

In the first part of these verses we see a striking example of our Lord's wisdom in dealing with those who said they wanted to be his disciples. The passage throws so much light on a subject frequently misunderstood in these days, that it deserves more than ordinary attention.

A certain teacher of the law offers to follow our Lord wherever he goes. It was a remarkable offer when we consider the class to which the man belonged, and the time at which it was made. But the offer receives a remarkable answer. It is not directly accepted nor yet flatly rejected. Our Lord only makes the solemn reply, "Foxes have holes and birds of the air have nests, but the Son of Man has no place to lay his head" (verse 20).

Another follower of our Lord next comes forward, and asks to be allowed to bury his father before going any further in the path of a disciple (verse 21). The request seems, at first sight, a natural and permissible one. But it draws from our Lord's lips a reply no less solemn than that already referred to: "Follow me, and let the dead bury their own dead" (verse 22).

There is something deeply impressive in both these sayings. They ought to be well weighed by all who claim to be Christians. They teach us plainly that people who show a desire to come forward and profess themselves true disciples of Christ should be warned plainly to count the cost before they begin. Are they prepared to endure hardship? Are they ready to carry the cross? If not, they are not yet fit to begin. They teach us plainly that there are times when a Christian must literally give up all for Christ's sake, and that even such duties as attending to a parent's funeral must be left to be performed by others. Such duties some will always be ready to attend to; and at no time can they be put in comparison with the greater duty of preaching the Gospel, and doing Christ's work in the world.

It would be good for the churches of Christ if these sayings of our Lord were remembered more than they are. It may be feared that the lesson they contain is too often overlooked by the ministers of the Gospel, and that thousands are admitted to full communion who are never warned to count the cost. Nothing, in fact, has done more harm to Christianity than the practice of filling the ranks of Christ's army with every volunteer who is willing to make a little profession, and to talk fluently of his "experience." It has been painfully forgotten that numbers alone do not make strength, and that there may be a great quantity of mere outward religion, while there is very little real grace. Let us remember this. Let us keep back nothing from young believers and inquirers after Christ: let us not enlist them on false pretences. Let us tell them plainly that there is a crown of glory at the end, but let us tell them no less plainly that there is a daily cross on the way.

The storm on the lake (8:23–27)

In these verses we learn that true saving faith is often mingled with much weakness and infirmity. It is a humbling lesson, but a very wholesome one.

We are told about our Lord and his disciples crossing the sea of Galilee in a boat. A storm arises and the boat is in danger of being filled with water by the waves that break over it. Meanwhile our Lord is asleep. The frightened disciples awake him, and cry to him for help. He hears their cry and stills the waters with a word so that it is "completely calm" (verse 26). At the same time he gently reproves the anxiety of his disciples: "You of little faith, why are you so afraid?" (verse 26).

What a vivid and instructive picture we have here of the hearts of thousands of believers! How many have faith and love enough to forsake all for Christ's sake, and to follow him wherever he goes, and yet are full of fears in the hour of trial! How many have grace enough to turn to Jesus in every trouble, crying, "Lord save us," and yet not grace enough to lie still and believe in the darkest hour that all is well!

Let the prayer, "Lord, increase our faith," always form part of our daily requests. Perhaps we never know the weakness of our faith until we are placed in the furnace of trial and anxiety. Blessed and happy is the person who finds by experience that his faith can stand the fire, and that he can say with Job, "though he slay me, yet will I hope in him" (Job 13:15).

We have great reason to thank God that Jesus, our great High Priest, is very compassionate and tender-hearted. He knows our frame: he considers our infirmities. He does not cast off his people because of defects. He has pity even on those he reproves. The prayer even of "little faith" is heard and gets an answer.

The region of the Gadarenes (8:28–34)

The subject of these seven verses is deep and mysterious. The driving out of demons is here described with special fullness. It is one of those passages which throw strong light on a dark and difficult point.

1. There is a devil

First, let us settle it firmly in our minds that there is such a being as the devil. It is an awful truth, and one too much overlooked. There is an unseen spirit always near us, very powerful and full of endless malice against our souls. From the beginning of creation he has labored to injure mankind. Until the Lord comes the second time and binds him, he will never stop tempting, and practicing mischief. In the days when our Lord was upon earth, it is clear that he had special power over the bodies of certain men and women, as well as over their souls. Even in our own times there may be more of this bodily possession than some suppose, though confessedly in a far less degree than when Christ came in the flesh. But that the devil is ever near us, and ever ready to ply our hearts with temptations, ought never to be forgotten.

2. The devil's power is limited

Second, let us settle it firmly in our minds that the power of the devil is limited. Mighty as he is, there is someone mightier still. Even though he is set on doing harm in the world, he can only work by permission. These verses show us that the evil spirits know they can only go to and fro and ravage the earth until the time allowed them by the Lord of lords. "Have you come here to torture us," they say, "before the appointed time?" (verse 29). Even their request shows us that they could not even hurt one of the pigs of the Gadarenes unless Jesus the Son of God allowed them: "Send us into the herd of pigs," they say (verse 31).

3. Christ delivers from the devil's power

Third, let us settle it in our minds that our Lord Jesus Christ is our great deliverer from the power of the devil. He can redeem us not only from all sin, and this present evil world, but from the devil. It was prophesied long ago that he would crush the serpent's head (Genesis 3:15). He began to crush that head when he was born of the Virgin Mary; he triumphed over that head when he died upon the cross; he showed his complete dominion over Satan by "healing all who were under the power of the devil" when he was on earth (Acts 10:38). Our great remedy, in all the assaults of the devil, is to cry to the Lord Jesus, and to seek his help. He can break the chains that Satan throws round us, and set us free. He can drive out every demon that plagues our hearts, as surely as in the days of old. It would be miserable indeed to know that there is a devil always near us, if we did not also know that Christ is "able to save completely those who come to God through him, because he always lives to intercede for them" (Hebrews 7:25).

4. The worldliness of the Gadarenes

Fourth, let us not leave this passage without observing the painful worldliness of the Gadarenes, among whom this miracle of driving out demons was performed. They pleaded with the Lord Jesus to "leave their region" (verse 34): they had no heart to feel for anything but the loss of their pigs. They did not care that two fellow-creatures, two immortal souls, had been freed from Satan's bondage; they did not care that among them stood a greater force than the devil, Jesus the Son of God. They cared for nothing but the fact that their pigs were drowned and "their hope of making money was gone" (Acts 16:19). They ignorantly regarded Jesus as one who stood between them and their profits, and they only wished to be rid of him.

There are only too many like these Gadarenes. There are thousands who care not one jot for Christ, or Satan, so long as they can make a little more money, and have a little more of the good things of this world. From this spirit may we be delivered! Against this spirit may we ever watch and pray! It is very common: it is awfully infectious. Let us recollect every morning that we have souls to be saved, and that we shall one day die, and after that be judged. Let us beware of loving the world more than Christ.

Matthew
Chapter 9

A paralytic healed; the calling of Matthew *(9:1–13)*

1. Jesus' knowledge of people's thoughts
Let us notice, in the first part of this passage, our Lord's knowledge of people's thoughts.

Some of the teachers of the law found fault with the words which Jesus spoke to a paralytic: they said secretly among themselves, "This fellow is blaspheming!" (verse 3). They probably supposed that no one knew what was going on in their minds. They had yet to learn that the Son of God could read hearts and discern spirits. Their malicious thought was publicly exposed and they were put to shame openly. Jesus knew their thoughts (verse 4).

There is an important lesson for us here. "Everything is uncovered and laid bare before the eyes of him to whom we must give account" (Hebrews 4:13). Nothing can be concealed from Christ. What do we think of in private, when no one sees us? What do we think of in church when we seem grave and serious? What are we thinking of at this moment while reading these words? Jesus knows. Jesus sees. Jesus records. Jesus will one day summon us to give account. It is written that "God will judge men's secrets through Jesus Christ, as my gospel declares" (Romans 2:16). Surely we ought to be very humble when we consider these things: we ought to thank God daily that the blood of Christ can cleanse from all sin; we ought often to cry, "May the words of my mouth and the meditation of my heart be pleasing in your sight" (Psalm 19:14).

2. The call of Matthew to be a disciple

Second, let us notice the wonderful call of the apostle Matthew to be Christ's disciple.

We find the man, who afterwards was the first to write a Gospel, sitting at the tax collector's booth (verse 9). We see him absorbed in his worldly calling, and possibly thinking of nothing but money and gain; but suddenly the Lord Jesus calls on him to follow him, and become his disciple. At once Matthew obeys. He hastens, and does not delay to keep Christ's commands (Psalm 119:60). He gets up and follows him.

We should learn from Matthew's case that with Christ nothing is impossible. He can take a tax collector and make him an apostle. He can change any heart, and make all things new. Let us never despair of anyone's salvation. Let us pray on, and speak on, and work on, in order to do good to souls, even to the souls of the worst. "The voice of the Lord is powerful" (Psalm 29:4). When he says by the power of the Spirit, "follow me," he can make the hardest and most sinful obey.

We should observe Matthew's decision. He waited for nothing. He did not wait until he found it "convenient" (Acts 24:25); and consequently he reaped a great reward. He wrote a book which is known all over the earth. He became a blessing to others as well as blessed in his own soul. He left a name behind him which is better known than the names of princes and kings. The richest man of the world is soon forgotten when he dies; but as long as the world stands millions will know the name of Matthew the tax collector.

3. The mission of Jesus Christ

Third, let us notice our Lord's precious declaration about his own mission.

The Pharisees found fault with him because he allowed tax collectors and "sinners" to be in his company. In their proud blindness they fancied that a teacher sent from heaven ought to have no dealings with such people. They were wholly ignorant of the grand design for which the Messiah was to come into the world, to be a Saviour, a Physician, a healer of sin-sick souls; and they drew from our Lord's lips a severe rebuke, accompanied by the blessed words, "I have not come to call the righteous, but sinners" (verse 13).

Let us make sure that we thoroughly understand the doctrine that these words contain. The first thing needed in order to have an interest in Christ is to feel deeply our own corruption, and to be willing to come to him for deliverance. We are not to keep away from Christ, as many ignorantly do, because we feel bad and wicked and unworthy; we are to remember that sinners are those he came into the world to save, and that if we feel we are sinners, that is good. Happy is he who really comprehends that one principal qualification for coming to Christ is a deep sense of sin!

Finally, if by the grace of God we really understand the glorious truth that sinners are those whom Christ came to call, let us make sure that we never forget it. Let us not dream that true Christians can ever attain such a state of perfection in this world as not to need the mediation and intercession of Jesus. Sinners we are in the day we first come to Christ. Poor needy sinners we continue to be so long as we live, drawing all the grace we have every hour out of Christ's fullness. We shall find ourselves sinners in the hour of our death, and shall die as much indebted to Christ's blood as on the day when we first believed.

New wine; a ruler's daughter raised to life (9:14–26)

1. Jesus the bridegroom

Let us mark, in this passage, the gracious name by which the Lord Jesus speaks of himself. He calls himself "the bridegroom" (verse 15).

What the bridegroom is to the bride, the Lord Jesus is to the souls of all who believe in him. He loves them with a deep and everlasting love. He takes them into union with himself: they are "one with Christ and Christ in them." He pays all their debts to God; he supplies all their daily needs; he sympathizes with them in all their troubles; he bears with all their infirmities, and does not reject them for a few weaknesses. He regards them as part of himself: those that persecute and injure them are persecuting him. The glory that he has received from his Father they will one day share with him, and where he is, they will be. These are the privileges of all true Christians, who are the Lamb's wife (Revelation 19:7). This is the dowry to which faith admits us. By it God joins our poor sinful souls to one precious Husband; and those God thus joins together will never be separated. Blessed indeed are they that believe.

2. A wise principle

Second, let us notice what a wise principle the Lord Jesus lays down for the treatment of young disciples.

There were some who found fault with our Lord's followers because they did not fast as John the Baptist's disciples did. Our Lord defends his disciples with an argument full of deep wisdom. He shows that it would not be fitting for them to fast so long as he, their Bridegroom, was with them. But he does not stop there. He goes on to show, by two parables, that young beginners in the school of Christianity must be dealt with gently. They must be taught what they are able to bear: they must not be expected to receive everything at once. To neglect this rule would be as unwise as to "pour new wine into old wineskins" (verse 17), or to sew "a patch of unshrunk cloth on an old garment" (verse 16).

There is a mine of deep wisdom in this principle, and everyone would do well to remember it in the spiritual teaching of those who are young in experience. We must be careful not to attach an excessive importance to the lesser things of religion; we must not be in a hurry to require a minute conformity to one rigid rule in things immaterial, until the first principles of repentance and faith have been thoroughly learned. To guide us in this matter, we have great need to pray for grace and Christian common sense. Tact in dealing with young disciples is a rare gift, but a very useful one. To know what to insist on as absolutely necessary from the first – and what to reserve, as a lesson to be learned when the learner has come to more perfect knowledge – is one of the highest attainments of a teacher of souls.

3. Encouragement to the humblest faith

Third, let us notice what encouragement our Lord gives to the humblest faith.

We read in this passage that a woman sorely afflicted with disease came behind our Lord in the crowd, and "touched the edge" of his garment in the hope that by so doing she would be healed (verses 20–21). She said not a word to obtain help; she made no public confession of faith; but she had confidence that if she could only "touch his cloak" she would be made well (verse 21). And so it happened. There lay hidden in that act of hers a seed of precious faith, which obtained our

Lord's commendation. She was made whole at once, and returned home in peace. To use the words of a good old writer, "she came trembling, and went back triumphing."

Let us treasure this story in our minds; it may perhaps help us mightily in some hour of need. Our faith may be feeble; our courage may be small; our grasp of the Gospel, and its promises, may be weak and trembling – but, after all, the grand question is, Do we really trust only in Christ? Do we look to Jesus, and only to Jesus, for pardon and peace? If so, that is good. If we may not touch his cloak, we can touch his heart. Such faith saves the soul. Weak faith is less strengthening than strong faith: weak faith will carry us to heaven with far less joy than full assurance; but weak faith gives an interest in Christ as surely as strong faith. The person who only touches the edge of Christ's cloak will never perish.

4. Christ's almighty power

Fourth, let us notice in this passage our Lord's almighty power. He restores to life someone who was dead.

How wonderful that sight must have been! Who that has ever seen the dead can forget the stillness, the silence, the coldness, when the breath has left the body? Who can forget the awful feeling that a mighty change has taken place, and a mighty gulf been placed between ourselves and the departed? But look! Our Lord goes to the room where the dead person lies, and calls the spirit back to its earthly shelter. The pulse once more beats; the eyes once more see; the breath once more comes and goes. The ruler's daughter is once more alive, and restored to her father and mother. This was omnipotence indeed! No one could have done this except the one who first created man, and who has all power in heaven and earth.

This is the kind of truth we can never know too well. The more clearly we see Christ's power, the more likely we are to achieve Gospel peace. Our position may be trying; our hearts may be weak; the world may be difficult to journey through; our faith may seem too small to carry us home; but let us take courage when we think on Jesus, and let us not be cast down. He who is for us is greater than all those who are against us. Our Saviour can raise the dead; our Saviour is almighty.

Two blind men healed; Christ's compassion on the crowds; the disciples' duty (9:27-38)

There are four lessons in this passage which deserve close attention. Let us mark them each in succession.

1. Strong faith where least expected

First, let us notice that strong faith in Christ may sometimes be found where it might least have been expected. Who would have thought that two blind men would have called our Lord the "Son of David" (verse 27)? They could not, of course, have seen the miracles that he did: they could only know him by common report. But the eyes of their understanding were enlightened, if their bodily eyes were dark. They saw the truth which teachers of the law and Pharisees could not see; they saw that Jesus of Nazareth was the Messiah. They believed that he was able to heal them.

An example like this shows us that we must never despair of anyone's salvation merely because he lives in a position unfavorable to his soul. Grace is stronger than circumstances: the life of religion does not depend merely upon outward advantages. The Holy Spirit can give faith, and keep faith in active exercise, without book-learning, without money, and with scanty means of grace. Without the Holy Spirit someone may know all mysteries, and live in the full blaze of the Gospel, and yet be lost. We shall see many strange sights at the last day. Poor cottagers will be found to have believed in the Son of David, while rich men, full of university learning, will prove to have lived and died, like the Pharisees, in hardened unbelief. Many that are "last will be first, and the first will be last" (Matthew 20:16).

2. Christ's experience of sickness

Second, let us notice that our Lord Jesus Christ has had great experience of disease and sickness. He "went through all the towns and villages" doing good (verse 35). He was an eye-witness of all the ills that flesh is heir to; he saw ailments of every kind, sort and description; he was brought in contact with every form of bodily suffering. None were too loathsome for him to attend to: none were too frightful for him to cure. He was a healer of "every disease and sickness" (verse 35).

There is much comfort to be drawn from this fact. We are each dwelling in a poor frail body. We never know how much suffering we may have to watch as we sit by the bedsides of beloved relatives and friends; we never know what racking complaint we ourselves may have to submit to before we lie down and die. But let us arm ourselves in good time with the precious thought that Jesus is specially fitted to be the sick man's friend. The great High Priest, to whom we must apply for pardon and peace with God, is eminently qualified to sympathize with an aching body, as well as to heal an ailing conscience. The eyes of the one who is King of kings often used to look with pity on the diseased. The world cares little for the sick, and often keeps aloof from them; but the Lord Jesus cares especially for the sick: he is the first to visit them and say, "I stand at the door and knock." Happy are those who hear his voice and open the door (Revelation 3:20)!

3. Christ's concern for neglected souls

Third, let us mark our Lord's tender concern for neglected souls. "He saw the crowds" of people when he was on earth, scattered about "like sheep without a shepherd" (verse 36), and he was moved with compassion. He saw them neglected by those who, for the time, ought to have been teachers. He saw them ignorant, hopeless, helpless, dying and unfit to die. The sight moved him to deep pity. That loving heart could not see such things and not feel.

Now what are our feelings when we see such a sight? This is the question that should arise in our minds. There are many like this to be seen on every side. There are millions of idolaters and heathen on earth – millions of deluded Muslims – millions of superstitious Roman Catholics; there are thousands of ignorant and unconverted Protestants near our own doors. Do we feel tenderly concerned about their souls? Do we deeply pity their spiritual destitution? Do we long to see that destitution relieved? These are serious inquiries, and ought to be answered. It is easy to sneer at missions to the heathen, and those who work for them; but the man who does not feel for the souls of all unconverted people can surely not have "the mind of Christ" (1 Corinthians 2:16).

4. A solemn duty

Fourth, let us mark that there is a solemn duty incumbent on all Christians who want to do good to the unconverted part of the world. They are to pray for more men to be raised up to work for the conversion of souls. It seems as if it was to be a daily part of our prayers. "Ask the Lord of the harvest, therefore, to send out workers into his harvest field" (verse 38).

If we know anything of prayer, let us make it a point of conscience never to forget this solemn charge of our Lord's. Let us settle it in our minds that it is one of the surest ways of doing good and stemming evil. Personal working for souls is good; giving money is good; but praying is best of all. By prayer we reach God, and without God work and money alike are in vain. By prayer we obtain the Holy Spirit's aid. Money can pay agents; universities can give learning; bishops may ordain; congregations may elect: but only the Holy Spirit can make ministers of the Gospel, and raise up lay workers in the spiritual harvest who need not be ashamed. Never, never may we forget that if we want to do good to the world, our first duty is to pray!

Matthew
Chapter 10

The commissioning of the first Christian preachers *(10:1–15)*

This chapter is one of particular solemnity. Here is the record of the first ordination which ever took place in the Church of Christ. The Lord Jesus chooses and sends forth the twelve apostles. Here is an account of the first charge ever delivered to newly ordained Christian ministers. The Lord Jesus himself delivers it. Never was there so important an ordination! Never was there so solemn a charge!

There are three lessons which stand out prominently on the face of the first fifteen verses of this chapter. Let us take them in order.

1. All ministers are not necessarily good
First, we are taught that all ministers are not necessarily good people. We see our Lord choosing Judas Iscariot to be one of his apostles (verse 4). Jesus knew all hearts; we cannot doubt that he knew well the characters of the men he chose; and he includes in the list of his apostles one who was a traitor!

We shall do well to bear this fact in mind. Orders do not confer the saving grace of the Holy Spirit: ordained men are not necessarily converted. We are not to regard them as infallible, either in doctrine or in practice; we are not to make popes or idols of them, and put them in Christ's place without noticing it. We are to regard them as human like ourselves (Acts 14:15), liable to the same weaknesses, and daily requiring the same grace. We are not to think it impossible for them to do very bad things; we must not expect them to be above the reach of harm from flattery, covetousness, and the world. We are to test their teaching against the Word of God, and to follow them so far as they follow

Christ, but no further. Above all, we ought to pray for them that they may be successors, not of Judas Iscariot, but of James and John. It is a serious responsibility to be a minister of the Gospel! Ministers need many prayers.

2. Christ's ministers are to do good

Second, we are taught that the great work of a minister of Christ is to do good. He is sent to seek "lost sheep," to proclaim good news, to relieve those who are suffering, to diminish sorrow, and to increase joy. His life is meant to be one of giving rather than receiving (verse 8).

This is a high standard, and a very special one. Let it be well weighed and carefully examined. It is plain, for one thing, that the life of a faithful minister of Christ cannot be one of ease. He must be ready to spend body and mind, time and strength, in the work of his calling: laziness and frivolity are bad enough in any profession, but worst of all in that of a watchman for souls. It is plain, too, that the position of the ministers of Christ is not what ignorant people sometimes assign to them, and which they, unhappily, sometimes claim for themselves. They are not so much ordained to rule as to serve; they are not so much intended to have dominion over the Church, as to meet its needs and to serve its members (2 Corinthians 1:24). Happy would it be for the cause of true religion if these things were better understood! Half the diseases of Christianity have arisen from mistaken notions about the minister's office.

3. The danger of neglecting the offers of the Gospel

Third, we are taught that it is a most dangerous thing to neglect the offers of the Gospel. It will prove "more bearable for Sodom and Gomorrah on the day of judgment" than for those who have heard Christ's truth, and not received it (verse 15).

This is a doctrine fearfully overlooked, and one that deserves serious consideration. Men are apt to forget that it does not require great open sins to be sinned in order to ruin a soul forever. They have only to go on hearing without believing, listening without repenting, going to church without going to Christ, and by and by they will find themselves in hell! We will all be judged according to our light; we will have to give account of our use of religious privileges: to hear of the "great salvation" (Hebrews 2:3) and yet neglect it, is one of the worst sins man can commit (John 16:9).

What are we doing ourselves with the Gospel? This is the question which everyone who reads this passage should put to his conscience. Let us assume that we are decent and respectable in our lives, correct and moral in all the relations of life, regular in our formal attendance on the means of grace. That is all very well so far as it goes, but is this all that can be said of us? Are we really receiving the love of the truth? Is Christ dwelling in our hearts by faith? If not, we are in fearful danger; we are far more guilty than the people of Sodom, who never heard the Gospel at all; we may awake to find that in spite of our regularity and morality and correctness, we have lost our souls to all eternity. It will not save us to have lived in the full sunshine of Christian privileges, and to have heard the Gospel faithfully preached every week. We must experience acquaintance with Christ; we must receive his truth personally; we must be united with him in life; we must become his servants and disciples. Without this, the preaching of the Gospel only adds to our responsibility, increases our guilt, and will at length sink us more deeply into hell. These are hard sayings! But the words of Scripture, which we have read, are plain and unmistakable. They are all true.

Instructions to the first Christian preachers *(10:16–23)*

The truths contained in these verses should be pondered by all who try to do good in the world. To the selfish man who cares for nothing but his own ease or comfort, there may seem to be little in them. To the minister of the Gospel, and to everyone who seeks to save souls, these verses ought to be full of interest. No doubt there is much in them which applies especially to the days of the apostles; but there is much also which applies to all times.

1. Have moderate expectations
First, we see that those who want to do good to souls must be moderate in their expectations. They must not think that universal success will attend their labors. They must reckon on meeting with much opposition; they must make up their minds to be hated (verse 22), persecuted,

and ill-used, and that too by their nearest relatives. They will often find themselves "like sheep among wolves" (verse 16).

Let us bear this in mind continually. Whether we preach, or teach, or visit from house to house, whether we write to give counsel, or whatever we do, let it be a settled principle with us not to expect more than Scripture and experience warrant. Human nature is far more wicked and corrupt than we think: the power of evil is far greater than we suppose. It is vain to imagine that everybody will see what is good for them, and believe what we tell them: that would be to expect what we shall not find, and would only end in disappointment. Happy is that laborer for Christ who knows these things as he starts and does not have to learn them by bitter experience! Here is the hidden reason why many have turned back, when they once seemed full of zeal to do good. They began with extravagant expectations; they did not "count the cost." They fell into the mistake of the great German Reformer who confessed he forgot at one time that "Old Adam was too strong for young Melanchthon."

2. Pray for wisdom

Second, we see that those who want to do good must pray for wisdom, good sense and a sound mind. Our Lord tells his disciples to be "as shrewd as snakes and as innocent as doves" (verse 16). He tells them that when they are persecuted in one place, they may legitimately "flee to another" (verse 23).

There are few of our Lord's instructions which it is so difficult to use correctly as this one. There is a line marked out for us between two extremes, but it is a line that requires great skill to define. To avoid persecution by holding our tongues and keeping our religion entirely to ourselves is one extreme: we are not to err in that direction. To court persecution and thrust our religion upon everyone we meet, without regard to place, time or circumstances, is another extreme. In this direction also we are warned not to err, any more than in the other. Truly we may say, "Who is equal to such a task?" (2 Corinthians 2:16). We need to cry to "the only God" (1 Timothy 1:17) for wisdom.

The extreme into which most men are liable to fall in the present day is that of silence, cowardice, and letting others alone. Our so-called prudence is apt to degenerate into a compromising line of conduct or downright unfaithfulness. We are only too ready to suppose that it is no use trying to do good to certain people: we excuse ourselves from efforts to benefit their souls by saying it would be indiscreet, or inexpedient, or would give needless offense, or would even do positive harm. Let us all watch and be on our guard against this spirit; laziness and the devil are often the true explanation of it. To give way to it is pleasant to flesh and blood, no doubt, and saves us much trouble: but those who give way to it often throw away great opportunities of usefulness.

On the other hand, it is impossible to deny that there is such a thing as a righteous and holy zeal, which is "not based on knowledge" (Romans 10:2). It is quite possible to create much needless offense, commit great blunders and stir up much opposition which might have been avoided by a little prudence, wise management and exercise of judgment. Let us all be sure that we are not guilty in this respect. We may be sure there is such a thing as Christian wisdom, which is quite distinct from Jesuitical subtlety or carnal policy. Let us seek this wisdom. Our Lord Jesus does not require us to throw aside our common sense when we undertake to work for him. There will be offense enough connected with our religion, do what we will; but let us not increase it without cause. Let us try to "be very careful" how we live, "not as unwise but as wise" (Ephesians 5:15).

It is to be feared that believers in the Lord Jesus do not sufficiently pray for the Spirit of knowledge, judgment, and a sound mind. They are apt to fancy that if they have grace, they have all they need. They forget that a gracious heart should pray that it may be full of wisdom, as well as of the Holy Spirit (Acts 6:3). Let us all remember this. Great grace and common sense are perhaps one of the rarest combinations: that they may go together is strikingly proved by the life of David and the ministry of the apostle Paul. In this, however, as in every other respect, our Lord Jesus Christ himself is our most perfect example: no one was ever so faithful as he, but no one was ever so truly wise. Let us make him our pattern and walk in his steps.

Warnings to the first Christian preachers (10:24–33)

To do good to souls in this world is very hard. All who try it find this out by experience: it needs a large stock of courage, faith, patience and perseverance. Satan will fight vigorously to maintain his kingdom; human nature is desperately wicked: to do harm is easy; to do good is hard.

The Lord Jesus knew this well, when he sent his disciples out to preach the Gospel for the first time. He knew what was in front of them, even if they did not. He took care to supply them with a list of encouragements in order to cheer them when they felt cast down. Weary missionaries abroad, or fainting ministers at home, disheartened schoolteachers and desponding district visitors would do well to study these nine verses often. Let us mark what they contain.

1. Do not expect a better reception than the Master

First, those who try to do good to souls must not expect to fare better than their great Master. "A student is not above his teacher, nor a servant above his master" (verse 24). The Lord Jesus was slandered and rejected by those whom he came to benefit. There was no error in his teaching; there was no defect in his method of imparting instruction, yet many hated him and called him Beelzebub (verse 25). Few believed him and cared for what he said. Surely we have no right to be surprised if we, whose best efforts are mingled with much imperfection, are treated in the same way as Christ. If we let the world alone, it will probably let us alone; but if we try to do it spiritual good, it will hate us as it did our Master.

2. Look forward to the day of judgment

Second, those who try to do good must look forward with patience to the day of judgment. "There is nothing concealed that will not be disclosed, or hidden that will not be made known" (verse 26). They must be content in this present world to be misunderstood, misrepresented, vilified, slandered and abused. They must not cease to work because their motives are mistaken and their characters fiercely assailed. They must remember continually that all will be set right at the last day: the secrets of all hearts will be revealed then. "He will make your righteousness shine like the dawn, the justice of your cause like the noonday sun" (Psalm 37:6). The purity of their intentions, the wisdom of their labors, and the rightfulness of their cause will at length be clear to all the world. Let us work on steadily and quietly. People may not understand us, and may vehemently oppose us, but the day of judgment is getting closer. We shall be vindicated at last. The Lord, when he comes again, "will bring to light what is hidden in darkness and will expose the motives of men's hearts. At that time each will receive his praise from God" (1 Corinthians 4:5).

3. Fear God more than people

Third, those who try to do good must fear God more than people. People can hurt the body, but their enmity must stop there: they can go no further. God "can destroy both soul and body in hell" (verse 28). We may be threatened with the loss of reputation, property and all that makes life enjoyable if we go on in the path of religious duty: we must not mind such threats when our course is plain. Like Daniel and the three children, we must submit to anything rather than displease God and wound our consciences. People's anger may be hard to bear, but God's anger is much harder; fear of other people does indeed bring a snare, but we must make it give way to the expulsive power of a stronger principle, namely the fear of God. It was a fine saying of good Colonel Gardiner, "I fear God, and therefore there is none else that I need fear."

4. Remember God's providential care

Fourth, those who try to do good must keep before their minds the providential care of God over them. Nothing can happen in this world without his permission. There is no such thing in reality as chance, accident or luck. "The very hairs" of their heads "are all numbered" (verse 30). The path of duty may sometimes lead them into great danger; health and life may seem to be in peril if they go forward. Let them take comfort in the thought that everything around them is in God's hand. Their bodies, their souls, their reputations are all in his safekeeping: no disease can seize them, no hand can hurt them, unless he allows. They may say boldly to every fearful thing they meet with, "You would have no power over me if it were not given to you from above" (John 19:11).

5. Remember the day of judgment

Fifth, those who try to do good should continually remember the day when they will meet their Lord to receive their final reward. If they want him to acknowledge them, and confess them before his Father's throne, they must not be ashamed to own and "acknowledge him" before the people of this world (verse 32). To do it may cost us much. It may bring us laughter, mockery, persecution and scorn; but let us not be laughed out of heaven. Let us recollect the great and dreadful day of account, and let us not be afraid to show men that we love Christ, and want them to know and love him also.

Let these encouragements be treasured up in the hearts of all who labor in Christ's cause, whatever their position may be. The Lord knows their trials, and has spoken these things for their comfort. He cares for all his believing people, but for none so much as those who work for his cause, and try to do good. May we seek to be of that number! Every believer may do something if he tries. There is always something for everyone to do. May we each have an eye to see it and a will to do it!

Cheering words to the first Christian preachers (10:34–42)

In these verses the great head of the church winds up his first charge to those whom he sends forth to make known his Gospel. He declares three great truths, which form a fitting conclusion to the whole discourse.

1. The Gospel will not always bring peace

First, he tells us to remember that his Gospel will not cause peace and agreement wherever it comes. "I did not come to bring peace, but a sword" (verse 34). The object of his first coming on earth was not to set up a millennial kingdom in which all would be of one mind, but to bring in the Gospel, which would lead to conflicts and divisions. We have no right to be surprised if we see this continually fulfilled: we are not to think it strange if the Gospel tears families apart and causes estrangement between the nearest relations. It is sure to do so in many cases, because of the deep corruption of the human heart. So long as one person believes, and another remains unbelieving, so long as one is resolved to keep his sins, and another is desirous to give them up, the result of the preaching of the Gospel must be division. For this the Gospel is not to blame, but the human heart.

There is deep truth in all this, which is constantly forgotten and overlooked. Many talk vaguely about "unity," "harmony" and "peace" in the church of Christ, as if they were things that we ought always to expect, and for the sake of which everything ought to be sacrificed! Such persons would do well to remember the words of our Lord. No doubt unity and peace are mighty blessings; we ought to seek them, pray for them and give up everything in order to obtain them, except truth and a good conscience. But it is an idle dream to suppose that the churches of Christ will enjoy much unity and peace before the millennium comes.

2. True Christians must face trouble

Second, our Lord tells us that true Christians must be ready to face trouble in this world. Whether we are ministers or hearers, whether we teach or are taught, it makes little difference: we must carry a "cross" (verse 38). We must be content to lose even life itself for Christ's sake. We must submit to the loss of people's favor, we must endure hardships, we must deny ourselves in many things or we shall never reach heaven at last. So long as the world, the devil and our own hearts are what they are, these things must be so.

We shall find it most useful to remember this lesson ourselves, and to impress it upon others. Few things do so much harm in religion as exaggerated expectations. People look for a degree of worldly comfort in Christ's service which they have no right to expect. When they do not find what they were expecting, they are tempted to give up religion in disgust. Happy is he who thoroughly understands that though Christianity holds out a crown in the end, it brings also a cross on the way.

3. God rewards the least service

Third, our Lord cheers us by saying that the least service done to those who work in his cause is observed and rewarded by God. Anyone who gives so little as "a cup of cold water to one of these little ones because he is my disciple . . . will certainly not lose his reward" (verse 42).

There is something very beautiful in this promise. It teaches us that the eyes of the great Master are always on those who labor for him and try to do good. Perhaps they seem to work on unnoticed and unregarded; the proceedings of preachers, missionaries and teachers and visitors of the poor may appear very trifling and insignificant compared with the movements of kings and parliaments, armies and statesmen; but they are not insignificant in the eyes of God. He notices who opposes his servants, and who helps them; he observes who is kind to them, as Lydia was to Paul (Acts 16:15); and who throws difficulties in their way, as Diotrephes did in the way of John (3 John 9). All their daily experience is recorded as they labor on in his harvest: everything is written down in his great book of remembrance, and will be brought to light at the last day. The chief butler forgot Joseph, when he was restored to his place; but the Lord Jesus never forgets any of his people. He will say to many who little expect it, on the resurrection morning: "I was hungry and you gave me something to eat, I was thirsty and you gave me something to drink" (Matthew 25:35).

Let us ask ourselves, as we close the chapter, in what light we regard Christ's work and Christ's cause in the world. Are we helpers of it or hinderers? Do we in any way aid the Lord's "prophets" and "righteous men" (verse 41)? Do we assist his "little ones" (verse 42)? Do we impede his laborers, or do we cheer them on? These are serious questions. People who give the "cup of cold water" whenever they have opportunity do wisely and well. People who work actively in the Lord's vineyard do better still. May we all strive to leave the world a better world than it was when we were born! This is to have the mind of Christ. This is to find out the value of the lessons this wonderful chapter contains.

Matthew
Chapter 11

Christ's testimony about John the Baptist (11:1–15)

1. John the Baptist's message
The first thing that demands our attention in this passage is the message which John the Baptist sends to our Lord Jesus Christ. He "sent his disciples to ask him, 'Are you the one who was to come, or should we expect someone else?'"

This question did not arise from doubt or unbelief on the part of John. We do that holy man injustice if we interpret it in such a way. It was asked for the benefit of his disciples: it was meant to give them an opportunity of hearing from Christ's own lips the evidence of his divine mission. No doubt John the Baptist felt that his own ministry was ended; something within him told him that he would never come out of Herod's prison, but would surely die. He remembered the ignorant jealousies that had already been shown by his disciples towards the disciples of Christ. He took the most likely course to dispel these jealousies forever: he sent his followers to "hear and see" for themselves (verse 4).

The conduct of John the Baptist in this matter affords a striking example to ministers, teachers and parents when they come near the end of their course. Their chief concern should be about the souls of those they are going to leave behind them; their great desire should be to persuade them to cling to Christ. The death of those who have guided and instructed us on earth ought always to have this effect. It should make us hold more firmly on to him who does not die any more "lives forever," and "has a permanent priesthood" (Hebrews 7:24).

2. Christ's testimony to John

The second thing that demands our notice in this passage is the high testimony which our Lord gives to the character of John the Baptist. No mortal ever received such commendation as Jesus here bestows on his imprisoned friend. "Among those born of women there has not risen anyone greater than John the Baptist" (verse 11). In time past John had boldly acknowledged Jesus publicly as the Lamb of God; now Jesus openly declares John to be more than a prophet.

There were some, no doubt, who were disposed to think lightly of John the Baptist, partly from ignorance of the nature of his ministry, partly from misunderstanding the question he had sent. Our Lord Jesus silences such cavilers by the declaration he here makes: he tells them not to suppose that John was a timid, vacillating, unstable man, "a reed swayed by the wind" (verse 7). If they thought he was, they were utterly mistaken. He was a bold, unflinching witness to the truth. Jesus tells them not to suppose that John was at heart a worldly man, fond of kings' courts and delicate living; if they thought he was, they were making a great mistake. He was a self-denying preacher of repentance, who would risk the anger of a king rather than not reprove his sins. In short, Jesus would have them know that John was "more than a prophet" (verse 9). He was one to whom God had given more honor than to all the Old Testament prophets. Certainly they prophesied about Christ, but they died without seeing him; John not only prophesied of him, but saw him face to face. They foretold that the days of the Son of Man would certainly come, and the Messiah appear; John was an actual eyewitness of those days, and an honored instrument in preparing people for them. The prophets predicted that the Messiah would be "led like a lamb to the slaughter" (Isaiah 53:7) and "cut off" (Daniel 9:26); John pointed to him and said, "Look, the Lamb of God, who takes away the sin of the world!" (John 1:29).

There is something very beautiful and comforting to true Christians in this testimony which our Lord bears to John the Baptist. It shows us the tender interest which our great Head feels in the lives and characters of all his members; it shows us what honor he is ready to give the work and labor that they go through in his cause. It is a sweet foretaste of the acknowledgment which he will make of them before the assembled world when he presents them faultless on the last day before his Father's throne.

Do we know what it is to work for Christ? Have we ever felt cast down and dispirited, as if we were doing no good, and no one cared for us? Are we ever tempted to feel, when laid aside by sickness, or withdrawn by providence, "I have labored in vain, and spent my strength for nothing"? Let us meet such thoughts by the recollection of this passage. Let us remember there is one who daily records all we do for him and sees more beauty in his servants' work than his servants do themselves. The same tongue which bore testimony to John in prison will bear testimony to all his people on the last day. He will say, "Come, you who are blessed by my Father; take your inheritance, the kingdom prepared for you since the creation of the world" (Matthew 25:34). And then his faithful witnesses will discover, to their wonder and surprise, that there was never a word spoken on their Master's behalf which does not receive a reward.

The unreasonableness of unbelievers; the danger of not using the light (11:16–24)

These sayings of the Lord Jesus were occasioned by the state of the Jewish nation when he was on earth. But they speak loudly to us also, as well as to the Jews. They throw great light on some parts of the natural human character; they teach us the perilous state of many immortal souls in the present day.

1. The unreasonableness of unconverted people
The first part of these verses shows us the unreasonableness of many unconverted people in the things of religion. The Jews, in our Lord's time, found fault with every teacher whom God sent among them. First came John the Baptist preaching repentance: an austere man, a man who withdrew himself from society and lived an ascetic life. Did this satisfy the Jews? No! They found fault and said, "He has a demon" (verse 18). Then came Jesus the Son of God preaching the Gospel: living as other men lived, and practicing none of John the Baptist's special austerities. And did this satisfy the Jews? No! They found fault again,

and said, "Here is a glutton and a drunkard, a friend of tax collectors and 'sinners'" (verse 19). In short, they were as perverse and hard to please as wayward children.

It is a sad fact that there are always thousands of people who claim to be Christians but are just as unreasonable as these Jews. They are equally perverse and equally hard to please: whatever we teach and preach, they find fault; whatever our manner of life, they are dissatisfied. Do we tell them of salvation by grace, and justification by faith? At once they cry out against our doctrine as licentious and Antinomian. Do we tell them of the holiness which the Gospel requires? At once they exclaim that we are too strict, pedantic and over-righteous. Are we cheerful? They accuse us of levity. Are we serious? They call us gloomy and sour. Do we keep aloof from balls and races and plays? They denounce us as puritanical, exclusive and narrow-minded. Do we eat and drink and dress like other people, and attend to our worldly callings, and go into society? They sneeringly insinuate that they see no difference between us and those who make no religious profession at all, and that we are no better than other people. What is all this but the conduct of the Jews over again? "We played the flute for you, and you did not dance; we sang a dirge, and you did not mourn" (verse 17). The one who spoke these words knew the hearts of men!

The plain truth is that true believers must not expect unconverted men to be satisfied either with their faith or their practice. If they do, they expect what they will not find. They must be prepared for objections, cavils and excuses, however holy their own lives may be. As Quesnel so rightly says, "Whatever measures good men take, they will never escape the censures of the world. The best way is not to be concerned at them." After all, what does Scripture say? "The sinful mind is hostile to God" (Romans 8:7). "The man without the Spirit does not accept the things that come from the Spirit of God" (1 Corinthians 2:14). This is the explanation of the whole matter.

2. The wickedness of deliberate impenitence
The second part of these verses shows us the exceeding wickedness of willful impenitence. Our Lord declares (verse 22) that it will be "more

bearable for Tyre and Sidon on the day of judgment" than for those towns where people had heard his sermons, and seen his miracles, but had not repented.

There is something very solemn in this saying. Let us look at it carefully. Let us think for a moment what dark, idolatrous, immoral, profligate places Tyre and Sidon must have been. Let us call to mind the unspeakable wickedness of Sodom. Let us remember that the cities named by our Lord – Korazin, Bethsaida and Capernaum – were probably no worse than other Jewish towns, and, at all events, were far better and more moral than Tyre, Sidon and Sodom. And then let us observe that the people of Korazin, Bethsaida and Capernaum are to be in the lowest hell because they had heard the Gospel and yet did not repent, because they had great religious advantages and did not use them. How awful this sounds!

Surely these words ought to make the ears of everyone tingle, if they hear the Gospel regularly, and yet remain unconverted. How great is the guilt of a person like this before God! How great is the danger in which he daily stands! Moral, decent and respectable as his life may be, he is actually more guilty than an idolatrous Tyrian or Sidonian, or a miserable inhabitant of Sodom! They had no spiritual light: he has, and neglects it. They heard no Gospel: he hears, but does not obey it. Their hearts might have been softened if they had enjoyed his privileges: Tyre and Sidon "would have repented" (verse 21), Sodom "would have remained to this day" (verse 23). His heart under the full blaze of the Gospel remains hard and unmoved. There is only one painful conclusion to be drawn: his guilt will be found greater than theirs at the last day. The remark of an English bishop is true, that "among all the aggravations of our sins, there is none more heinous than the frequent hearing of our duty."

May we all think often about Korazin, Bethsaida and Capernaum! Let us settle it in our minds that it will never do to be content with merely hearing and liking the Gospel. We must go further than this, we must actually "repent . . . and turn to God" (Acts 3:19). We must actually take hold of Christ, and become one with him. Till then we are in awful danger. It will prove more tolerable to have lived in Tyre, Sidon and Sodom than to have heard the Gospel in our own country and at last die unconverted.

Christ's greatness; the fullness of Gospel invitations *(11:25–30)*

There are few passages in the four Gospels more important than this. There are few which contain so many precious truths in so short a compass. May God give us an eye to see, and a heart to feel their value!

1. A childlike and teachable frame of mind

First, let us learn the excellence of a childlike and teachable frame of mind. Our Lord says to his Father, "You have hidden these things from the wise and learned, and revealed them to little children" (verse 25).

It is not for us to attempt to explain why some receive and believe the Gospel, while others do not. The sovereignty of God in this matter is a deep mystery: we cannot fathom it. But one thing, at all events, stands out in Scripture as a great practical truth to be remembered always. Those from whom the Gospel is hidden are generally "the wise in their own eyes, and clever in their own sight"; those to whom the Gospel is revealed are generally humble, simple-minded, and willing to learn. The words of the Virgin Mary are continually being fulfilled: "He has filled the hungry with good things but has sent the rich away empty" (Luke 1:53).

Let us watch against pride in every shape, pride of intellect, pride of wealth, pride in our own goodness, pride in our own deserts. Nothing is so likely to keep a man out of heaven, and prevent him seeing Christ, as pride. So long as we think we are something we shall never be saved. Let us pray for and cultivate humility; let us seek to know ourselves aright, and to find out our place in the sight of a holy God. The beginning of the way to heaven is to feel that we are on the way to hell, and to be willing to be taught by the Spirit. One of the first steps in saving Christianity is to be able to say with Saul, "Lord, what will you have me do?" (see Acts 9:6). There is hardly a sentence of our Lord's so frequently repeated as this: "He who humbles himself will be exalted" (Luke 18:14).

2. The greatness and majesty of Jesus Christ

Second, let us learn from these verses the greatness and majesty of our Lord Jesus Christ.

The language of our Lord on this subject is deep and wonderful. He says, "All things have been committed to me by my Father. No one knows the Son except the Father, and no one knows the Father except the Son and those to whom the Son chooses to reveal him" (verse 27). We may truly say, as we read these words, "Such knowledge is too wonderful for me, too lofty for me to attain" (Psalm 139:6). We see something of the perfect union which exists between the first and second Persons of the Trinity; we see something of the immeasurable superiority of the Lord Jesus to all who are nothing more than human. But when we have said all this, we must confess that there are heights and depths in this verse which are beyond our feeble comprehension. We can only admire them in the spirit of little children, but the half, we must feel, remains untold.

Let us, however, draw from these words the great practical truth that all power over everything that concerns our soul's interests is placed in our Lord Jesus Christ's hands. "All things have been committed to" him. He carries the keys: to him we must go for admission into heaven. He is the door: through him we must enter. He is the Shepherd: we must hear his voice and follow him if we do not want to perish in the wilderness. He is the Physician: we must apply to him if we want to be healed of the plague of sin. He is the bread of life: we must feed on him if we want to have our souls satisfied. He is the light: we must follow him if we do not want to wander in darkness. He is the fountain: we must wash in his blood if we want to be cleansed and made ready for the great day of account. Blessed and glorious are these truths! If we have Christ, we have all things (1 Corinthians 3:22).

3. The breadth and the Gospel invitations

Third, let us learn from this passage the breadth and fullness of the invitations of Christ's Gospel.

The three last verses of the chapter, which contain this lesson, are indeed precious. They meet the trembling sinner who asks, "Will Christ reveal his Father's love to someone like me?" with the most gracious encouragement. They are verses which deserve to be read with special attention. For 1900 years they have been a blessing to the world, and have done good to myriads of souls. There is not a sentence in them which does not contain a mine of thought.

We should notice whom Jesus invites. He does not address those who feel themselves righteous and worthy. He addresses "all you who are weary and burdened" (verse 28). It is a wide description; it comprises multitudes in this weary world. All who feel a load on their heart which they want to be free of, a load of sin or a load of sorrow, a load of anxiety or a load of remorse – all, whoever they may be and whatever their past lives, all these people are invited to come to Christ.

We should notice what a gracious offer Jesus makes: "I will give you rest. . . . You will find rest for your souls" (verses 28–29). How cheering and comforting are these words! Unrest is one great characteristic of the world: hurry, vexation, failure, disappointment stare us in the face on every side. But here is hope: there is an ark of refuge for the weary, as truly as there was for Noah's dove. There is rest in Christ, rest of conscience, and rest of heart, rest built on pardon of all sin, rest flowing from peace with God.

We should note what a simple request Jesus makes to the weary and burdened ones. "Come to me. . . . Take my yoke upon you and learn from me" (verses 28–29). He imposes no hard conditions; he does not say anything about work to be done first, or establishing whether we deserve his gifts: he only asks us to come to him just as we are, with all our sins, and to submit ourselves like little children to his teaching. "Do not go," he seems to say, "to other people for relief. Do not wait for help to come from any other quarter. Just as you are, this very day, come to me."

We should note what an encouraging account Jesus gives of himself. He says, "I am gentle and humble in heart" (verse 29). How true that is. The experience of all the saints of God has often proved it. Mary and Martha at Bethany, Peter after his fall, the disciples after the resurrection, Thomas after his cold unbelief, all tasted the gentleness and humility of Christ. It is the only place in Scripture where the "heart" of Christ is actually named. It is a saying never to be forgotten.

4. Serving Jesus

Fourth, we should note the encouraging account that Jesus gives of his service. He says, "My yoke is easy and my burden is light" (verse 30). No doubt there is a cross to be carried, if we follow Christ; no doubt there are trials to be endured, and battles to be fought; but the comforts of the Gospel far outweigh the cross. Compared to the service of the world and sin, compared to the yoke of Jewish ceremonies and the bondage of human superstition, Christ's service is in the highest sense easy and light. His yoke is no more a burden than the feathers are to a bird; his commands are not burdensome (1 John 5:3); his ways are pleasant ways, and all his paths are peace (see Proverbs 3:17).

And now comes the solemn inquiry, "Have we accepted this invitation for ourselves? Have we no sins to be forgiven, no griefs to be removed, no wounds of conscience to be healed?" Let us hear Christ's voice: he speaks to us as well as to the Jews. He says, "Come unto me." Here is the key to true happiness; here is the secret of having a light heart. Everything turns and hinges on an acceptance of this offer of Christ.

May we never be satisfied till we know and feel that we have come to Christ by faith for rest, and do still come to him for fresh supplies of grace every day! If we have come to him already, let us learn to cling to him more closely. If we have never come to him yet, let us begin to come today. His word shall never be broken: "whoever comes to me I will never drive away" (John 6:37).

Matthew
Chapter 12

The true doctrine of the Sabbath *(12:1–13)*

The one great subject which stands out prominently in this passage of Scripture is the Sabbath day. It is a subject on which strange opinions prevailed among the Jews in our Lord's time. The Pharisees had added to the teaching of Scripture about it, and overlaid the true character of the day with the traditions of men. It is a subject on which diverse opinions have often been held in the churches of Christ, and wide differences exist at the present time. Let us see what we may learn about it from our Lord's teaching in these verses.

1. Christ does not end the Sabbath
First, let us learn from this passage that our Lord Jesus Christ does not do away with the observance of a weekly Sabbath day, either here or elsewhere in the four Gospels. We often find his opinion expressed about Jewish errors on the subject of the Sabbath; but we do not find a word to teach us that his disciples were not to keep a Sabbath at all.

It is of much importance to observe this. The mistakes that have arisen from a superficial consideration of our Lord's sayings on the Sabbath question are neither few nor small; thousands have rushed to the hasty conclusion that Christians have nothing to do with the fourth commandment, and that it is no more binding on us than the Mosaic law about sacrifices. There is nothing in the New Testament to justify any such conclusion.

The plain truth is that our Lord did not abolish the law of the weekly Sabbath: he only freed it from incorrect interpretations, and purified it from human additions. He did not tear out of the decalogue the fourth commandment: he only stripped it of the miserable traditions with which the Pharisees had incrusted the day, and by which they had made it not a blessing but a burden. He left the fourth commandment where he found it, a part of the eternal law of God, of which not the smallest letter, not the least stroke of a pen, was ever to pass away. May we never forget this!

2. Christ allows works of necessity and mercy on the Sabbath

Second, let us learn from this passage that our Lord Jesus Christ allows all works of real necessity and mercy to be done on the Sabbath day.

This is a principle which is abundantly established in the passage of Scripture we are now considering. We find our Lord justifying his disciples for plucking the heads of grain on a Sabbath. It was an act permitted in Scripture (Deuteronomy 23:25). They "were hungry" and in need of food (verse 1), therefore they were not to blame. We find him maintaining the lawfulness of healing a sick man on the Sabbath day (verses 11–12). The man was suffering from disease and pain. In such a case it was no breach of God's commandment to afford relief. We ought never to rest from doing good.

The arguments by which our Lord supports the lawfulness of any work of necessity and mercy on the Sabbath are striking and unanswerable. He reminds the Pharisees, who charge him and his disciples with breaking the law, how David and his men, for want of other food, had eaten the bread of the Presence out of the tabernacle. He reminds them how the priests in the temple are obliged to do work on the Sabbath by slaying animals and offering sacrifices (verse 5). He reminds them how even a sheep would be helped out of a pit on the Sabbath, rather than be allowed to suffer and die, by any one of themselves (verse 11). Above all, he lays down the great principle that no ordinance of God is to be pressed so far as to make us neglect the plain duties of love. "I desire mercy, not sacrifice" (verse 7). The first tablet of the law is not to be so interpreted as to make us break the second. The fourth commandment is not to be so explained so that we are unkind and unmerciful to our neighbor. There is deep wisdom in all this. We are reminded of the saying, "No one ever spoke the way this man does" (John 7:46).

In leaving the subject, let us beware that we are never tempted to take low views of the sanctity of the Christian Sabbath. Let us take care that we do not make our gracious Lord's teaching an excuse for profaning the Sabbath. Let us not abuse the liberty which he has so clearly marked out for us, and pretend that we do things on the Sabbath from "necessity and mercy," which in reality we do for our own selfish gratification.

There is great reason for warning people on this point. The mistakes of the Pharisee about the Sabbath were in one direction; the mistakes of the Christian are in another. The Pharisee pretended to add to the holiness of the day; the Christian is too often disposed to take away from that holiness, and to keep the day in an idle, profane, irreverent manner. May we all watch our own conduct on this subject! Saving Christianity is closely bound up with Sabbath observance. May we never forget that our great aim should be to "keep the Sabbath holy" (see Exodus 20:8). Works of necessity may be done: "It is lawful to do good" (verse 12) and show mercy; but to give the Sabbath to idleness, pleasure-seeking, or the world, is utterly unlawful. It is contrary to the example of Christ, and a sin against a plain commandment of God.

Wickedness of the Pharisees; Christ's character *(12:14–21)*

1. The wickedness of the human heart
The first thing which demands our notice in this passage is the desperate wickedness of the human heart, which it exemplifies. Silenced and defeated by our Lord's arguments, the Pharisees plunged deeper and deeper into sin. They "went out and plotted how they might kill Jesus" (verse 14).

What evil had our Lord done, that he should be so treated? None, none at all. No charge could be brought against his life. He was holy, harmless, undefiled, and separate from sinners; his days were spent in doing good. No charge could be brought against his teaching. He had proved it to be consistent with Scripture and reason, and no reply had been made to his proofs. But it mattered little how perfectly he lived or taught: he was hated.

This is human nature appearing in its true colors! The unconverted heart hates God, and will show its hatred whenever it dares, and has a favorable opportunity. It will persecute God's witnesses; it will dislike all who have anything of God's mind and are renewed after his image. Why were so many of the prophets killed? Why were the names of the apostles cast out as evil by the Jews? Why were the early martyrs slain? Why were John Hus, Jerome of Prague, Ridley and Latimer burned at the stake? Not for any sins that they had sinned, not for any wickedness they had committed. They all suffered because they were godly men. And human nature, unconverted, hates godly men because it hates God.

It must never surprise true Christians if they meet with the same treatment that the Lord Jesus met with. "Do not be surprised, my brothers, if the world hates you" (1 John 3:13). They will not escape natural human enmity by the utmost consistency or the closest walk with God. They need not torture their consciences by fancying that if they were only more faultless and consistent, everybody would surely love them. That would be a mistake. They should remember that there was only one perfect man on earth, and that he was not loved but hated. It is not the infirmities of believers that the world dislikes, but their godliness; it is not the remains of the old nature that excite the world's enmity, but seeing the new nature. Let us remember these things, and be patient. The world hated Christ, and the world will hate Christians.

2. Christ's character

The second thing which demands our notice in this passage is the encouraging description of our Lord Jesus Christ's character, which St. Matthew draws from the prophet Isaiah. "A bruised reed he will not break, and a smoldering wick he will not snuff out" (verse 20).

What are we to understand by the bruised reed and smoldering wick? The language of the prophet no doubt is figurative. What is it that these two expressions mean? The simplest explanation seems to be that the Holy Spirit is here describing people whose grace is at present weak, whose repentance is feeble, and whose faith is small. Towards such persons the Lord Jesus Christ will be very tender and compassionate. Weak as the bruised reed is, it will not be broken; small as the spark of fire may be within the smoldering wick, it will not be quenched. It is a standing truth in the kingdom of grace that weak grace, weak faith and weak repentance are all precious in our Lord's sight. Mighty as he is, he "does not despise men" (Job 36:5).

The doctrine here laid down is full of comfort and consolation. There are thousands in every church of Christ to whom it ought to speak peace and hope. There are some in every congregation hearing the Gospel who are ready to despair of their own salvation because their strength seems so small. They are full of fears and despondency because their knowledge, faith, hope and love appear so dwarfish and diminutive. Let them drink comfort out of this text; let them know that weak faith gives a man as real and true an interest in Christ as strong faith, though it may not give him the same joy. There is life in an infant as truly as in an adult; there is fire in a spark as truly as in a burning flame. The least degree of grace is an everlasting possession. It comes down from heaven; it is precious in our Lord's eyes. It will never be overthrown.

Does Satan make light of the beginnings of repentance towards God, and faith towards our Lord Jesus Christ? No, indeed he does not! He is very angry because he sees his time is short. Do the angels of God think lightly of the first signs of penitence and feeling after God in Christ? No, indeed, "there is rejoicing" among them when they see it (Luke 15:10)! Does the Lord Jesus only regard faith and repentance with interest if they are strong and mighty? No, indeed! As soon that "bruised reed," Saul of Tarsus, begins to cry to him, he sends Ananias to him, saying: "he is praying" (Acts 9:11). We make a great mistake if we do not encourage the very first movements of a soul towards Christ. Let the ignorant world scoff and mock, if it wants to; we may be sure that "bruised reeds" and "smoldering wicks" are very precious in our Lord's eyes.

May we all lay these things to heart, and use them in time of need, both for ourselves and others! It should be a standing maxim in our religion, that a spark is better than utter darkness, and little faith better than no faith at all. "Who despises the day of small things?" (Zechariah 4:10.) It is not despised by Christ. It ought not to be despised by Christians.

Blasphemy; sins against knowledge; idle words (12:22–37)

This passage of Scripture contains "things hard to be understood." The sin against the Holy Spirit in particular has never been fully explained by the most learned divines. It is not difficult to show from Scripture what the sin is not, but it is difficult to show clearly what it is. We must not be surprised. The Bible would not be the book of God, if it had not deep places here and there, which we have no line to fathom. Let us rather thank God that there are lessons of wisdom to be gathered, even out of these verses, which the unlearned may easily understand.

1. The prejudiced blaspheme against religion

First, let us gather from them that there is nothing too blasphemous for hardened and prejudiced people to say against religion. Our Lord casts out a devil, and at once the Pharisees declare that he does it "by . . . the prince of demons" (verse 24).

This was an absurd charge. Our Lord shows that it was unreasonable to suppose that the devil would help to pull down his own kingdom, and "Satan drive out Satan" (verse 26). But there is nothing too absurd and unreasonable for men to say when they are thoroughly set against religion. The Pharisees are not the only people who have lost sight of logic, good sense and temper when they have attacked the Gospel of Christ.

Strange as this charge may sound, it is one that has often been made against the servants of God. Their enemies have been obliged to confess that they are doing a work, and producing an effect on the world. The results of Christian labor stare them in the face and they cannot deny them. What then can they say? They say the very thing that the Pharisees said of our Lord, "It is the devil." The early heretics used language of this kind about Athanasius, the Roman Catholics spread reports of this sort about Martin Luther. Such things will be said as long as the world stands.

We must never be surprised to hear of dreadful charges being made against the best of men, without cause. "If they called the Master of the house Beelzebub, how much more shall they call them of his household?" It is an old device. When the Christian's arguments cannot be answered, and the Christian's works cannot be denied, the last resource of the wicked is to try to blacken the Christian's character. If this is our lot, let us bear it patiently. Having Christ and a good conscience, we may be content; false charges will not keep us out of heaven. Our character will be cleared at the last day.

2. Impossible to be neutral in religion

Second, let us gather from these verses the impossibility of neutrality in religion. "He who is not with me is against me, and he who does not gather with me scatters," says our Lord (verse 30).

There are many people in every age of the church, who need to have this lesson pressed upon them. They endeavor to steer a middle course in religion; they are not so bad as many sinners, but still they are not saints. They feel the truth of Christ's Gospel when it is brought before them; but they are afraid to acknowlege what they feel. Because they have these feelings, they flatter themselves they are not so bad as others, and yet they shrink from the standard of faith and practice which the Lord Jesus sets up. They are not boldly fighting on Christ's side, and yet they are not openly against him. Our Lord warns all such people that they are in a dangerous position. There are only two parties in religious matters, there are only two camps, there are only two sides. Are we with Christ, and working in his cause? If not, we are against him. Are we doing good in the world? If not, we are doing harm.

The principle here laid down is one which it concerns us all to remember. Let us settle it in our minds that we shall never have peace and do good to others unless we are thorough-going and decided in our Christianity. The way of Gamaliel never yet brought happiness and usefulness to anyone, and never will.

3. Sins against knowledge

Third, let us gather from these verses the exceeding sinfulness of sins against knowledge.

This is a practical conclusion which appears to flow naturally from our Lord's words about the blasphemy against the Holy Spirit. Difficult as these words undoubtedly are, they seem fairly to prove that there are degrees in sin. Offenses arising from ignorance of the true mission of the Son of man will not be punished so heavily as offenses committed against the noontide light of the dispensation of the Holy Spirit. The brighter the light, the greater the guilt of the person who rejects it; the clearer a person's knowledge of the nature of the Gospel, the greater the sin in willfully refusing to repent and believe.

The doctrine which is taught here is one that does not stand alone in Scripture. We read in the letter to the Hebrews: "It is impossible for those who have once been enlightened . . . if they fall away, to be brought back to repentance. . . . If we deliberately keep on sinning after we have received the knowledge of the truth, no sacrifice for sins is left, but only a fearful expectation of judgment" (Hebrews 6:4, 6; 10:26–27). It is a doctrine of which we find sad proofs in every place. The unconverted children of godly parents, the unconverted servants of godly families and the unconverted members of evangelical congregations are the hardest people on earth to impress. They seem past feeling. The same fire which melts the wax hardens the clay. It is a doctrine, moreover, which receives awful confirmation from the stories of some whose last ends were eminently hopeless. Pharaoh, Saul, Ahab, Judas Iscariot, the Emperor Julian and Francis Spira are fearful illustrations of our Lord's meaning. In each of these cases there was a combination of clear knowledge and deliberate rejection of Christ. In each there was light in the head, but hatred of truth in the heart. And the end of each seems to have been "blackest darkness . . . forever" (Jude 13).

May God give us a will to use our knowledge, whether it be little or great! May we beware of neglecting our opportunities, and of not making the best use of our privileges! Have we light? Then let us live fully up to our light. Do we know the truth? Then let us walk in the truth. This is the best safeguard against the unpardonable sin.

4. Carefulness about our daily words

Fourth, let us gather from these verses the immense importance of carefulness about our daily words. Our Lord tells us that people "will have to give account on the day of judgment for every careless word they have spoken" (verse 36). And he adds, "By your words you will be acquitted, and by your words you will be condemned" (verse 37).

There are few of our Lord's sayings which are so heart-searching as this. There is nothing, perhaps, to which most people pay less attention than their words. They go through their daily work, speaking and talking without thought or reflection, and seem to fancy that if they *do* what is right, it matters very little what they *say*.

But is it so? Are our words so utterly trifling and unimportant? We dare not say so with such a passage of Scripture as this before our eyes. Our words are the evidence of the state of our hearts, as surely as the taste of the water is an evidence of the state of the spring. "Out of the overflow of the heart the mouth speaks" (verse 34). The lips only utter what the mind conceives. Our words will form one subject of inquiry at the day of judgment: we shall have to give account of our sayings, as well as of our doings. Truly these are very solemn considerations. If there were no other text in the Bible, this passage ought to convince us that we are all "guilty before God," and need a righteousness better than our own, namely the righteousness of Christ (see Philippians 3:9).

Let us be humble as we read this passage and recollect time past. How many idle, foolish, vain, light, frivolous, sinful and unprofitable things we have all said! How many words we have used which, like thistle-down, have flown far and wide and sown mischief in the hearts of others that will never die! How often when we have met our friends, "our conversation," to use an old saint's expression, "has only made work for repentance." There is deep truth in the remark of Burkitt, "A profane scoff or atheistical jest may stick in the minds of those who hear it, after the tongue that spake it is dead. A word spoken is physically transient, but morally permanent." "The tongue," says Solomon, "has the power of life and death" (Proverbs 18:21).

Let us be watchful as we read this passage about words, when we look forward to our days yet to come; let us resolve, by God's grace, to be more careful over our tongues, and more particular about our use of them; let us pray daily that our "conversation be always full of grace" (Colossians 4:6). Let us say every morning with holy David, "I will watch my ways and keep my tongue from sin" (Psalm 39:1). Let us cry with him to the Strong One for strength, and say: "Set a guard over my mouth, O LORD; keep watch over the door of my lips" (Psalm 141:3). Well indeed might St. James say, "If anyone is never at fault in what he says, he is a perfect man" (James 3:2).

The power of unbelief (12:38–42)

This is one of those places which strikingly illustrate the truth of Old Testament history. Our Lord speaks of the Queen of the South as a real, true person, who had lived and died (verse 42). He refers to the story of Jonah, and his miraculous preservation in the huge fish's belly, as undeniable matters of fact (verse 40). Let us remember this if we hear people professing to believe the writers of the New Testament, and yet sneering at the things recorded in the Old Testament as if they were fables. Such people forget that in so doing they pour contempt upon Christ himself. The authority of the Old Testament and the authority of the New stand or fall together; the same Spirit who inspired the evangelists to write of Christ also inspired men to write of Solomon and Jonah. These are not unimportant points in this day: let them be well fixed in our minds.

The practical lesson which demands our attention in these verses is the amazing power of unbelief.

We should mark how the scribes and Pharisees call upon our Lord to show them more miracles. "Teacher, we want to see a miraculous sign from you" (verse 38). They pretended that they only wanted more evidence in order to be convinced and become disciples: they shut their eyes to the many wonderful works which Jesus had already done. It was not enough for them that he had healed the sick, and cleansed the lepers, raised the dead, and driven out demons: they were not yet persuaded; they yet demanded more proof. They would not see what our Lord plainly pointed at in his reply – that they had no real *will* to believe. There was evidence enough to convince them, but they had no wish to be convinced.

There are many in the church of Christ who are exactly in the state of these teachers of the law and Pharisees. They flatter themselves that they only require a little more proof to become committed Christians. They fancy that if their reason and intellect could only be met with some additional arguments, they would at once give up all for Christ's sake, take up the cross, and follow him. But in the meantime they wait. Alas, for their blindness! They will not see that there is abundance of evidence on every side of them. The truth is that they do not want to be convinced.

May we all be on our guard against the spirit of unbelief: it is a growing evil in these latter days. Lack of simple childlike faith is an increasing feature of the times, in every rank of society. The true explanation of a hundred strange things that startle us in the conduct of leading men in churches and states is downright lack of faith. Men who do not believe all that God says in the Bible must necessarily take a vacillating and undecided line on moral and religious questions. "If you do not stand firm in your faith, you will not stand at all" (Isaiah 7:9).

The danger of an imperfect religious reformation *(12:43–45)*

The practical lesson which meets us in these verses is the immense danger of a partial and imperfect religious reformation.

We should note what an awful picture our Lord draws of the man to whom the unclean spirit returns after having once left him. How fearful are those words: "I will return to the house I left" (verse 44). How vivid that description: "It finds the house unoccupied, swept clean and put in order" (verse 44). How tremendous the conclusion: "It goes and takes with it seven other spirits more wicked than itself, and . . . the final condition of that man is worse than the first" (verse 45). It is a picture most painfully full of meaning. Let us scan it closely, and learn wisdom.

1. The Jewish church and nation

It is certain that we have in this picture the history of the Jewish church and nation at the time of our Lord's coming. They were at first called out of Egypt to be God's special people, yet they never seem to have wholly lost the tendency to worship idols. Afterwards they were redeemed from the captivity of Babylon, yet they never seem to have rendered to God a due return for his goodness. They had been aroused by John the Baptist's preaching, yet their repentance appears to have been only skin-deep. At the time when our Lord spoke they had become, as a nation, hardy and more perverse than ever. The grossness of idol-worship had given place to the deadness of mere formality: "seven other spirits worse than the first" had taken possession of them. Their last state was rapidly becoming worse than the first: another forty years, and their iniquity came to the full. They madly plunged into a war with Rome; Judea became a very Babel of confusion; Jerusalem was taken; the temple was destroyed: the Jews were scattered over the face of the earth.

2. The Christian churches

Again it is highly probable that we have in this picture the history of the whole body of Christian churches. They were set free from heathen darkness by the preaching of the Gospel, yet they have never really lived up to their light. Many of them were revived at the time of the Protestant Reformation, yet they have none of them made a right use of their privileges, or "gone on to perfection": they have all more or less stopped short and rested on their oars. They have all been too ready to be satisfied with mere external amendments. And now there are painful symptoms in many quarters that the "evil spirit" has returned to his house, and is preparing an outbreak of unfaithfulness and false doctrine, such as the churches have never yet seen. Between unbelief in some quarters, and formal superstition in others, everything seems ripe for some fearful manifestation of antichrist. It may well be feared that "the final condition" of the professing Christian churches will prove "worse than the first."

3. The individual soul

Saddest and worst of all, we have in this picture the history of many an individual's soul. There are people who seemed at one time of their lives to be under the influence of strong religious feelings: they reformed their ways; they laid aside many things that were bad; they took up many things that were good. But they stopped there, and went no further, and by and by gave up religion altogether. The evil spirit returned to their hearts, and found them "unoccupied, swept clean and put in order." They are now worse than they ever were before. Their consciences seem seared; their sense of religious things appears entirely destroyed – they are like people given over to a reprobate mind. One would say it was "impossible" for them to be "brought back to repentance" (Hebrews 6:4–6). No one proves so hopelessly wicked as those who after experiencing strong religious convictions have gone back again to sin and the world.

If we love life, let us pray that these lessons may be deeply impressed on our minds. Let us never be content with a partial reformation of life, without thorough conversion to God, and mortification of the whole body of sin. It is a good thing to try to drive sin out of our hearts, but let us take care that we also receive the grace of God in its place. Let us make sure that we not only get rid of the old tenant, the devil, but have also got the Holy Spirit dwelling in us.

Christ's love of his disciples (12:46–50)

The practical lesson which meets us in these verses is the tender affection with which the Lord Jesus regards his true disciples.

We should note how he speaks about everyone who does the will of his Father in heaven. He says they are "my brother and sister and mother" (verse 50). What gracious words these are! Who can conceive the depth of our dear Lord's love towards his blood relatives? It was a pure, unselfish love. It must have been a mighty love, a love that passes man's understanding. Yet here we see that all his believing people are counted as his relatives: he loves them, feels for them, cares for them as members of his family, bone of his bone, and flesh of his flesh.

There is a solemn warning here to all who mock and persecute true Christians on account of their religion. They do not consider what they are doing; they are persecuting the near relatives of the King of kings. They will find on the last day that they have mocked those whom the Judge of all regards as his "brother and sister and mother."

There is rich encouragement here for all believers. They are far more precious in their Lord's eyes than they are in their own. Their faith may be feeble, their repentance weak, their strength small: they may be poor and needy in this world; but there is a glorious "whoever" in the last verse of this chapter which ought to cheer them. "Whoever" believes is a near relative of Christ: the Elder Brother will provide for him in time and eternity, and never let him be cast away. There is not one "young sister" in the family of the redeemed, whom Jesus does not remember (Song of Songs 8:8). Joseph provided richly for all his relatives (Genesis 47:11–12), and the Lord Jesus will provide for his.

Matthew
Chapter 13

This chapter is remarkable for the number of parables it has. Seven striking illustrations of spiritual truth are here drawn by the great head of the church from the book of nature. By doing so he shows us that religious teaching may draw help from everything in creation. Those that would "find just the right words" (Ecclesiastes 12:10) should not forget this.

The parable of the sower (13:1–23)

The parable of the sower, which begins this chapter, is one of those parables which can have a very wide application. Its truth is continually being proved under our own eyes. Wherever the Word of God is preached or expounded and people are assembled to hear it, the sayings of our Lord in this parable are found to be true. It describes what goes on, as a general rule, in all congregations.

1. The work of the preacher
First, let us learn from this parable that the work of the preacher resembles that of the sower.

Like the sower, the preacher must sow good seed if he wants to see fruit. He must sow the pure Word of God, and not the traditions of the church or the doctrines of men. Without this, his labor will be vain. He may go to and fro, and seem to say much, and to work busily in his weekly ministerial duty, but there will be no harvest of souls for heaven, no living results, and no conversions.

Like the sower, the preacher must be diligent. He must spare no pains; he must use every possible means to make his work prosper; he must patiently sow by every stream (Isaiah 32:20), and sow in hope. He must "be prepared in season and out of season" (2 Timothy 4:2), undeterred by difficulties and discouragements; "whoever watches the wind will not plant" (Ecclesiastes 11:4). No doubt his success does not entirely depend on his labor and diligence, but without labor and diligence success will not be obtained.

Like the sower, the preacher cannot give life. He can scatter the seed committed to his charge, but he cannot command it to grow: he may offer the word of truth to a people, but he cannot make them receive it and bear fruit. To give life is God's solemn prerogative: "The Spirit gives life" (John 6:63). God alone can "make things grow" (1 Corinthians 3:7).

Let these things sink down into our hearts. It is no light thing to be a real minister of God's Word. To be an idle, formal workman in the church is easy; to be a faithful sower is very hard. Preachers ought to be specially remembered in our prayers.

2. Hearing without benefit

Second, let us learn from this passage that there are various ways of hearing the Word of God without benefit.

We may listen to a sermon with a heart like the hard "path" (verse 4): careless, thoughtless, and unconcerned. Christ crucified may be set before us most movingly, and we may hear of his sufferings with utter indifference, as a subject in which we have no interest. As fast as the words fall on our ears, the devil may pluck them away, and we may go home as if we had not heard a sermon at all. Alas, there are many such hearers! It is as true of them as of the idols of old, "They have . . . eyes, but they cannot see; they have ears, but cannot hear" (Psalm 135:16–17). Truth seems to have no more effect on their hearts than water on a stone.

We may listen to a sermon with pleasure, while the impression produced on us is only temporary and short-lived. Our hearts, like the "rocky places" (verse 5), may yield a plentiful crop of warm feelings and good resolutions; but all this time there may be no deeply-rooted work in our souls, and the first cold blast of opposition or temptation may cause our seeming religion to wither away. Alas, there are many such hearers! The mere love of sermons is no sign of grace. Thousands of baptized people are like the Jews of Ezekiel's day: "To them you are nothing more than one who sings love songs with a beautiful voice and plays an instrument well, for they hear your words but do not put them into practice" (Ezekiel 33:32).

We may listen to a sermon and approve of every word it contains, and yet get no benefit from it because of the absorbing influence of this world. Our hearts, like the thorny ground (verse 7), may be choked with a rank crop of cares, pleasures and worldly plans. We may really like the Gospel, and wish to obey it, and yet insensibly give it no chance of bearing fruit, by allowing other things to fill a place in our affections, until they occupy our whole hearts. Alas, there are many such hearers! They know the truth well: they hope one day to be committed Christians; but they never come to the point of giving up all for Christ's sake. They never make up their minds to "seek first his kingdom" – and so die in their sins.

These are points that we ought to weigh well. We should never forget that there are more ways than one of hearing the Word without profit. It is not enough that we come to hear: we may come and be indifferent. It is not enough that we are not indifferent hearers: our impressions may be only temporary and ready to perish. It is not enough that our impressions are not merely temporary; but they may be continually yielding no result, because we obstinately cling to the world. Truly "the heart is deceitful above all things and beyond cure. Who can understand it?" (Jeremiah 17:9).

3. Only one evidence

Third, let us learn from this parable that there is only one evidence of hearing the Word rightly. That evidence is to bear "a crop" (verse 8).

The crop here spoken of is the fruit of the Spirit. Repentance towards God, faith towards the Lord Jesus Christ, holiness of life and character, prayerfulness, humility, love, spiritual mindedness – these are the only satisfactory proofs that the seed of God's Word is doing its proper work in our souls. Without such proofs our religion is vain, however noble our claims: it is no better than a resounding gong or a clanging cymbal. Christ has said, "I chose you and appointed you to go and bear *fruit*" (John 15:16).

There is no part of the whole parable more important than this. We must never be content with a barren orthodoxy, and coldly maintaining correct theological views; we must not be satisfied with clear knowledge, warm feelings, and decently claiming to be Christians; we must see to it that the Gospel we claim to love produces positive "fruit" in our hearts and lives. This is real Christianity. These words of St. James should often ring in our ears: "Do not merely listen to the word, and so deceive yourselves. Do what it says" (James 1:22).

Let us not leave these verses without asking ourselves the important question, "How do we hear?" We live in a Christian country; we probably go to a place of worship Sunday after Sunday, and hear sermons. In what spirit do we hear them? What effect have they upon our characters? Can we point to anything that deserves the name of "fruit"?

We may rest assured that to reach heaven at last it needs something more than going to church regularly on Sundays and listening to preachers. The Word of God must be received into our hearts, and become the mainspring of our conduct: it must produce practical impressions on our inner being, that will appear in our outward behavior. If it does not do this, it will only add to our condemnation on the day of judgment.

The parable of the weeds (13:24–43)

The parable of the weeds, which occupies the most of these verses, is one of special importance in the present day. It is well suited to correcting the extravagant expectations many Christians have of the effect of missions abroad, and of preaching the Gospel at home. May we give it the attention which it deserves!

1. Good and evil will always be found together

First, this parable teaches us that good and evil will always be found together in the professing church, until the end of the world.

The visible church is pictured as a mixed body: it is a vast "field" in which "wheat" and "weeds" grow side by side (verses 24–26). We must expect to find believers and unbelievers, converted and unconverted, "the sons of the kingdom" and "the sons of the evil one" (verses 38–39), all mingled together in every congregation of baptized people.

The purest preaching of the Gospel will not prevent this. In every age of the church the same state of things has existed: it was the experience of the early Fathers; it was the experience of the Reformers; it is the experience of the best ministers at the present time. There has never been a visible church or a religious assembly of which the members have all been "wheat." The devil, that great enemy of souls, has always taken care to sow "weeds."

The most strict and prudent discipline will not prevent this: Episcopalians, Presbyterians and Independents all alike find it to be so. Do what we will to purify a church, we shall never succeed in obtaining a perfectly pure fellowship: weeds will be found among the wheat; hypocrites and deceivers will creep in. Worst of all, if we are extreme in our efforts to obtain purity we do more harm than good: we run the risk of encouraging many a Judas Iscariot, and breaking many a bruised reed. In our zeal to pull up the weeds (verse 28), we are in danger of rooting up the wheat with them (verse 29). Such zeal is not based on knowledge and has often done much harm. Those who do not care what happens to the wheat provided they can root up the weeds show little of the mind of Christ – and after all, there is deep truth in the charitable saying of Augustine, "Those who are weeds today may be wheat tomorrow."

Are we inclined to look for the conversion of the whole world by the labors of missionaries and ministers? Let us place this parable before us, and beware of such an idea. We shall never see all the inhabitants of earth, "the wheat" of God, in the present order of things: the weeds and wheat will "grow together until the harvest" (verse 30). The kingdoms of this world will never become the kingdom of Christ, and the millennium will never begin until the King himself returns.

Are we ever tried by the scoffing argument of unbelievers that Christianity cannot be a true religion because there are so many false Christians? Let us recall this parable, and remain unmoved. Let us tell them that this state of things does not surprise us at all. Our Master prepared us for it 1900 years ago. He foresaw and foretold that his church would be a field containing not only "wheat" but "weeds."

Are we ever tempted to leave the Protestant church for another, because we see many of its members unconverted? Let us remember this parable, and take care what we do. We shall never find a perfect church. We may spend our lives in migrating from communion to communion, and pass our days in perpetual disappointment: go where we will, and worship where we may, we shall always find "weeds."

2. The godly and the ungodly will be separated

Second, the parable teaches us that there is to be a day of separation between the godly and the ungodly members of the visible church, at the end of the world.

The present mixed state of things is not to be forever: the wheat and the weeds are to be divided at last. The Lord Jesus will "send out his angels" (verse 41) on the day of his second coming, and gather all who claim to be Christians into two great companies. Those mighty harvesters will make no mistake: they will discern with unerring judgment between the righteous and the wicked, and place every one in his own lot. The saints and faithful servants of Christ will receive glory, honor and eternal life; the worldly, the ungodly, the indifferent and the unconverted will be thrown "into the fiery furnace" (verse 42).

There is something particularly solemn in this part of the parable. The meaning allows for no mistake: our Lord himself explains it in words of unusual clearness, as if he wants to impress it deeply on our minds. Well may he say at the conclusion, "He who has ears, let him hear" (verse 43).

Let the ungodly tremble when they read this parable; let them see in its fearful language their own certain doom, unless they repent and turn to God. Let them know that they are sowing misery for themselves if they continue to neglect God. Let them reflect that their end will be to be gathered among the bundles of "weeds," and be burned. Surely such a prospect ought to make us think! As Baxter truly says, "We must not misinterpret God's patience with the ungodly."

Let believers in Christ take comfort when they read this parable; let them see that there is happiness and safety prepared for them in the great and dreadful day of the Lord. The voice of the archangel and the trumpet call of God will proclaim no terror for them: they will summon them to join what they have long desired to see – a perfect church and a perfect fellowship of saints. How beautiful will the whole body of believers appear when finally separated from the wicked! How pure will the wheat look in God's barn when the weeds are eventually taken away! How brightly will grace shine when no longer dimmed by incessant contact with the worldly and unconverted! The righteous are little known in the present day: the world sees no beauty in them, even as it saw none in their Master. The world does not know us because "it did not know him" (1 John 3:1). But the righteous will one day "shine like the sun in the kingdom of their Father" (verse 43). To use the words of Matthew Henry, "their sanctification will be perfected, and their justification will be published." "When Christ, who is your life, appears, then you also will appear with him in glory" (Colossians 3:4).

The parables of the treasure, the pearl, and the net *(13:44–50)*

The parables of the "treasure hidden in a field" (verse 44) and the "merchant looking for fine pearls" (verses 45–46) appear intended to convey the same lesson. They vary, no doubt, in one striking way: the "treasure" was found by someone who does not seem to have sought it; the "pearl" was found by one who was actually looking for pearls. But the conduct of the finders, in both cases, was precisely alike: both "sold all they had" to make the thing they had found their own property; and it is exactly at this point that the instruction of both parables agrees.

1. Giving up everything to win eternal life
These two parables are meant to teach us that those who are really convinced of the importance of salvation will give up everything to win Christ and eternal life.

What was the conduct of the two men our Lord describes? One was persuaded that there was a "treasure hidden in a field," which would amply repay him if he bought the field, however great the price. The other was persuaded that the "pearl" he had found was so immensely valuable that he wanted to buy it at any cost. Both were convinced that they had found a thing of great value: both were satisfied that it was worth a great sacrifice now to make this thing their own. Others might wonder at them; others might think them foolish for paying such a sum of money for the "field" and "pearl," but they knew what they were about. They were sure that they were getting a bargain.

We see, in this simple picture, the conduct of a true Christian explained. He is what he is, and does what he does in his religion, because he is thoroughly persuaded that it is worthwhile. He comes out from the world; he puts off the old man; he leaves the vain companions of his past life. Like Matthew, he gives up everything, and like Paul, he considers "everything a loss" (Philippians 3:8) for Christ's sake. And why? Because he is convinced that Christ will make amends to him for all he gives up. He sees in Christ an endless "treasure," he sees in Christ a precious "pearl": to win Christ he will make any sacrifice. This is true faith. This is the stamp of a genuine work of the Holy Spirit.

We see in these two parables the real clue to the conduct of many unconverted people. They are what they are in religion because they are *not fully persuaded* that it is worthwhile to be different. They flinch from decision; they shrink from taking up the cross; they hesitate between two opinions; they will not commit themselves. They will not come forward boldly on the Lord's side. And why? Because they have not faith. They are not sure that "the treasure" is there; they are not satisfied that "the pearl" is worth so much. They cannot yet make up their minds to "sell everything" so that they may win Christ. And so, too often, they perish forever! When people will venture nothing for Christ's sake, we must draw the sorrowful conclusion that they have not got the grace of God.

2. The true nature of the church

The parable of the net let down into the lake (verses 47–50) has some points in common with that of the weeds. It is intended to instruct us on the true nature of the visible church of Christ.

The preaching of the Gospel was the letting down of a large net into the middle of the lake of this world; the professing church which it was to gather together was to be a mixed body. Within the folds of the net there were to be fish of every kind, both good and bad; within the pale of the church there were to be Christians of various sorts, unconverted as well as converted, false as well as true. The separation of good and bad was sure to come at last, but not before the end of the world. Such was the account which the great Master gave to his disciples of the churches which they were to found.

It is of the utmost importance to have the lessons of this parable deeply engraved on our minds. There is hardly any point in Christianity on which greater mistakes exist than the nature of the visible church. There is none, perhaps, on which mistakes are so perilous to the soul.

Let us learn from this parable that all congregations of people who claim to be Christians ought to be regarded as mixed bodies: they are all assemblies containing "good fish and bad," converted and unconverted, children of God and children of the world, and ought to be described and addressed as such. To tell all baptized people that they are born again, and have the Spirit, and are members of Christ, is utterly unwarrantable. Such a mode of address may flatter and please; it is not likely to profit or save. It is sadly going to promote self-righteousness, and lull sinners to sleep; it overthrows the plain teaching of Christ, and is ruinous to souls. Do we ever hear such doctrine? If we do, let us remember "the net."

Finally, let it be a settled principle with us never to be satisfied with mere outward church membership. We may be inside the net, and yet not be in Christ. The waters of baptism are poured on myriads who are never washed in the water of life; the bread and wine are eaten and drunk by thousands at the Lord's table, who never feed on Christ by faith. Are we converted? Are we among the "good fish"? This is the grand question! It is one which must be answered at last. The net will soon be "pulled . . . up on the shore" (verse 48), and the true character of everyone's religion at length be exposed. There will be an eternal separation between the good fish and the bad: there will be a "fiery furnace" for "the wicked" (verses 49–50). Surely, as Baxter says, "these plain words more need belief and consideration than exposition."

Christ's treatment in his own country; the danger of unbelief (13:51–58)

1. A striking question

The first thing which we ought to notice in these verses is the striking question with which our Lord concludes the seven wonderful parables of this chapter: "Have you understood all these things?" (verse 51).

111

Personal application has been called the "soul" of preaching. A sermon without application is like a letter posted without an address: it may be well written, correctly dated and properly signed, but it is useless, because it never reaches its destination. Our Lord's inquiry is an admirable example of real heart-seaching application: "Have you understood?"

The mere outward practice of hearing a sermon can benefit no one, unless they comprehend what it means: they might just as well listen to the blowing of a trumpet, or the beating of a drum. The intellect must be set in motion, and the heart impressed: ideas must be received into the mind; the seeds of new thoughts must be carried off. Without this the hearing is in vain.

It is important to see this clearly; there is a vast amount of ignorance about it. Thousands go regularly to places of worship and think they have done their religious duty, but never carry away an idea, or receive an impression. Ask them, when they return home on a Sunday evening, what they have learned, and they cannot tell you a word. Examine them at the end of a year on the religious knowledge they have attained, and you will find them as ignorant as the heathen.

Let us watch our souls in this matter. Let us take with us to church not only our bodies, but our minds, our reason, our hearts and our consciences. Let us often ask ourselves, "What have I got from this sermon? What have I learned? What truths have been impressed on my mind?" Intellect, no doubt, is not everything in religion; but it does not therefore follow that it is nothing at all. The heart is unquestionably the main point: but we must never forget that the Holy Spirit generally reaches the heart through the mind. Sleepy, idle, inattentive hearers are never likely to be converted.

2. The treatment Jesus received

Second, we ought to notice in these verses the strange treatment which our Lord received in his own country.

He came to the town of Nazareth, where he had been brought up, and "began teaching the people in their synagogue" (verse 54). His teaching, no doubt, was the same as it always was: "No one ever spoke the way this man does" (John 7:46). But it had no effect on the people of Nazareth. They were "amazed" (verse 54), but their hearts were unmoved. They said, "Isn't this the carpenter's son? Isn't his mother's name Mary?" (verse 55). They despised him, because they were so familiar with him. "They took offense at him" (verse 57). And they drew from our Lord the solemn remark, "Only in his hometown and in his own house is a prophet without honor" (verse 57).

Let us see a melancholy page of human nature unfolded to our view in this story. We are all apt to despise mercies if we are accustomed to them, and have them cheap. The Bibles and religious books which are so plentiful, the means of grace of which we have so abundant a supply, the preaching of the Gospel which we hear every week – all are liable to be undervalued. It is sadly true that, in religion more than anything else, "familiarity breeds contempt." People forget that truth is truth, however old and hackneyed it may sound – and despise it because it is old. Alas, by so doing they provoke God to take it away!

Do we wonder that the relatives, servants and neighbors of godly people are not always converted? Do we wonder that the parishioners of eminent ministers of the Gospel are often their hardest and most impenitent hearers? Let us wonder no more. Let us note the experience of our Lord at Nazareth, and learn wisdom.

Do we ever fancy that if we had only seen and heard Jesus we would have been faithful disciples? Do we think that if we had only lived near him, and been eyewitnesses of his ways, we would not have been undecided, wavering and half-hearted about religion? If we do, let us think so no longer. Let us observe the people of Nazareth, and learn wisdom.

3. The ruinous nature of a lack of faith

Third, we should notice in these verses the ruinous nature of unbelief. The chapter ends with the fearful words, "He did not do many miracles there because of their lack of faith" (verse 58).

We see in this single phrase the secret of the everlasting ruin of multitudes of souls! They perish forever, because they *will not* believe. There is nothing else on earth or heaven that prevents their salvation: their sins, however many, might all be forgiven; the Father's love is ready to receive them; the blood of Christ is ready to cleanse them; the power of the Spirit is ready to renew them. But a great barrier bars the way: their lack of faith. "You refuse to come to me," says Jesus, "to have life" (John 5:40).

May we all be on our guard against this accursed sin! It is the old root-sin which caused the fall of man. Cut down in the true child of God by the power of the Spirit, it is always ready to bud and sprout again. There are three great enemies against which God's children should daily pray: pride, worldliness, and a lack of faith. Of these three none is greater than a lack of faith.

Matthew
Chapter 14

The martyrdom of John the Baptist *(14:1–12)*

We have in this passage a page out of God's book of martyrs: the story of the death of John the Baptist. The wickedness of King Herod, the bold reproof which John gave him, the consequent imprisonment of the faithful reprover, and the disgraceful circumstances of his death are all written for our learning. "Precious in the sight of the LORD is the death of his saints" (Psalm 116:15).

The story of John the Baptist's death is told more fully by St. Mark than by St. Matthew. For the present it seems sufficient to draw two general lessons from St. Matthew's narrative, and to fasten our attention exclusively upon them.

1. The power of conscience

First, let us learn from these verses the great power of conscience.

King Herod hears "the reports about Jesus" (verse 1), and says to his servants, "This is John the Baptist; he has risen from the dead!" (verse 2). He remembered his own wicked dealings with that holy man, and his heart failed within him. His heart told him that he had despised his godly counsel, and committed a foul and abominable murder; and his heart told him that, though he had killed John, there would yet be a reckoning day. He and John the Baptist would yet meet again. Bishop Hall puts it well: "A wicked man needs no other tormentor, especially for sins of blood, than his own heart."

There is a conscience in all men by nature. Let this never be forgotten. Fallen, lost, desperately wicked as are all born into the world, God has taken care to leave himself a witness in our hearts. It is a poor, blind guide, without the Holy Spirit: it can save no one; it leads no one to Christ: it may be "seared" and trampled under foot. But there is such a thing as conscience in every man, accusing or defending him; and Scripture and experience alike declare it (Romans 2:15). Conscience can make even kings miserable when they have willfully rejected its advice; it can fill the princes of this world with fear and trembling, as it did Felix, when Paul preached. They find it easier to imprison and behead the preacher, than to bind his sermon, and silence the voice of his reproof in their own hearts. God's witnesses may be put off the way, but their testimony often lives and works on long after they are dead. God's prophets do not live forever, but their words often survive them (2 Timothy 2:9; Zechariah 1:5).

Let the thoughtless and ungodly remember this, and not sin against their consciences. Let them "be sure that their sins will find them out" (Numbers 32:23). They may laugh, and jest, and mock at religion for a little time. They may cry, "Who is afraid? Where is the mighty harm of our ways?" They may depend upon the fact they are sowing misery for themselves, and will reap a bitter crop sooner or later. Their wickedness will overtake them one day: they will find, like Herod, how "evil and bitter it is" to "forsake the LORD your God" (Jeremiah 2:19).

Let ministers and teachers remember that there is a conscience in people, and let them work on boldly. Instruction is not always thrown away because it seems to bear no fruit at the time it is given; teaching is not always in vain, though we fancy that it is unheeded, wasted and forgotten. There is a conscience in the hearers of sermons; there is a conscience in the children at our schools. Many a sermon and lesson will yet rise again, when he who preached or taught it is in the grave like John the Baptist. Thousands know that we are right, and, like Herod, dare not confess it.

2. No reward in this world

Second, let us learn that God's children must not look for their reward in this world.

If ever there was a case of godliness unrewarded in this life, it was that of John the Baptist. Let us think for a moment what a remarkable man he was during his short career, and then think to what end he came. Look at the one who was "a prophet of the Most High" (Luke

1:76), and greater than anyone born of women (Matthew 11:11), imprisoned like a criminal! See him cut off by a violent death before the age of thirty-four; the "burning light" quenched, the faithful preacher murdered for doing his duty – and this to gratify the hatred of an adulterous woman, and at the command of a capricious tyrant! Truly there was an event here, if there ever was one in the world, which might make an ignorant person say, "What is the good of serving God?"

But these are the sort of things which show us that there will one day be a judgment. The God of the spirits of all humanity shall at last set up an assize and reward every one according to his works. The blood of John the Baptist and James the Apostle and Stephen, of Polycarp, Hus, Ridley and Latimer, shall yet be required. It is all written in God's book. "The earth will disclose the blood shed upon her; she will conceal her slain no longer" (Isaiah 26:21). The world shall yet know that there is a God that judges the earth. "If you see the poor oppressed in a district, and justice and rights denied, do not be surprised at such things; for one official is eyed by a higher one, and over them both are others higher still" (Ecclesiastes 5:8).

Let all true Christians remember that their best things are yet to come. Let us think it nothing strange if we have sufferings in this present time. It is a probationary period: we are still at school. We are learning patience, longsuffering, gentleness and meekness, which we could hardly learn if we had our good things now. But there is an eternal holiday yet to begin. For this let us wait quietly; it will make amends for all. "Our light and momentary troubles are achieving for us an eternal glory that far outweighs them all" (2 Corinthians 4:17).

The miracle of the loaves and fishes *(14:13–21)*

These verses contain one of our Lord Jesus Christ's greatest miracles: the feeding of "five thousand men, besides women and children" (verse 21) with five loaves and two fishes. Of all the miracles worked by our Lord, not one is so often mentioned in the New Testament as this. Matthew, Mark, Luke and John all dwell upon it. It is plain that this event in the story of our Lord is intended to receive special attention. Let us give it that attention, and see what we may learn.

1. A proof of Christ's divine power

First, this miracle is an unanswerable proof of our Lord's divine power.

To satisfy the hunger of more than five thousand people with so small a portion of food as five loaves and two fishes would clearly be impossible without a supernatural multiplication of the food. It was a thing that no magician, impostor or false prophet would ever have attempted. Such a person might possibly pretend to cure a single sick person, or to raise a single dead body, and by trickery might persuade weak people that he succeeded; but such a person would never attempt such a mighty work as that which is here recorded. He would know well that he could not persuade 10,000 men, women and children that they were full when they were hungry. He would be exposed as a cheat and impostor on the spot.

Yet this is the mighty work which our Lord actually performed, and by performing it gave a conclusive proof that he was God. He called into being what did not before exist: he provided visible, tangible, material food for more than 5,000 people, out of a supply which in itself would not have satisfied fifty. Surely we must be blind if we do not see in this the hand of him who "gives food to every creature" (Psalm 136:25), and made the world and all that is in it. To create is something only God can do.

We ought to hold firmly on to passages such as this. We should treasure up in our minds every evidence of our Lord's divine power. The cold, orthodox, unconverted man may see little in the story: the true believer should store it in his memory. Let him think of the world, the devil and his own heart, and learn to thank God that his Saviour, the Lord Jesus Christ, is almighty.

2. A sign of Christ's compassion

Second, this miracle is a striking example of our Lord's compassion toward people.

Jesus "saw a large crowd" in a remote place, ready to faint for hunger. He knew that many in that multitude had no true faith and love towards himself: they followed him because it was fashionable, or from curiosity or some equally low motive (John 6:26). But our Lord had pity on all of them: all of them shared the food miraculously provided. All of them were "satisfied" (verse 20) and none went away hungry.

Let us see in this the heart of our Lord Jesus Christ toward sinners. He is always the same. He is now as he was long ago, "the LORD, the LORD, the compassionate and gracious God, slow to anger, abounding in love and faithfulness" (Exodus 34:6). He does not deal with people according to their sins, or reward them according to their iniquities. He loads even his enemies with benefits. No one will be so without excuse as those who are found impenitent at last: "God's kindness leads you toward repentance" (Romans 2:4). In all his dealings with people on earth, he showed himself one who delights to show mercy (Micah 7:18). Let us strive to be like him. "We ought," says an old writer, "to have abundance of pity and compassion on diseased souls."

3. A sign of the sufficiency of the Gospel
Third, this miracle is a living sign of the sufficiency of the Gospel to meet the spiritual needs of all mankind.

There can be little doubt that all our Lord's miracles have a deep figurative meaning, and teach great spiritual truths. They must be handled reverently and discreetly. Care must be taken that we do not, like many of the Fathers, see allegories where the Holy Spirit meant none to be seen. But, perhaps, if there is any miracle worked by Christ which has a clear figurative meaning, in addition to the plain lessons which may be drawn from its surface, it is that which is now before us.

What does this hungry multitude in a remote place represent to us? It is a symbol of all mankind. The human race is a large group of perishing sinners, famishing in the midst of a wilderness world – helpless, hopeless, and on the way to ruin. We have all gone astray like lost sheep (Isaiah 53:6); we are by nature far away from God. Our eyes may not be opened to the full extent of our danger, but in reality we are "wretched, pitiful, poor, blind and naked" (Revelation 3:17). There is but a step between us and everlasting death.

What do these loaves and fishes represent, apparently so inadequate to meet the necessities of the case, but by miracle made sufficient to feed 10,000 people? They are a symbol of the doctrine of Christ crucified for sinners, as their vicarious substitute, and making atonement by his death for the sin of the world. To human nature that doctrine seems weakness itself. Christ crucified was "a stumbling block to Jews, and foolishness to Gentiles" (1 Corinthians 1:23). And yet Christ crucified has proved that "the bread of God is he who comes down from heaven and gives life to the world" (John 6:33). The story of the cross has amply met the spiritual needs of mankind wherever it has been preached. Thousands of every rank, age and nation are witnesses that it is "the power of God and the wisdom of God" (1 Corinthians 1:24). They have eaten of it and been "satisfied," they have found it "real food and . . . real drink" (John 6:55).

Let us ponder these things well. There are great depths in all our Lord Jesus Christ's recorded dealings upon earth, which no one has ever fully fathomed. There are mines of rich instruction in all his words and ways, which no one has thoroughly explored. Many a passage in the Gospels is like the cloud which Elijah's servant saw (1 Kings 18:44). The more we look at it, the greater it will appear. There is an inexhaustible fullness in Scripture. Other writings seem comparatively poor and threadbare when we become familiar with them; but the more we read the Bible the richer we shall find it.

Christ walking on the sea (14:22–36)

The story in these verses is one of singular interest. The miracle here recorded brings out in strong light the character both of Christ and his people. The power and mercy of the Lord Jesus, and the mixture of faith and unbelief in his best disciples, are beautifully illustrated.

1. Christ's power over created things
First, we learn from this miracle what absolute dominion our Saviour has over all created things. We see him "walking on the lake" (verse 25) as if it were dry land. Those angry waves, which tossed the ship of his disciples to and fro, obey the Son of God and become a solid floor under his feet. That liquid surface, which was agitated by the least breath of wind, bears up the feet of our Redeemer like a rock. To our poor, weak minds, the whole event is utterly incomprehensible. The picture of two feet walking on the sea is said by Doddridge to have been the Egyptian emblem of an impossible thing; the scientist will tell us that for material flesh and blood to walk on water is a physical impossibility. Enough for us to know that it was done. Enough for us to

remember that to him who created the seas at the beginning, it must have been perfectly easy to walk over their waves when he pleased.

There is encouragement here for all true Christians. Let them know that there is nothing created which is not under Christ's control. All things serve him (see Mark 4:41). He may allow his people to be tried for a period, and to be tossed to and fro by storms of trouble; he may be later than they wish in coming to their aid, and not draw near till the "fourth watch of the night" (verse 25), but never let them forget that winds, and waves and storms are all Christ's servants. They cannot move without Christ's permission. "Mightier than the thunder of the great waters, mightier than the breakers of the sea – the LORD on high is mighty" (Psalm 93:4). Are we ever tempted to cry with Jonah, "You hurled me into the deep, into the very heart of the seas, and the current swirled about me" (Jonah 2:3)? Let us remember they are his billows. Let us wait patiently. We may yet see Jesus coming to us, and walking on the water.

2. The power Jesus can give to believers

Second, we learn from this miracle what power Jesus can bestow on those who believe in him. We see Simon Peter coming down out of the ship and walking on the water, like his Lord. What a wonderful proof this was of our Lord's divinity! To walk on the sea himself was a mighty miracle; but to enable a poor weak disciple to do the same, was a mightier miracle still.

There is a deep meaning in this part of the story: it shows us what great things our Lord can do for those who hear his voice and follow him. He can enable them to do things which at one time they would have thought impossible. He can carry them through difficulties and trials which, without him, they would never have dared to face. He can give them strength to walk through fire and water unharmed, and to get the better of every foe. Moses in Egypt, Daniel in Babylon, the saints in Nero's household, are all examples of his mighty power. Let us fear nothing, if we are in the path of duty. The waters may seem deep; but if Jesus says, "Come" (verse 29), we have no cause to be afraid. "Anyone who has faith in me will do what I have been doing. He will do even greater things than these" (John 14:12).

3. The trouble disciples bring on themselves by unbelief

Third, let us learn from this miracle how much trouble disciples bring upon themselves by unbelief. We see Peter walking boldly on the water for a little way; but by and by when he sees the wind boisterous (verse 30) he is afraid, and begins to sink. The weak flesh gets the better of the willing spirit. He forgets the wonderful proofs of his Lord's goodness and power, which he had just received. He did not consider that the same Saviour who had enabled him to walk one step, must be able to hold him up forever; he did not reflect that he was nearer to Christ when once on the water, than he was when he first left the ship. Fear took away his memory, alarm confused his reason. He thought of nothing but the winds and waves and his immediate danger, and his faith gave way. "Lord," he cried, "save me!" (verse 30).

What a lively picture we have here of the experience of many believers! How many there are who have enough faith to take the first step in following Christ, but not enough faith to go on as they began. They take fright at the trials and dangers which seem to be in their way. They look at the enemies that surround them, and the difficulties that seem likely to beset their path: they look at them more than at Jesus, and at once their feet begin to sink, their hearts faint within them, their hope vanishes away: their comforts disappear. And why is all this? Christ is not altered: their enemies are not greater than they were. It is just because, like Peter, they have ceased to look to Jesus, and have given way to unbelief. They are taken up with thinking about their enemies, instead of thinking about Christ. May we lay this to heart, and learn wisdom!

4. Christ's mercy to believers

Fourth, let us learn from this miracle how merciful our Lord Jesus Christ is to weak believers. We see him stretching out his hand immediately to save Peter, as soon as Peter cried to him. He does not leave him to reap the fruit of his own unbelief, and to sink in the deep waters: he only seems to consider his trouble, and to think of nothing so much as delivering him from it. The only word he utters is the gentle reproof, "You of little faith, why did you doubt?" (verse 31).

We should mark, in this concluding part of the miracle, the exceeding gentleness of Christ. He can bear with much, and forgive much when he sees true grace in someone's heart. As a mother deals gently with her infant, and does not cast it away because it is wayward and obstinate, so does the Lord Jesus deal gently with his people. He loved and pitied them before conversion, and after conversion he loves and pities them still more. He knows their feebleness, and bears long with them. He wants us to know that doubting does not prove that a person has no faith, but only that his faith is small; and even when our faith is small, the Lord is ready to help us. "When I said, 'My foot is slipping,' your love, O LORD, supported me" (Psalm 94:18).

How much there is in all this to encourage people to serve Christ! Where is the person who ought to be afraid to begin running the Christian race, with such a Saviour as Jesus? If we fall, he will raise us again. If we err, he will bring us back. But his mercy will never be taken from us altogether. He has said, "Never will I leave you; never will I forsake you" (Hebrews 13:5), and he will keep his word. May we only remember that while we do not despise little faith we must not sit down content with it. Our prayer must always be, "Lord, increase our faith."

Matthew
Chapter 15

The teachers of the law and Pharisees; the danger of traditions
(15:1–9)

We have in these verses a conversation between our Lord Jesus Christ
and certain teachers of the law and Pharisees. The subject of it may
seem, at first sight, of little interest in modern days; but it is not so in
reality. The principles of the Pharisees are principles that never die.
There are truths laid down here which are of deep importance.

1. Hypocrites and the outward things in religion
First, we learn that hypocrites generally attach great importance to
mere outward things in religion.

The complaint of the teachers of the law and Pharisees in this place
is a striking case in point. They brought an accusation to our Lord
against his disciples, but what was its nature? It was not that they were
covetous or self-righteous. It was not that they were untruthful or
uncharitable. It was not that they had broken any part of the law of
God. But the disciples of Jesus "break the tradition of the elders. They
don't wash their hands before they eat!" (verse 2). They did not
observe a rule of merely human authority, which some old Jew had
invented! This was the sum total of their offense!

Do we see nothing of the spirit of the Pharisees in the present day?
Unhappily we see only too much. There are thousands of people who
claim to be Christians who seem to care nothing about the religion of
their neighbors provided that it agrees in outward matters with their
own. Does their neighbor worship according to their particular form?
Can he repeat their shibboleth, and talk a little about their favorite

doctrines? If he can, they are satisfied, though there is no evidence that he is converted. If he cannot, they are always finding fault, and cannot speak peaceably of him, though he may be serving Christ better than themselves. Let us beware of this spirit: it is the very essence of hypocrisy. Let our principle be, "The kingdom of God is not a matter of eating and drinking, but of righteousness, peace and joy in the Holy Spirit" (Romans 14:17).

2. The danger of adding to the Word of God

Second, we learn from these verses the great danger of attempting to add anything to the Word of God. Whenever a man takes upon him to make additions to the Scriptures, he is likely to end with valuing his own additions above Scripture itself.

We see this point brought out most strikingly in our Lord's answer to the charge of the Pharisees against his disciples. He says, "And why do you break the command of God for the sake of your tradition?" (verse 3). He strikes boldly at the whole system of *adding* anything to God's perfect Word as being necessary to salvation. He exposes the mischievous tendency of the system by an example. He shows how the vaunted traditions of the Pharisees were actually destroying the authority of the fifth commandment. In short, he establishes the great truth, which ought never to be forgotten, that there is an inherent tendency in all traditions to "nullify the word of God" (verse 6). The authors of these traditions may have meant no such thing; their intentions may have been pure. But it is evidently the doctrine of Christ that there is a tendency in all religious institutions of mere human authority to usurp the authority of God's Word. Bucer, in a solemn remark, says that "a man is rarely to be found who pays an excessive attention to human inventions in religion who does not put more trust in them than in the grace of God."

And have we not seen melancholy proof of this truth in the history of the church of Christ? Unhappily we have seen only too much. As Baxter says, "Men think God's laws too many and too strict, and yet make more of their own, and are precise for keeping them." Have we never read how some have exalted canons, rubrics, and ecclesiastical laws above the Word of God, and have punished disobedience to them with far greater severity than open sins like drunkenness and swearing?

Have we never heard of the extravagant importance which the Church of Rome attaches to monastic vows, and vows of celibacy, and keeping feasts and fasts, insomuch that she seems to place them far above family duties, and the Ten Commandments? Have we never heard of people who make more ado about eating meat in Lent than about gross impurity of life, or murder? Have we never observed in our own land, how many seem to make adherence to episcopacy the weightiest matter in Christianity, and to regard "churchmanship," as they call it, as far outweighing repentance, faith, holiness and the graces of the Spirit? These are questions which can only receive one sorrowful answer. The spirit of the Pharisees still lives, after 1900 years: the disposition to "nullify the word of God for the sake of your tradition" (verse 6) is to be found among Christians, as well as among Jews: the tendency practically to exalt human inventions above God's Word is still fearfully prevalent. May we watch against it and be on our guard! May we remember that no tradition or human institution in religion can ever excuse the neglect of relative duties, or justify disobedience to any plain command of God's Word.

3. God desires the worship of the heart

Third, we learn from these verses that the religious worship which God desires is the worship of the heart. We find our Lord establishing this by a quotation from Isaiah: "These people honor me with their lips, but their hearts are far from me" (verse 8).

The heart is the principal thing in the relation of husband and wife, of friend and friend, of parent and child. The heart must be the principal point to which we attend in all the relations between God and our souls. What is the first thing we need in order to be Christians? A new heart. What is the sacrifice God asks us to bring to him? A broken and contrite heart (Psalm 51:17). What is the true circumcision? The circumcision of the heart (Romans 2:29). What is genuine obedience? To obey from the heart. What is saving faith? To believe with the heart. Where ought Christ to dwell? To dwell in our hearts through faith (Ephesians 3:17). What is the chief request that Wisdom makes to everyone? "My son, give me your heart" (Proverbs 23:26).

Let us leave the passage with honest self-inquiry as to the state of our own hearts. Let us settle it in our minds that all formal worship of God, whether in public or private, is utterly in vain so long as our "hearts are far from" him (verse 8). The bent knee, the bowed head, the loud Amen, the daily chapter, the regular attendance at the Lord's table, are all useless and unprofitable so long as our affections are nailed to sin, or pleasure, or money, or the world. The question of our Lord must first be answered satisfactorily, before we can be saved. He says to everyone, "Do you love me?" (John 21:17).

False teachers; the heart the source of sin *(15:10–20)*

There are two striking sayings of the Lord Jesus in this passage. One is about false doctrine: the other is about the human heart. Both of them deserve the closest attention.

As far as false doctrine is concerned, our Lord declares that it is a duty to oppose it, that its final destruction is sure, and that its teachers ought to be forsaken. He says, "Every plant that my heavenly Father has not planted will be pulled up by the roots. Leave them" (verses 13–14).

It is clear, from examination of the passage, that the disciples were surprised at our Lord's strong language about the Pharisees and their traditions. They had probably been accustomed from their youth to regard the Pharisees as the wisest and best of men. They were startled to hear their Master denouncing them as hypocrites, and charging them with transgressing the commandment of God. "Do you know," they said, "that the Pharisees were offended?" (verse 12). To this question we are indebted for our Lord's explanatory declaration, a declaration which perhaps has never received the notice it deserves.

The plain meaning of our Lord's words is that false doctrine like that of the Pharisees was a plant to which no mercy should be shown. It was a "plant which his heavenly Father had not planted," and a plant which it was a duty to "pull up by the roots," whatever offense it might cause. To spare it was no charity, because it was injurious to the souls of men. It mattered nothing that those who planted it were high in office, or learned: if it contradicted the Word of God it ought to be opposed, refuted and rejected. His disciples must therefore understand that it was right to resist all teaching that was unscriptural, and to "leave" and forsake all instructors who persisted in it. Sooner or later they would find that all false doctrine will be completely overthrown and put to shame, and that nothing will stand but what is built on the Word of God.

There are lessons of deep wisdom in this saying of our Lord, which serve to throw light on the duty of many a professing Christian. Let us mark them well, and see what they are. It was practical obedience to this saying which produced the blessed Protestant Reformation. Its lessons deserve close attention.

1. The duty of boldness in resisting false teaching

First, do we not see here the duty of boldness in resisting false teaching? Beyond doubt we do. No fear of giving offense, no dread of ecclesiastical censure, should make us hold our peace when God's truth is in peril. If we are true followers of our Lord, we ought to be outspoken, unflinching witnesses against error. "Truth," says Musculus, "must not be suppressed because men are wicked and blind."

2. The duty of forsaking false teachers

Second, do we not see again the duty of forsaking false teachers if they will not give up their delusions? Beyond doubt we do. No false delicacy, no mock humility should make us shrink from leaving the teaching of any minister who contradicts God's Word. It is at our peril if we submit to unscriptural teaching: our blood will be on our own heads. To use the words of Whitby, "It never can be right to follow the blind into the ditch."

3. The duty of patience

Third, do we not see the duty of patience, when we see false teaching abound? Beyond doubt we do. We may take comfort in the thought that it will not stand long: God himself will defend the cause of his own truth; sooner or later every heresy "will be pulled up by the roots." We are not to fight with worldly weapons, but wait, and preach, and protest, and pray. Sooner or later, as Wycliffe said, "the truth shall prevail."

With respect to the human heart our Lord declares in these verses that it is the true source of all sin and defilement. The Pharisees taught that holiness depended on food and drink, on washing the body and purifications. They held that all who observed their traditions on these matters were pure and clean in God's sight, and that all who neglected them were impure and unclean. Our Lord overthrew this miserable doctrine by showing his disciples that the real source of all defilement was not on the outside, but on the inside. "Out of the heart," he says, "come evil thoughts, murder, adultery, sexual immorality, theft, false testimony, slander. These are what make a man 'unclean'" (verses 19–20). People who want to serve God aright need something far more important than washing the body: they must seek to have a "clean heart."

What an awful picture we have here of human nature, and drawn too by someone who "knew what was in a man" (John 2:25)! What a fearful catalogue this is of the contents of our own hearts! What a melancholy list of seeds of evil our Lord has exposed, lying deep down within every one of us and ready at any time to spring into active life! What can the proud and self-righteous say, when they read such a passage as this? This is no sketch of the heart of a robber or murderer: it is the true and faithful account of the hearts of all mankind. May God grant that we may ponder it well and learn wisdom!

Let it be a settled resolution with us that in all our religion the state of our hearts shall be the main thing. Let it not content us to go to church and observe the forms of religion: let us look far deeper than this, and desire to have a heart "right before God" (Acts 8:21). The right heart is a heart sprinkled with the blood of Christ, and renewed by the Holy Spirit, and purified by faith. Never let us rest till we find within ourselves the witness of the Spirit, that God has created in us a pure heart (Psalm 51:10), and made us a new creation (2 Corinthians 5:17).

Finally, let it be a settled resolution with us to "guard" our hearts above all else (Proverbs 4:23) all the days of our lives. Even after renewal they are weak: even after putting on the new man they are deceitful. Let us never forget that our chief danger is from within. The world and the devil combined, cannot do us so much harm as our own hearts will, if we do not watch and pray. Happy is he who daily remembers the words of Solomon: "He that trusteth in his own heart is a fool" (Proverbs 28:26, KJV).

The Canaanite woman *(15:21–28)*

Another of our Lord's miracles is recorded in these verses. The circumstances are particularly full of interest; let us take them in order, and see
what they are. Every word in these narratives is rich in instruction.

1. Faith found where least expeceted

First, we see that true faith may sometimes be found where it might
have been least expected.

A Canaanite woman cries to our Lord for help, on behalf of her
daughter. "Lord, Son of David, have mercy on me!' she says (verse 22).
Such a prayer would have showed great faith had she lived in Bethany
or Jerusalem; but when we find that she came from the "region of Tyre
and Sidon" (verse 21), such a prayer may well fill us with surprise. It
ought to teach us that it is grace, not place, which makes people believers. We may live in a prophet's family, like Gehazi, the servant of
Elisha, and yet continue impenitent, unbelieving and fond of the
world. We may dwell in the midst of superstition and dark idolatry,
like the girl in Naaman's house, and yet be faithful witnesses for God
and his Christ. Let us not despair of anyone's soul merely because his
lot is cast in an unfavorable position. It is possible to dwell in the coasts
of Tyre and Sidon, and yet sit down in the kingdom of God.

2. Affliction can be a blessing

Second, we see that affliction sometimes proves a blessing to a person's
soul.

The Canaanite woman, no doubt, had been sorely tried. She had seen
her darling child vexed with a demon, and been unable to relieve her;
but yet that trouble brought her to Christ, and taught her to pray.
Without it she might have lived and died in careless ignorance, and
never seen Jesus at all. Surely it was good for her to be afflicted (Psalm
119:71).

Let us mark this well. There is nothing which shows our ignorance
so much as our impatience under trouble. We forget that every cross is
a message from God, and intended to do us good in the end. Trials are
intended to make us think – to wean us from the world – to send us to
the Bible – to drive us to our knees. Health is a good thing; but sickness

is far better, if it leads us to God. Prosperity is a great mercy; but adversity is a greater one if it brings us to Christ. Anything, anything is better than living in indifference and dying in sin. Better a thousand times to be afflicted like the Canaanite woman and, like her, flee to Christ, than live at ease like the rich "fool" (Luke 12:20), and die at last without Christ and without hope.

3. Christ's people are often less compassionate than Christ

Third, we see that Christ's people are often less gracious and compassionate than Christ himself.

The woman about whom we are reading found small favor with our Lord's disciples. Perhaps they regarded an inhabitant of the region of Tyre and Sidon as unworthy of their Master's help. At any rate they said, "Send her away" (verse 23).

There is too much of this spirit among many who claim to be believers. They are apt to discourage inquirers after Christ, instead of helping them forward. They are too ready to doubt the reality of a beginner's grace because it is small, and to treat him as the disciples treated Saul when he first came to Jerusalem after his conversion, "not believing that he really was a disciple" (Acts 9:26). Let us beware of giving way to this spirit: let us seek to have more of the mind that was in Christ. Like him, let us be gentle and kind and encouraging in all our treatment of those who are seeking to be saved: above all, let us tell people continually that they must not judge Christ by Christians. Let us assure them that there is far more in that gracious Master than there is in the best of his servants. Peter and James and John may say to the afflicted soul, "Send her away," but such a word never came from the lips of Christ. He may sometimes keep us long waiting, as he did this woman, but he will never send us away empty.

4. Perseverance in prayer

Fourth, we see what encouragement there is to persevere in prayer, both for ourselves and others.

It is hard to conceive a more striking illustration of this truth than we have in this passage. The prayer of this afflicted mother at first seemed entirely unnoticed: Jesus "did not answer a word" (verse 23). Yet she prayed on. The saying which then came from our Lord's lips sounded discouraging: "I was sent only to the lost sheep of Israel" (verse 24). Yet she prayed on: "Lord, help me!" (verse 25). The second saying of our Lord was even less encouraging than the first: "It is not right to take the children's bread and toss it to their dogs" (verse 26). Yet "hope deferred" did not make her "heart sick" (Proverbs 13:12). Even then she was not silenced: even then she finds a plea for some "crumbs" of mercy to be granted to her. And her importunity obtained at length a gracious reward: "Woman, you have great faith! your request is granted" (verse 28).

That promise has never been broken: "Seek and you will find" (Matthew 7:7).

Prayer for ourselves

Let us remember this story when we pray for ourselves. We are sometimes tempted to think that we receive no benefit from our prayers, and that we may as well give them up altogether. Let us resist the temptation: it comes from the devil. Let us believe, and pray on. Against our besetting sins, against the spirit of the world, against the wiles of the devil, let us pray on and not faint. For strength to do duty, for grace to bear our trials, for comfort in every trouble, let us devote ourselves to prayer (Colossians 4:2). Let us be sure that no time is so well spent in every day as that which we spend upon our knees. Jesus hears us, and in his own good time will give an answer.

Prayer for others

Let us remember this story when we intercede for others. Have we children whose conversion we desire? Have we relations and friends about whose salvation we are anxious? Let us follow the example of this Canaanite woman, and lay the state of their souls before Christ. Let us name their names before him night and day, and never rest till we have an answer. We may have to wait many a long year: we may seem to pray in vain, and intercede without profit; but let us never give up while life lasts. Let us believe that Jesus has not changed, and that he who heard the Canaanite mother, and granted her request will also hear us, and one day give us an answer of peace.

Christ's miracles of healing *(15:29–39)*

The beginning of this passage contains three points which deserve our special attention. For the present let us dwell exclusively on them.

1. People take more care of their bodies than of their souls

First, let us note how much more people take pains about the relief of their physical diseases than about their souls. We read that "great crowds came to him, bringing the lame, the blind, the crippled, the mute and many others" (verse 30). Many of them, no doubt, had journeyed many miles, and were very tired. Nothing is so difficult and troublesome as to move sick people. But the hope of being healed was in sight: such hope is everything to a sick person.

We know little of human nature if we wonder at the conduct of these people. We need not wonder at all. They felt that health was the greatest of earthly blessings; they felt that pain was the hardest of all trials to bear. There is no arguing against sense. A man feels his strength failing; he sees his body wasting and his face becoming pale; he realizes that his appetite is leaving him. He knows, in short, that he is ill, and needs a physician. Show him a physician within reach, about whom it is said that he never fails to effect a cure, and he will go to him without delay.

Let us, however, not forget that our souls are far more diseased than our bodies, and let us learn a lesson from the conduct of these people. Our souls are afflicted with an illness far more deep-seated, far more complicated, far more hard to cure than any ailment that attacks the body. They are in fact plague-stricken by sin. They must be healed, and healed effectually, or perish everlastingly. Do we really know this? Do we feel it? Are we alive to our spiritual disease? Alas, there is but one answer to these questions! The bulk of mankind do not feel it at all. Their eyes are blinded. They are utterly unaware of their danger. For bodily health they crowd the waiting-rooms of doctors; for bodily health they take long journeys to find purer air; but for their souls' health they take no thought at all. Happy indeed is that man or woman who has found out his soul's disease! Such a person will never rest till he has found Jesus. Troubles will seem nothing to him. Life, life, eternal life is at stake! He will "consider everything a loss" that he may gain Christ and be healed (Philippians 3:8).

2. Christ's power in healing all who were brought to him

Second, let us mark the marvelous ease and power with which our Lord healed all who were brought to him. We read that "the people were amazed when they saw the mute speaking, the crippled made well, the lame walking and the blind seeing. And they praised the God of Israel" (verse 31).

See in these words a living picture of our Lord Jesus Christ's power to heal sin-diseased souls. There is no disease of the soul that he cannot cure. There is no form of spiritual complaint that he cannot overcome. The fever of lust, the paralysis of love of the world, the slow consumption of indolence and sloth, the heart-disease of unbelief, all, all give way when he sends out his Spirit on any human being. He can put a new song in a sinner's mouth, and make him speak with love of that Gospel which he once ridiculed and blasphemed. He can open the eyes of a person's understanding and make him see the kingdom of God; he can open a person's ears, and make him willing to hear his voice and to follow him wherever he goes. He can give power to someone who once walked in the broad way that leads to destruction, and guide his feet into the way of life. He can make hands that were once instruments of sin, serve him and do his will. The time of miracles is not yet over. Every conversion is a miracle. Have we ever seen a real instance of conversion? Let us know that we saw in it the hand of Christ. We should have seen nothing really greater if we had seen our Lord making the dumb to speak and the lame to walk, when he was on earth.

Do we want to know what to do if we desire to be saved? Do we feel soul-sick and want a cure? We must just go to Christ in faith, and seek forgiveness from him. He has not changed: 1900 years have made no difference to him. High at the right hand of God, he is still the Great Physician. He still "welcomes sinners" (Luke 15:2). He is still powerful to heal.

3. Christ's abundant compassion

Thirdly, let us note the abundant compassion of our Lord Jesus Christ. We read that "Jesus called his disciples to him and said, 'I have compassion for these people'" (verse 32). A great crowd of men and women is always a solemn sight. It should stir our hearts to feel that each is a dying sinner, and each has a soul to be saved. No one ever seems to have felt so much when he saw a crowd, as Christ did.

It is a curious and striking fact, that of all the feelings experienced by our Lord when upon earth, there is none so often mentioned as "compassion." His joy, his sorrow, his thankfulness, his anger, his wonder, his zeal, all are occasionally recorded. But none of these feelings are so frequently mentioned as "compassion." The Holy Spirit seems to point out to us that this was the distinguishing feature of his character, and the predominant feeling of his mind when he was among men. Nine times, excluding when it is mentioned in the parables, the Spirit has caused that word "compassion" to be written in the Gospels.

There is something very touching and instructive about this. Nothing is written by chance in the Word of God: there is a special reason for the selection of every single expression. That word "compassion," no doubt, was specially chosen for our benefit.

It ought to encourage all who are hesitating about beginning to walk in God's ways. Let them remember that their Saviour is full of "compassion." He will receive them graciously; he will forgive them freely; he will remember their former iniquities no more; he will supply all their need abundantly. Let them not be afraid. Christ's mercy is a deep well of which no one ever found the bottom.

It ought to comfort the saints and servants of the Lord when they feel weary. Let them call to mind that Jesus is "full of compassion." He knows what a world it is in which they live; he knows the body of a man and all its frailties; he knows the devices of their enemy, the devil. And the Lord pities his people: let them not be cast down. They may feel that weakness, failure and imperfection are stamped on all they do; but let them not forget that word which says, "His compassions never fail" (Lamentations 3:22).

Matthew
Chapter 16

The enmity of the Sadducees and Pharisees *(16:1–12)*

In these verses we find our Lord assailed by the untiring enmity of the Pharisees and Sadducees. As a general rule these two sects were at enmity between themselves; in persecuting Christ, however, they made common cause. Truly it was an unholy alliance! Yet how often we see the same thing in the present day. Men who hold opposing opinions will agree in disliking the Gospel, and will work together to oppose its progress. "There is nothing new under the sun" (Ecclesiastes 1:9).

1. Christ's repetition of words he had already used
The first point in this passage which deserves special note is the repetition which our Lord makes of words used by him on a former occasion. He says, "a wicked and adulterous generation looks for a miraculous sign, but none will be given it except the sign of Jonah" (verse 4). If we turn to Matthew 12:39, we shall find that he had said the very same thing once before.

This repetition may seem a trifling and unimportant matter in the eyes of some. But it is not so in reality. It throws light on a subject which has perplexed the minds of many sincere lovers of the Bible, and ought therefore to be specially observed.

This repetition shows us that our Lord was in the habit of saying the same things over again. He did not content himself with saying a thing once, and then never repeat it. It is evident that it was his custom to bring forward certain truths again and again, and so impress them more deeply on the minds of his disciples. He knew the weakness of our memories about spiritual things; he knew that what we hear twice, we remember better than what we hear once. He therefore brought out of his treasury old things as well as new.

Now what does all this teach us? It teaches us that we need not be so anxious to harmonize the narratives we read in the four Gospels, as many are disposed to be. It does not follow that the sayings of our Lord which we find to be the same in St. Matthew and St. Luke, were always used at the same time, or that the events with which they are connected must necessarily be the same. St. Matthew may be describing one event in our Lord's life; St. Luke may be describing another: and yet the words of our Lord, on both occasions, may have been precisely alike. To attempt to make out the two events to be one and the same because the same words are used has often led Bible students into great difficulties. It is far safer to hold the view here maintained that at different times our Lord often used the same words.

2. A solemn warning

The second point which deserves special note in these verses is the solemn warning which our Lord gives his disciples. His mind was evidently pained with false doctrines which he saw among the Jews, and the pernicious influence which they exercised. He seizes the opportunity to utter a caution. "Be careful. Be on your guard against the yeast of the Pharisees and Sadducees" (verse 6). Let us note what those words contain.

To whom was this warning addressed? To the twelve apostles, to the first ministers of the church of Christ, to men who had forsaken all for the Gospel's sake! Even they are warned! The best of men are only men, and at any time may fall into temptation. "If you think you are standing firm, be careful that you don't fall!" (1 Corinthians 10:12). If we love life, and would see good days, let us never think that we do not need that hint: "Be careful. Be on your guard."

Against what does our Lord warn his apostles? Against the "teaching" (verse 12) of the Pharisees and Sadducees. The Pharisees, we are frequently told in the Gospels, were self-righteous formalists; the Sadducees were skeptics, freethinkers, and half unbelievers. Yet even Peter, James, and John must beware of their doctrines! Truly the best and holiest of believers should be on their guard!

By what image does our Lord describe the false teaching against which he cautions his disciples? He calls them yeast. Like yeast, they might seem a small thing compared to the whole body of truth; like yeast, once admitted they would work secretly and noiselessly; like yeast, they would gradually change the whole character of the religion with which they were mixed. How much is often contained in a single word! It was not merely the open danger of heresy but "yeast" of which the apostles were to beware.

There is much in all this that calls loudly for the close attention of all who claim to be Christians. The caution of our Lord in this passage has been shamefully neglected. It would have been well for the church of Christ if the warnings of the Gospel had been as much studied as its promises.

Let us then remember that this saying of our Lord's about the "yeast of the Pharisees and Sadducees" (verse 11) was intended for all time. It was not meant only for the generation to which it was spoken; it was meant for the perpetual benefit of the church of Christ. He who spoke it saw prophetically the future history of Christianity. The Great Physician knew well that Pharisaic doctrines and Sadducee doctrines would prove the two great wasting diseases of his church until the end of the world. He would have us know that there will always be Pharisees and Sadducees in the ranks of Christians. Their succession will never fail; their generation will never become extinct. Their name may change, but their spirit will always remain. Therefore he cries to us, "Be careful. Be on your guard!"

Finally, let us make a personal use of this caution, by keeping up a holy jealousy over our own souls. Let us remember that we live in a world where Pharisaism and Sadduceeism are continually striving for the mastery in the church of Christ. Some want to add to the Gospel, and some want to take away from it; some would bury it, and some would pare it down to nothing; some would stifle it by heaping on additions, and some would bleed it to death by subtraction from its truths. Both parties agree only in one respect: both would kill and destroy the life of Christianity if they succeeded in having their own way. Against both errors let us watch and pray, and stand on guard. Let us not add to the Gospel, to please the modern Pharisee; let us not subtract from the Gospel, to please the modern Sadducee. Let our principle be "the truth, the whole truth, and nothing but the truth": nothing added to it, and nothing taken away.

Peter's noble confession *(16:13–20)*

There are words in this passage which have led to painful differences and divisions among Christians. People have striven and contended about their meaning till they have lost sight of all charity, and yet have failed to carry conviction to one another's minds. Let it suffice us to glance briefly at the controversial words, and then pass on to more practical lessons.

What then are we to understand, when we read that remarkable saying of our Lord's, "You are Peter, and on this rock I will build my church" (verse 18)? Does it mean that the apostle Peter himself was to be the foundation on which Christ's church was to be built? Such an interpretation, to say the least, appears exceedingly improbable. To speak of an erring, fallible child of Adam as the foundation of the spiritual temple is very unlike the ordinary language of Scripture. Above all, no reason can be given why our Lord should not have said, "I will build my church on *you*," if such had been his meaning, instead of saying, "I will build my church on *this rock*."

The true meaning of the "rock" in this passage appears to be the truth of our Lord's messiahship and divinity, which Peter had just confessed. It is as though our Lord had said, "You are rightly called by the name Peter, or stone, for you have confessed that mighty truth on which, as on a rock, I will build my church."

[There is nothing modern, or especially Protestant, in this view. It was held by Chrysostom long ago. It was taught by Ferus, a famous Roman Catholic preacher of the Franciscan order, at Mainz in the sixteenth century, in his homilies on St. Matthew.

It may be well to mention here that it is a complete delusion to suppose that the Scriptures can be interpreted according to the "unanimous consent of the Fathers." There is no such unanimous consent! It is a mere high-sounding phrase, utterly destitute of any foundation in facts. The Fathers disagree as much in explaining Scripture as Whitby and Gill, or Matthew Henry and D'Oyly and Mant.]

But what are we to understand when we read the promise which our Lord makes to Peter: "I will give you the keys of the kingdom of heaven" (verse 19)? Do these words mean that the right of admitting souls to heaven was to be placed in Peter's hands? The idea is preposterous. Such an office is the special prerogative of Christ himself (Revelation 1:18). Do the words mean that Peter was to have any primacy or superiority over the rest of the apostles? There is not the slightest proof that such a meaning was attached to the words in New Testament times, or that Peter had any rank or dignity above the rest of the twelve.

The true meaning of the promise to Peter appears to be that he was to have the special privilege of first opening the door of salvation, both to the Jews and Gentiles. This was fulfilled to the letter when he preached on the day of Pentecost to the Jews, and when he visited the Gentile Cornelius at his own house. On each occasion he used "the keys," and threw open the door of faith. He seems to have been aware of this himself. "God," he says, "made a choice among you that the Gentiles might hear from my lips the message of the gospel and believe" (Acts 15:7).

Finally, what are we to understand when we read the words, "whatever you bind on earth will be bound in heaven, and whatever you loose on earth will be loosed in heaven" (verse 19)? Does this mean that the apostle Peter was to have any power to forgive sins, and absolve sinners? Such an idea is derogatory to Christ's special office, as our great High Priest. It is a power which we never find Peter, or any of the apostles, once exercising. They always refer people to Christ.

The true meaning of this promise appears to be that Peter and his brothers the apostles were to be specially commissioned to teach with authority the way of salvation. As the Old Testament priest declared authoritatively whose leprosy was cleansed, so the apostles were appointed to "declare and pronounce" authoritatively whose sins were forgiven. Beside this, they were to be specially inspired to lay down rules and regulations for the guidance of the church on disputed questions. Some things they were to "bind" or forbid; others they were to "loose" or allow. The decision of the Council at Jerusalem that the Gentiles need not be circumcised was one example of the exercise of this power (Acts 15:19); but it was a commission specially confined to the apostles. In discharging it they had no successors. With them it began, and with them it expired.

We will leave these controversial words here: enough perhaps has been said about them for our personal edification. Let us only remember that, in whatever sense men take them, they have nothing to do with the Church of Rome. Let us now turn our attention to points which more immediately concern our own souls.

1. The noble confession which Peter makes
In the first place, let us admire the noble confession which the apostle Peter makes in this passage. He says, in reply to our Lord's question, "Who do you say I am?" (verse 15): "You are the Christ, the Son of the living God" (verse 16).

At first sight, a careless reader may see nothing very remarkable about these words of the apostle. It may be thought extraordinary that they should call forth such strong commendation from our Lord. But such thoughts arise from ignorance. People forget that it is a widely different thing to believe in Christ's divine mission when we dwell amid professing Christians, and to believe in it when we dwell amid hardened and unbelieving Jews. The glory of Peter's confession lies in this, that he made it when few were with Christ and many against him. He made it when the rulers of his own nation, the scribes, priests and Pharisees, were all opposed to his Master; he made it when our Lord was in the "very nature of a servant" (Philippians 2:7), without wealth, without royal dignity, without any visible mark of a King. To make such a confession at such a time, required great faith and great decision of character. The confession itself, as Brentius says, "was an epitome of all Christianity, and a compendium of true doctrine about religion." Therefore our Lord said, "Blessed are you, Simon son of Jonah" (verse 17). We shall do well to copy that zeal and affection which Peter displayed. We are perhaps too much disposed to underrate this holy man, because of his occasional instability, and his threefold denial of his Lord. This is a great mistake. With all his faults, Peter was a fervent, single-minded servant of Christ; with all his imperfections, he has given us a pattern that many Christians would be wise to follow. Zeal like his may have its ebbs and flows, and sometimes lacks steadiness of purpose; zeal like his may be ill-directed, and sometimes makes sad mistakes. But zeal like his is not to be despised. It wakes up the sleepy; it stirs the sluggish; it provokes others to action. Anything is better than sluggishness, luke-warmness and torpor in the church of Christ. It would have been happy for Christendom had there been more Christians like Simon Peter and Martin Luther.

2. What Christ means when he speaks of his church
Second, let us take care that we understand what our Lord means when he speaks of his church.

The church which Jesus promises to build on a rock is the "blessed company of all faithful people." It is not the visible church of any one nation, country or place: it is the whole body of believers of every age, language and people. It is a church composed of all who are washed in Christ's blood, clothed in Christ's righteousness, renewed by Christ's Spirit, joined to Christ by faith, and letters of Christ in life; it is a church of which every member is baptized with the Holy Spirit, and is really and truly holy; it is a church which is one body. Everyone who belongs to it is of one heart and one mind, and holds the same truths, and believes the same doctrines as necessary to salvation. It is a church which has only one head: that head is Jesus Christ himself. "He is the head of the body" (Colossians 1:18).

Let us beware of mistakes on this subject. Few words are so much misunderstood as the word "church"; few mistakes have so much injured the cause of pure religion. Ignorance on this point has been a fertile source of bigotry, sectarianism and persecution. Men have wrangled and contended about Episcopal, Presbyterian and Independent churches as if it were necessary to salvation to belong to some particular party, and as if, belonging to that party, we must of course belong to Christ. All this time they have lost sight of the one true church, outside of which there is no salvation at all. It will matter nothing at the last day where we have worshiped, if we are not found members of the true church of God's elect.

3. The promises Christ makes to his church
Third, let us note the glorious promises which our Lord makes to his church. He says: "The gates of Hades will not overcome it" (verse 18).

The meaning of this promise is that the power of Satan will never destroy the people of Christ. He who brought sin and death into the first creation by tempting Eve will never bring ruin on the new creation by overthrowing believers. The mystical body of Christ shall never perish or decay. Though often persecuted, afflicted, distressed and brought low, it will never come to an end. It will outlive the wrath of Pharaohs and Roman Emperors. Visible churches, like Ephesus, may come to nothing, but the true church never dies. Like the bush that Moses saw, it may burn, but will not be consumed. *Every* member of it will be brought safe to glory. In spite of falls, failures and short-comings, in spite of the world, the flesh and the devil, no member of the true church will ever perish (John 10:28).

Peter rebuked *(16:21–23)*

In the beginning of these verses we find our Lord revealing to his disciples a great and startling truth. That truth was his approaching death on the cross. For the first time he places before their minds the astounding announcement that "He must go to Jerusalem and suffer . . . and . . . be killed" (verse 21). He had not come on earth to take a kingdom, but to die. He had not come to reign and be served, but to shed his blood as a sacrifice, to give his life as a ransom for many (Matthew 20:28).

It is almost impossible for us to conceive how strange and incomprehensible these tidings must have seemed to his disciples. Like most of the Jews, they could form no idea of a suffering Messiah. They did not understand that Isaiah 53 had to be fulfilled literally; they did not see that the sacrifices of the law were all meant to point them to the death of the true Lamb of God. They thought of nothing but the second glorious coming of Messiah, which is yet to take place at the end of the world. They thought so much of the Messiah's crown, that they lost sight of his cross. We shall do well to remember this: a right understanding of this matter throws strong light on the lessons which this passage contains.

1. Spiritual ignorance in Christ's true disciples
First, we learn from these verses that there may be much spiritual ignorance even in a true disciple of Christ.

We cannot have a clearer proof of this than the conduct of the apostle Peter in this passage. He tries to dissuade our Lord from suffering on the cross. "Never, Lord!" he says. "This shall never happen to you!" (verse 22). He did not see the full purpose of our Lord's coming into the world. His eyes were blinded to the necessity of our Lord's death. He actually did what he could to prevent that death taking place at all! And yet we know that Peter was a converted man; he really believed that Jesus was the Messiah. His heart was right in the sight of God.

These things are meant to teach us that we must neither regard good men as infallible because they are good men, nor yet suppose they have no grace because their grace is weak and small. One brother may possess singular gifts, and be a bright and shining light in the church of Christ; but let us not forget that he is a man, and as a man liable to commit great mistakes. Another brother's knowledge may be scanty: he may fail to judge rightly on many points of doctrine; he may err both in word and deed. But has he faith and love towards Christ? Is he holding on to the head? If so, let us deal patiently with him. What he does not see now, he may see later on. Like Peter, he may now be in the dark, and yet, like Peter, enjoy one day the full light of the Gospel.

2. The importance of the doctrine of Christ's atoning death

Second, let us learn from these verses that there is no doctrine of Scripture so deeply important as the doctrine of Christ's atoning death.

We cannot have clearer proof of this than the language used by our Lord in rebuking Peter. He addresses him by the awful name of "Satan" (verse 23), as if he were an adversary, and doing the devil's work in trying to prevent his death. He says to him, whom he had so recently called "blessed," "Get behind me, Satan! You are a stumbling block to me" (verse 23). He tells the man whose noble confession he had just commended so highly, "You do not have in mind the things of God, but the things of men." Stronger words than these never fell from our Lord's lips. The error that drew from such a loving Saviour such a stern rebuke to such a true disciple, must have been a mighty error indeed.

The truth is that our Lord wants us to regard the crucifixion as the central truth of Christianity. Right views of his vicarious death, and the benefits resulting from it, lie at the very foundation of Bible religion.

Never let us forget this. On matters of church government, and the form of worship, people may differ from us and still reach heaven in safety. On the matter of Christ's atoning death as the way of peace, truth is only one. If we are wrong here, we are ruined forever. Error on many points is only a skin disease; error about Christ's death is a disease of the heart. Here let us take our stand: let nothing move us from this ground. The sum of all our hopes must be that Christ "died for us" (1 Thessalonians 5:10). Give up that doctrine, and we have no solid hope at all.

The necessity of self-denial and the value of the soul *(16:24–28)*

In order to see the connection of these verses we must remember the mistaken impressions of our Lord's disciples as to the purpose of his coming into the world. Like Peter they could not bear the idea of the crucifixion. They thought that Jesus had come to set up an earthly kingdom; they did not see that he had to suffer and die. They dreamed of worldly honors and temporal rewards in their Master's service; they did not understand that true Christians, like Christ, must be made "perfect through suffering" (Hebrews 2:10). Our Lord corrects these misapprehensions in words of special solemnity, which we shall do well to lay up in our hearts.

1. Trouble and self-denial

First, let us learn from these verses that we must be ready to face trouble and self-denial if we follow Christ.

Our Lord dispels the fond dreams of his disciples by telling them that his followers must take up the cross (verse 24). The glorious kingdom they were expecting was not about to be set up immediately. They must be ready to face persecution and affliction if they intended to be his servants: they must be content to lose their lives (verse 25) if they wanted to have their souls saved.

It is good for us all to see this point clearly. We must not conceal from ourselves that true Christianity brings with it a daily cross in this life, while it offers us a crown of glory in the life to come. The self must be crucified daily; the devil must be resisted daily; the world must be overcome daily. There is a war to be waged, and a battle to be fought. All this is the inseparable accompaniment of true religion: heaven is not to be won without it. Never was there a truer word than the old saying, "No cross, no crown!" If we have never found this out by experience, our souls are in a poor condition.

2. Precious souls

Second, let us learn from these verses that there is nothing so precious as a human soul.

Our Lord teaches this lesson by asking one of the most solemn questions that the New Testament contains. It is a question so well known, and so often repeated, that people often lose sight of its searching character; but it is a question that ought to sound in our ears like a trumpet whenever we are tempted to neglect our eternal interests: "What good will it be for a man if he gains the whole world, yet forfeits his soul?" (verse 26).

There can only be one answer to this question. There is nothing on earth, or under the earth, that can make amends to us for the loss of our souls. There is nothing that money can buy, or people can give, to be named in comparison with our souls. The world and all that it contains is temporal: it is all fading, perishing and passing away. The soul is *eternal:* that one single word is the key to the whole question. Let it sink down deeply into our hearts. Are we wavering in our religion? Do we fear the cross? Does the way seem too narrow? Let our Master's words ring in our ears: "What good will it be for a man?" and let us doubt no more.

3. Rewards at the second coming

Third, let us learn that the second coming of Christ is the time when his people shall receive their rewards. "The Son of Man is going to come in his Father's glory with his angels, and then he will reward each person according to what he has done" (verse 27).

There is deep wisdom in this saying of our Lord's when viewed in connection with the preceding verses. He knows the human heart: he knows how soon we are ready to be cast down and, like Israel of old, to be "impatient on the way" (Numbers 21:4). He therefore holds out to us a gracious promise. He reminds us that he has yet to come a second time, as surely as he came the first time. He tells us that this is the time when his disciples will receive their good things. There will be glory, honor and reward in abundance one day for all who have served and loved Jesus; but it is to be in the dispensation of the second advent, and not of the first. The bitter must come before the sweet, the cross before the crown. The first advent is the dispensation of the crucifixion; the second advent is the dispensation of the kingdom. We must submit to take part with our Lord in his humiliation if we desire to share in his glory.

And now let us not leave these verses without serious self-inquiry as to the matters which they contain. We have heard of the necessity of taking up the cross and denying ourselves: have we taken it up, and are we carrying it daily? We have heard of the value of the soul: do we live as if we believed it? We have heard of Christ's second advent: do we look forward to it with hope and joy? Happy is the person who can give a satisfactory answer to these questions!

Matthew
Chapter 17

The transfiguration *(17:1–13)*

These verses contain one of the most remarkable events in our Lord's earthly ministry, the event commonly called the transfiguration. The order in which it is recorded is beautiful and instructive. The latter part of the last chapter showed us the cross; here we are graciously allowed to see something of the coming reward. The hearts which have just been saddened by a plain statement of Christ's sufferings are at once gladdened by a vision of Christ's glory. Let us note this. We often lose much by not tracing the connection between chapter and chapter in the Word of God.

There are some mysterious things, no doubt, in the vision here described. It must be like this. We are as yet in the body. Our senses are conversant with gross and material things; our ideas and perceptions about glorified bodies and dead saints must necessarily be vague and imperfect. Let us content ourselves with endeavoring to mark out the practical lessons which the transfiguration is meant to teach us.

1. A pattern of the glory to come
First, we have in these verses a striking pattern of the glory in which the Lord Jesus Christ and his people will appear when he comes for the second time.

There can be little question that this was one main object of this wonderful vision. It was meant to encourage the disciples by giving them a glimpse of good things yet to come. That face which "shone like the sun" and those clothes "as white as the light" (verse 2) were intended to give the disciples some idea of the majesty in which Jesus will appear to the world when he comes for the second time, and all his saints with him. The corner of the veil was lifted up to show them their Master's true dignity. They were taught that if he did not yet appear to the world in the guise of a King, it was only because the time for putting on his royal robes had not yet come. It is impossible to draw any other conclusion from St. Peter's language when writing on the subject. He says, with clear reference to the transfiguration, "we were eyewitnesses of his majesty" (2 Peter 1:16).

It is good for us to have the coming glory of Christ and his people deeply impressed on our minds. We are sadly apt to forget it. There are few visible indications of it in the world: "At present we do not see everything subject to him" (Hebrews 2:8). Sin, unbelief and super-stition abound. Thousands are practically saying, "We don't want this man to be our king" (Luke 19:14). What Christ's people will be has not yet been made known (1 John 3:2): their crosses, their tribulations, their weaknesses, their conflicts, are all plain enough, but there are few signs of their future reward. Let us beware of giving way to doubts in this matter: let us silence such doubts by reading over the story of the transfiguration. There is laid up for Jesus, and all that believe in him, such glory as the human heart never conceived. It is not only promised, but part of it has actually been seen by three competent witnesses. One of them says, "We have seen his glory, the glory of the One and Only, who came from the Father" (John 1:14). Surely that which has been seen may well be believed.

2. Proof of bodily resurrection and life after death
Second, we have in these verses an unanswerable proof of the resurrec-tion of the body, and the life after death. We are told that Moses and Elijah appeared visibly in glory with Christ: they were seen in a bodily form. They were heard talking with our Lord. Fourteen hundred and eighty years had rolled round since Moses died and was buried; more than 900 years had passed away since Elijah was taken "up to heaven in a whirlwind" (2 Kings 2:1), yet here they are seen alive by Peter, James and John!

Let us lay firm hold on this part of the vision. It deserves close atten-tion. We must all feel, if we ever think at all, that the state of the dead is a wonderful and mysterious subject. One after another we bury them out of our sight; we lay them in their narrow beds and see them no more, and their bodies become dust. But will they really live again? Shall we really see them any more? Will the grave really give back the dead at the last day? These are the questions that will occasionally come across the minds of some, in spite of all the plainest statements in the Word of God.

Now we have in the transfiguration the clearest evidence that the dead will rise again. We find two men appearing on earth, in their bodies, who had long been separate from the land of the living, and in them we have a pledge of the resurrection of all. All that have ever lived upon earth will again be called to life, and render up their account: not one will be found missing. There is no such thing as annihilation. All that have ever fallen asleep in Christ will be found in his safekeeping: patriarchs, prophets, apostles, martyrs, down to the humblest servant of God in our own day. "Though unseen to us they all live to God." "He is not the God of the dead, but of the living" (Luke 20:38). Their spirits live as surely as we live ourselves, and will appear hereafter in glorified bodies, as surely as Moses and Elijah on the mountain. These are indeed solemn thoughts! There is a resurrection, and men like Felix may well tremble. There is a resurrection, and men like Paul may well rejoice.

3. Testimony to Christ's superiority to mankind

Third, we have in these verses a remarkable testimony to Christ's infinite superiority over all that are born of woman.

This is a point which is brought out strongly by the voice from heaven which the disciples heard. Peter, bewildered by the heavenly vision and not knowing what to say, proposed to build three shelters, one for Christ, one for Moses and one for Elijah. He seemed, in fact, to place the law-giver and the prophet side by side with his divine Master, as if all three were equal. At once, we are told, the proposal was rebuked in a marked manner. A cloud covered Moses and Elijah, and they were seen no more. A voice at the same time came out of the cloud, repeating the solemn words used at our Lord's baptism, "This is my Son, whom I love; with him I am well pleased. Listen to him!" (verse 5). That voice was meant to teach Peter that there was One there far greater than Moses or Elijah.

Moses was a faithful servant of God; Elijah was a bold witness for the truth: but Christ was far above either one or the other. He was the Saviour to whom law and prophets were continually pointing; he was the true prophet to whom all were commanded to listen (Deuteronomy 18:15). Moses and Elijah were great men in their day, but Peter and his companions were to remember that in nature, dignity and office they were far below Christ. He was the true sun: they were the planets depending daily on his light. He was the root: they were the branches. He was the Master: they were the servants. Their goodness was all derived: his was original and his own. Let them honor Moses and the prophets as holy men, but if they wanted to be saved they must take Christ alone for their Master, and glory only in him. "Listen to him."

Let us see in these words a striking lesson to the whole church of Christ. There is a constant tendency in human nature to "listen to humans." Bishops, priests, deacons, popes, cardinals, councils, presbyterian preachers and independent ministers are continually exalted to a place which God never intended them to fill, and made practically to usurp the honor of Christ. Against this tendency let us all watch, and be on our guard. Let these solemn words of the vision always ring in our ears: "Listen to Christ."

The best of humanity are only human at their very best. Patriarchs, prophets, apostles, martyrs, fathers, reformers, puritans – all, all are sinners, who need a Saviour: holy, useful, honorable in their place, but sinners after all. They must never be allowed to stand between us and Christ. He alone is the Son, with whom the Father is well pleased; he alone is sealed and appointed to give the bread of life; he alone has the keys in his hands: "God over all, forever praised!" (Romans 9:5). Let us take heed that we hear his voice and follow him; let us value all religious teaching just in proportion as it leads us to Jesus. The sum and substance of saving religion is to "listen to Christ."

The healing of a boy with a demon *(17:14–21)*

We read in this passage another of our Lord's great miracles. He heals a boy who was possessed by a demon.

1. The influence Satan sometimes exercises over the young

The first thing we see in these verses is a living image of the awful influence sometimes exercised by Satan over the young. We are told of a certain man's son, who had "seizures" and was "suffering greatly" (verse 15). We are told of the evil spirit pressing him on to the destruction of body and soul: "He often falls into the fire or into the water" (verse 15). It was one of those cases of Satanic possession which, however common in our Lord's time, in our own day is rarely seen; but we can easily imagine that, when they did occur, they must have been particularly distressing to the relatives of the afflicted. It is painful enough to see the bodies of those we love wracked by disease: how much more painful must it have been to see body and mind completely under the influence of the devil! "Out of hell," says Bishop Hall, "there could not be greater misery."

But we must not forget that there are many instances of Satan's spiritual dominion over young people which are quite as painful, in their way, as the case described in this passage. There are thousands of young men who seem to have wholly given themselves to Satan's temptations, and to be led "captive to do his will" (2 Timothy 2:26). They cast off all fear of God, and all respect for his commands; they serve various lusts and pleasures; they refuse to listen to the advice of parents, teachers or ministers; they fling aside all regard for health, character or worldly respectability. They do all that lies in their power to ruin themselves, body and soul, for time and eternity: they are willing bond-slaves of Satan. Who has not seen such young men? They are to be seen in town and in country; they are to be found among rich and among poor. Surely such young men give sad proof that although Satan nowadays seldom has possession of people's bodies, he still exercises a fearful dominion over some men's souls.

Yet it must be remembered that we must never despair even about such young people as these. We must call to mind the almighty power of our Lord Jesus Christ. Bad as was the case of the boy of whom we read in these verses, he was "healed from that moment" when he was brought to Christ! Parents, teachers and ministers should go on praying for young people, even at their worst. Hard as their hearts seem now, they may yet be softened: desperate as their wickedness now appears, they may yet be healed. They may yet repent and turn to God, like John Newton, and their final condition prove better than their first. Who can tell? Let it be a settled principle with us when we read about our Lord's miracles never to despair of the conversion of any soul.

2. The weakening effect of unbelief

Second, we see in these verses a striking example of the weakening effect of unbelief. The disciples anxiously inquired of our Lord, when they saw the devil yielding to his power, "Why couldn't we drive it out?" (verse 19). They received an answer full of the deepest instruction: "Because you have so little faith" (verse 20). Did they want to know the secret of their own sad failure in the hour of need? It was lack of faith.

Let us ponder this point well and learn wisdom. Faith is the key to success in the Christian warfare. Unbelief is the sure road to defeat. Once let our faith languish and decay, and all our graces will languish with it. Courage, patience, long-suffering and hope will soon wither and dwindle away: faith is the root on which they all depend. The same Israelites who at one time went through the Red Sea in triumph, at another time shrunk from danger like cowards when they reached the borders of the promised land. Their God was the same who had brought them out of the land of Egypt; their leader was the same Moses who had worked so many wonders before their eyes; but their faith was not the same. They gave way to shameful doubts of God's love and power. "They were not able to enter, because of their unbelief" (Hebrews 3:19).

3. Satan's kingdom not to be pulled down without hard work

Third, we see in these verses that Satan's kingdom is not to be pulled down without diligence and effort. This seems to be the lesson of the verse which concludes the passage we are now considering: "This kind does not go out except by prayer and fasting" (verse 21, footnote). A gentle rebuke to the disciples appears to be implied in the words. Perhaps they had been too elated by past successes; perhaps they had been less careful in the use of means in their Master's absence than they were under their Master's eye. At any rate they receive a plain hint from our Lord that the warfare against Satan must never be lightly carried on. They are warned that no victories are to be won easily over the prince of this world. Without fervent prayer and diligent self-mortification, they would often meet with failure and defeat.

The lesson laid down here is one of deep importance. "I would," says Bullinger, "that this part of the Gospel pleased us as much as those parts which concede liberty." We are all apt to contract a habit of doing religious acts in a thoughtless, perfunctory way. Like Israel, puffed up with the fall of Jericho, we are ready to say to ourselves, "Only a few men are there" (Joshua 7:3); "There is no need to exert all our strength." Like Israel, we often learn by bitter experience that spiritual battles are not to be won without hard fighting. The ark of the Lord must never be handled irreverently; God's work must never be carelessly done.

May we all bear in mind our Lord's words to his disciples, and make practical use of them. In the pulpit and on the platform, in the Sunday school and in the district, in our use of family prayers and in reading our own Bibles, let us diligently watch our own spirit. Whatever we do, let us do it with all our might (Ecclesiastes 9:10). It is a fatal mistake to underrate our foes. He who is for us is greater than he who is against us, but, for all that, he that is against us is not to be despised. He is the "prince of this world" (John 12:31); he is a "strong man, fully armed" (Luke 11:21) keeping his house, who will not "go out" and part with his goods without a struggle. "Our struggle is not against flesh and blood, but against the rulers, against the authorities, against the powers" (Ephesians 6:12). We must take the whole armor of God, and not only take it, but use it too. We may be very sure that those who win most victories over the world, the flesh and the devil are those who pray most in private and beat their bodies and make them their slaves (1 Corinthians 9:27).

The fish and the temple tax *(17:22–27)*

These verses contain a situation in our Lord's story which is not recorded by any of the evangelists except St. Matthew. A remarkable miracle is worked in order to provide payment for the tax required for the service of the temple. There are three striking points in the narrative which deserve attentive observation.

1. Christ's perfect knowledge

First, let us observe our Lord's perfect knowledge of everything that is said and done in this world. We are told that "the collectors of the two-drachma tax came to Peter and asked, 'Doesn't your teacher pay the temple tax?' 'Yes, he does,' he replied" (verses 24–25). It is evident that our Lord was not present when the question was asked and the answer given; and yet no sooner did Peter come into the house than our Lord asked him, "What do you think, Simon? From whom do the kings of the earth collect duty and taxes?" (verse 25). He showed that he was as well acquainted with the conversation as if he had been listening or standing by.

There is something especially solemn in the thought that the Lord Jesus knows all things. There is an eye that sees all our daily conduct; there is an ear that hears all our daily words. All things are naked and opened to his eyes. Concealment is impossible; hypocrisy is useless. We may deceive ministers; we may impose upon our relations and neighbors: but the Lord sees us through and through. We cannot deceive Christ.

We ought to endeavor to make practical use of this truth. We should strive to live as in the Lord's sight and, like Abraham, to "walk before" him (Genesis 17:1). Let it be our daily aim to say nothing we would not like Christ to hear, and to do nothing we would not like Christ to see. Let us measure every difficult question about right and wrong by one simple test: "How would I behave if Jesus were standing by my side?" Such a standard is not extravagant and absurd. It is a standard that interferes with no duty or relation of life; it interferes with nothing but sin. Happy is he that tries to realize his Lord's presence, and to do all and say everything as to Christ.

2. Christ's power over creation

Second, let us observe our Lord's almighty power over all creation. He makes a fish his paymaster: he makes a dumb creature bring the tax money to meet the collector's demand. As Jerome says so well, "I know not which to admire most here, our Lord's foreknowledge or his greatness."

We see here a literal fulfillment of the Psalmist's words: "You made him ruler over the works of your hands; you put everything under his feet: all flocks and herds, and the beasts of the field, the birds of the air, and the fish of the sea, all that swim the paths of the seas" (Psalm 8:6–8).

Here is one among many proofs of the majesty and greatness of our Lord Jesus Christ. Only he who first created could at his will command the obedience of all his creatures. "By him all things were created" (Colossians 1:16). The believer who goes out to do Christ's work among the heathen may safely commit himself to his Master's keeping: he serves one who has all power, even over the beasts of the earth. How wonderful the thought that such an almighty Lord should condescend to be crucified for our salvation! How comforting the thought that when he comes again the second time he will gloriously reveal his power over all created things to the whole world: "the wolf and the lamb will feed together, and the lion will eat straw like the ox, but dust will be the serpent's food" (Isaiah 65:25).

3. Christ's willingness to make concessions rather than give offense

Third, let us observe in these verses our Lord's willingness to make concessions, rather than give offense. He might justly have claimed exemption from the payment of this temple tax. He, who was Son of God, might fairly have been excused from paying for the maintenance of his Father's house; he who was "greater than the temple" (Matthew 12:6) might have shown good cause for declining to contribute to the support of the temple. But our Lord does not do so. He claims no exemption. He desires Peter to pay the money demanded. At the same time he declares his reasons: it was to be done "so that we may not offend them" (verse 27). "A miracle is worked," says Bishop Hall, "rather than offend even a tax collector."

Our Lord's example in this case deserves the attention of all who call themselves Christians. There is deep wisdom in those seven words, "so that we may not offend them." They teach us plainly that there are matters in which Christ's people ought to sink their own opinions and submit to requirements which they may not thoroughly approve, rather than give offense and "hinder the gospel of Christ" (1 Corinthians 9:12). We should never give up God's rights, but we may sometimes safely give up our own. It may sound very fine and very heroic to be always standing out tenaciously for our rights! But it may well be doubted, with such a passage as this, whether such tenacity is always wise, and shows the mind of Christ. There are occasions when it shows more grace in a Christian to submit than to resist.

Let us remember this passage as *citizens and subjects*. We may not like all the political measures of our rulers; we may disapprove of some of the taxes they impose. But the big question after all is, Will it do any good to the cause of religion to resist the powers that be? Are their measures really injuring our souls? If not, let us hold our peace, "so that we may not offend them." "A Christian," says Bullinger, "never ought to disturb the public peace for things of mere temporary importance."

Let us remember this passage as *members of a church*. We may not like every detail of the forms and ceremonies used in our fellowship; we may not think that those who rule us in spiritual matters are always wise: but after all, are the points on which we are dissatisfied really of vital importance? Is any great truth of the Gospel at stake? If not, let us be quiet, "so that we may not offend them."

Let us remember this passage as *members of society*. There may be practices in the circles where our lot is cast, which to us as Christians are tiresome, useless and unprofitable: but are they matters of principle? Do they injure our souls? Will it do any good to the cause of religion if we refuse to comply with them? If not, let us patiently submit, "so that we may not offend them."

It would be good for the church and the world if these words of our Lord had been more studied, pondered and used! Who can tell the damage that has been done to the cause of the Gospel by morbid scrupulosity, and conscientiousness, falsely so called! May we all remember the example of the great apostle of the Gentiles: "we put up with anything rather than hinder the gospel of Christ" (1 Corinthians 9:12).

Matthew
Chapter 18

Conversion and humility; the reality of hell *(18:1–14)*

1. The necessity of conversion
The first thing that we are taught in these verses is the necessity of conversion, and of conversion shown in childlike humility. The disciples came to our Lord with the question, "Who is the greatest in the kingdom of heaven?" (verse 1). They spoke as if half-enlightened, and full of worldly expectations. They received an answer well calculated to awaken them from their day-dream. The answer contained a truth which lies at the very foundation of Christianity: "Unless you change and become like little children, you will never enter the kingdom of heaven" (verse 3).

Let these words sink down deeply in our hearts. Without conversion there is no salvation. We all need an entire change of nature: of ourselves we have neither faith, fear, nor love towards God. We "must be born again" (John 3:7). Of ourselves we are utterly unfit for dwelling in God's presence. Heaven would be no heaven to us if we were not "converted." It is true of all ranks, classes and orders of mankind: all are born in sin and are children of wrath, and all, without exception, need to be born again and made new creatures. A new heart must be given to us, and a new spirit put within us; old things must pass away, and all things must become new. It is a good thing to be baptized into the Christian church, and use Christian means of grace, but after everything, "are we converted?"

Do we want to know whether we are really converted? Do we want to we know the test by which we must try ourselves? The surest mark of true conversion is humility. If we have really received the Holy

Spirit, we will show it by a meek and childlike spirit. Like children, we shall think humbly about our own strength and wisdom, and be very dependent on our Father in heaven. Like children, we shall not seek great things in this world; but having food and clothing and a Father's love, we shall be content. Truly this is a heart-searching test! It exposes the unsoundness of many a so-called conversion. It is easy to be a convert from one party to another party, from one sect to another sect, from one set of opinions to another set of opinions: such conversions save no one's soul. What we all want is a conversion from pride to humility, from high thoughts about ourselves to lowly thoughts about ourselves, from self-conceit to self-abasement, from the mind of the Pharisee to the mind of the tax collector. A conversion of this kind we must experience if we hope to be saved. These are the conversions that are wrought by the Holy Spirit.

2. The sin of putting stumbling-blocks in the way of believers

Second, we are taught in these verses concerning the great sin of putting stumbling-blocks in the way of believers. The words of the Lord Jesus on this subject are especially solemn: "Woe to the world because of the things that cause people to sin! . . . Woe to the man through whom they come!" (verse 7).

We put stumbling-blocks in the way of men's souls whenever we do anything to keep them back from Christ, or to turn them out of the way of salvation, or to disgust them with true religion. We may do it directly, by persecuting, ridiculing, opposing or dissuading them from committed service of Christ; we may do it indirectly by living a life inconsistent with our religious profession, and by making Christianity loathsome and distasteful by our own conduct. Whenever we do anything of the kind, it is clear, from our Lord's words, that we commit a great sin.

There is something very fearful in the doctrine here laid down: it should make us search our hearts. It is not enough that we wish to do good in this world: are we are quite sure that we are not doing harm? We may not openly persecute Christ's servants, but are there any that we are injuring by our ways and our example? It is awful to think of the amount of harm that can be done by one person who claims to be a Christian but is inconsistent. They give a handle to the unbeliever; they supply the worldly with an excuse for remaining undecided; they check the inquirer after salvation; they discourage the saints. They are, in short, living sermons on behalf of the devil. The last day alone will reveal the wholesale ruin of souls that these things have occasioned in the church of Christ. One of Nathan's charges against David was, "You have made the enemies of the LORD show utter contempt" (2 Samuel 12:14).

3. The reality of punishment after death

Third, we are taught in these verses the reality of future punishment after death. Two strong expressions are used by our Lord on this point. He speaks of being "thrown into eternal fire" (verse 8). He speaks of being "thrown into the fire of hell" (verse 9).

The meaning of these words is clear and unmistakable. There is a place of unspeakable misery in the world to come, to which all who die impenitent and unbelieving must ultimately be consigned. There is revealed in Scripture a "raging fire" which sooner or later will devour all God's adversaries (Hebrews 10:27). The same sure Word which holds out a heaven to all who repent and turn to God, declares plainly that there will be a hell for all the ungodly.

Let no one deceive us with vain words upon this awful subject. People have appeared in these last days who profess to deny the eternity of future punishment, and repeat the devil's old argument, that we "will not surely die" (Genesis 3:4) Let none of their arguments move us, however plausible they may sound. Let us stand fast in the old paths. The God of love and mercy is also a God of justice: he will surely requite. The flood in Noah's day, and the burning of Sodom, were meant to show us what he will one day do. No lips have ever spoken so clearly about hell as those of Christ himself. Hardened sinners will find out, to their cost, that there is such a thing as the wrath of the Lamb (Revelation 6:16–17).

4. The value God sets on the least of believers

Fourth, we are taught in these verses the value that God sets on the least and lowest of believers. "Your Father in heaven is not willing that any of these little ones should be lost" (verse 14).

These words are meant for the encouragement of all true Christians, and not for little children only. The context in which they are found with the parable of the hundred sheep and one that went astray seems to place this beyond doubt. They are meant to show us that our Lord Jesus is a Shepherd who cares tenderly for every soul committed to his charge. The youngest, the weakest, the sickliest of his flock is as dear to him as the strongest: they will never perish. No one will ever snatch them out of his hand. He will lead them gently through the wilderness of this world; he will not drive them hard a single day, lest any die (Genesis 33:13). He will carry them through every difficulty; he will defend them against every enemy. The saying which he spoke will be literally fulfilled: "I have not lost one of those you gave me" (John 18:9). With such a Saviour, who need fear beginning to be a thorough Christian? With such a Shepherd who, having once begun, need fear being cast away?

Differences among Christians; church discipline *(18:15–20)*

These words of the Lord Jesus contain an expression which has often been misapplied. The command to "listen to the church" (verse 17) has been so interpreted as to contradict other passages of God's Word. It has been falsely applied to the authority of the whole visible church in matters of doctrine, and so been made an excuse for the exercise of much ecclesiastical tyranny. But the abuse of Scripture truths must not tempt us to neglect the use of them. We must not turn away altogether from any text, because some have perverted it and made it poison.

1. Rules for the healing of differences in the church
First, let us notice how admirable are the rules laid down by our Lord for the healing of differences among brothers and sisters.

If we have unhappily received any injury from a fellow-member of Christ's church, the first step to be taken is to "go and show him his fault, just between the two of you" (verse 15). He may have injured us unintentionally, as Abimelech did Abraham (Genesis 21:26); his conduct may admit an explanation, like that of the tribes of Reuben, Gad and Manasseh, when they built an altar as they returned to their own land (Joshua 22:24). At any rate, this friendly, faithful, straightforward way of dealing is the most likely course to win a brother, if he is to be won. "A gentle tongue can break a bone" (Proverbs 25:15). Who can tell but he may say at once, "I was wrong," and make ample reparation?

If, however, this course fails to produce any good effect, a second step is to be taken. We are to "take one or two others along" (verse 16), and tell our brother of his fault in their presence and hearing. Who can tell but his conscience may be stricken when he finds his misconduct made known, and he may be ashamed and repent? If not, we shall at all events have the testimony of witnesses that we did all we could to bring our brother to a right mind, and that he deliberately refused, when appealed to, to make amends.

Finally, if this second course proves useless, we are to refer the whole matter to the Christian congregation of which we are members: we are to "tell it to the church" (verse 17). Who can tell but the heart which has been unmoved by private remonstrances may be moved by the fear of public exposure? If not, there remains but one view to take of our brother's case: we must sorrowfully regard him as one who has shaken off all Christian principles, and will be guided by no higher motives than "a pagan or a tax collector" (verse 17).

The passage is a beautiful instance of the mingled wisdom and tender consideration of our Lord's teaching. What a knowledge it shows of human nature! Nothing does so much harm to the cause of religion as the quarrels of Christians: no stone should be left unturned, no trouble spared, in order to prevent their being dragged before the public. What a delicate thoughtfulness this shows for the sensitivity of poor human nature! Many a scandalous breach would be prevented if we were more ready to practice the rule of "just between the two of you." The church would indeed be happy if this portion of our Lord's teaching were more carefully studied and obeyed! Differences and divisions there will be, so long as the world stands; but many of them would be extinguished at once, if the course recommended in these verses was tried.

2. The exercise of discipline in a Christian congregation
Second, let us observe what a clear argument we have in these verses for the exercise of discipline in a Christian congregation.

Our Lord commands that disagreements between Christians, which cannot be otherwise settled, be referred to the decision of the church or Christian assembly to which they belong. "Tell it," he says (verse 17), "to the church." It is evident from this that he intends every cognizance of the moral conduct of its members, either by the action of the whole body collectively, or of heads and elders to whom its authority may be delegated. It is evident also that he intends every congregation to have the power of excluding disobedient and refractory members from participation in its ordinances. "If he refuses," he says, "to listen even to the church, treat him as you would a pagan and a tax collector." He says not a word about temporal punishment and civil disabilities. Spiritual penalities are the only penalty he permits the church to inflict; and when rightly inflicted, they are not to be lightly regarded. "Whatever you bind on earth will be bound in heaven" (Matthew 16:19). Such appears to be the substance of our Lord's teaching about ecclesiastical discipline.

It is vain to deny that the whole subject is surrounded with difficulties. On no point has the influence of the world weighed so heavily on the action of churches: on no point have churches made so many mistakes. No doubt the power of excommunication has been fearfully abused and perverted, and, as Quesnel says, "we ought to be more afraid of our sins than of all the excommunications in the world." Still it is impossible to deny, with this passage in mind, that church discipline is according to the mind of Christ, and, when wisely exercised, is calculated to promote a church's health and well-being. It can never be right that all sorts of people, however wicked and ungodly, should be allowed to come to the Lord's table. It is the clear duty of every Christian to use his influence to prevent such a state of things. A perfect communion can never be attained in this world, but purity should be our target. An increasingly high standard of qualification for full church membership will always be found as one of the best evidences of a prosperous church.

3. Christ's encouragement to those who meet in his name
Third, let us observe what gracious encouragement Christ holds out to those who meet together in his name. He says, "where two or three come together in my name, there am I with them" (verse 20). That saying is a striking proof of our Lord's divinity. God alone can be in more places than one at the same time.

There is comfort in these words for all who love to meet together for religious purposes. At every assembly for public worship, at every gathering for prayer and praise, at every missionary meeting, at every Bible reading, the King of kings is present, Christ himself attends. We may often be disheartened by the small number who are present on such occasions, compared with the number of those who meet for worldly ends; we may sometimes find it hard to bear the taunts and ridicule of an ill-natured world, which cries like the enemy of old, "What are those feeble Jews doing?" (Nehemiah 4:2). But we have no reason for despondency: we may boldly fall back on these words of Jesus. At all such meetings we have the company of Christ himself.

There is solemn rebuke in these words for all who neglect the public worship of God and never attend meetings for any religious purpose. They turn their backs on the society of the Lord of lords; they miss the opportunity of meeting Christ himself. It is no good saying that the proceedings of religious meetings are marked by weakness and infirmity, or that as much good is got by staying at home as going to church: the words of our Lord should silence such arguments at once. Surely men are not wise when they speak contemptuously of any gathering where Christ is present.

May we all ponder these things! If we have met together with God's people for spiritual purposes in times past, let us persevere, and not be ashamed. If we have hitherto despised such meetings, let us consider our ways, and learn wisdom.

The parable of the unforgiving servant *(18:21–35)*

In these verses the Lord Jesus deals with a deeply important subject, the forgiveness of injuries. We live in a wicked world, and it is vain to expect that we can escape ill-treatment, however carefully we may behave. To know how to conduct ourselves when we are ill-treated is of great moment to our souls.

1. We ought to forgive others to the uttermost
First, the Lord Jesus lays it down as a general rule that we ought to forgive others to the uttermost. Peter put the question, "How many times

shall I forgive my brother when he sins against me? Up to seven times?" (verse 21). Jesus replied: "I tell you, not seven times, but seventy-seven times" (verse 22).

The rule here laid down must of course be interpreted with sober-minded qualification. Our Lord does not mean that offenses against the law of the land and the good order of society are to be passed over in silence; he does not mean that we are to allow people to commit thefts and assaults with impunity. All that he means is that we are to study a general spirit of mercy and forgivingness towards our brothers and sisters. We are to bear much, and to put up with much, rather than quarrel; we are to overlook much, and submit to much, rather than have any strife; we are to lay aside everything like malice, strife, revenge and retaliation. Such feelings are only fit for pagans: they are utterly unworthy of a disciple of Christ.

What a happy world it would be if this rule of our Lord's was more known and better obeyed! How many of the miseries of mankind are occasioned by disputes, quarrels, lawsuits, and an obstinate tenacity about what men call "their rights"! How many of these might be altogether avoided if men were more willing to forgive, and more desirous for peace! Let us never forget that a fire cannot go on burning without fuel; just in the same way it takes two to make a quarrel. Let us each resolve, by God's grace, that we will never be one of these two. Let us resolve to return good for evil, and blessing for cursing, and so to melt down enmity, and change our foes into friends (Romans 12:20). It was a fine feature in Archbishop Cranmer's character, that if you did him an injury he was sure to be your friend.

2. Motives for a forgiving spirit

Second, our Lord supplies us with two powerful motives for exercising a forgiving spirit. He tells us a story of a man who owed an enormous sum to his master, and "was not able to pay" (verse 25). Nevertheless at the time of reckoning his master had compassion on him, and "canceled the debt" (verse 27). He tells us that this man, after being forgiven himself, refused to forgive a fellow-servant a trifling debt. He actually threw him into prison, and would not listen to any of his demands. He tells us how punishment overtook this wicked and cruel man, who, after receiving mercy, ought surely to have shown mercy to others. Finally, he concludes the parable with the impressive words, "This is how my heavenly Father will treat each of you unless you forgive your brother from your heart" (verse 35).

It is clear from this parable that one motive for forgiving others ought to be the recollection that we all need forgiveness at God's hands ourselves. Day after day we are coming short in many things, "leaving undone what we ought to do, and doing what we ought not to do." Day after day we require mercy and pardon. Our neighbors' offenses against us are mere trifles, compared with our offenses against God. Surely it ill becomes poor erring creatures like us to be extreme in marking what is done amiss by our brethren, or slow to forgive it.

Another motive for forgiving others ought to be the recollection of the day of judgment, and the standard by which we shall all be tried in that day. There will be no forgiveness in that day for unforgiving people. Such people would be unfit for heaven: they would not be able to value a dwelling-place to which "mercy" is the only title, and in which "mercy" is the eternal subject of song. Surely if we mean to stand at the right hand, when Jesus sits on the throne of his glory, we must learn, while we are on earth, to forgive.

Let these truths sink down deeply into our hearts. It is a melancholy fact that there are few Christian duties so little practiced as that of forgiveness: it is sad to see how much bitterness, unmercifulness, spite, hardness and unkindness there is among men. Yet there are few duties so strongly commanded in the New Testament Scriptures as this duty is, and few whose neglect so clearly shuts a man out of the kingdom of God.

Do we want to give proof that we are at peace with God, washed in Christ's blood, born of the Spirit, and made God's children by adoption and grace? Let us remember this passage; like our Father in heaven, let us be forgiving. Has anyone injured us? Let us this day forgive him. As Leighton says, "We ought to forgive ourselves little, and others much."

Do we want to do good to the world? Do we want to have any influence on others, and make them see the beauty of true religion? Let us remember this passage. Men who do not care for doctrines can understand a forgiving temper.

Do we want to grow in grace ourselves and become more holy in all our ways, words and works? Let us remember this passage. Nothing so grieves the Holy Spirit, and brings spiritual darkness over the soul, as giving way to a quarrelsome and unforgiving temper (Ephesians 4:30–32).

Matthew
Chapter 19

Christ's judgment about divorce *(19:1–12)*

In these verses we have the mind of Christ declared on two subjects of great moment. One is the relation of husband and wife; the other is the light in which we should regard little children in the matter of their souls.

It is difficult to overrate the importance of these two subjects: the well-being of nations and the happiness of society are closely connected with right views upon them. Nations are nothing but a collection of families. The good order of families depends entirely on keeping up the highest standard of respect for the marriage tie, and on the right training of children. We ought to be thankful that, on both these points, the great head of the church pronounced judgment so clearly.

With respect to marriage, our Lord teaches that the union of husband and wife ought never to be broken off, except for the greatest of all causes, namely, actual unfaithfulness.

In these days when our Lord was upon earth divorces were permitted among the Jews for the most trifling and frivolous causes. The practice, though tolerated by Moses to prevent worse evils – such as cruelty or murder – had gradually become an enormous abuse, and no doubt led to much immorality (Malachi 2:14–16). The remark made by our Lord's disciples shows the deplorably low state of public feeling on the subject. They said, "If this is the situation between a husband and wife, it is better not to marry" (verse 10). They meant, of course, "if a man may not put away his wife for a slight cause at any time, he had better not marry at all." Such language from the mouths of apostles sounds strange indeed!

Our Lord brings forward a completely different standard for the guidance of his disciples. He first founds his judgment on the original institution of marriage. He quotes the words used in the beginning of Genesis, where the creation of man and the union of Adam and Eve are described, as a proof that no relationship should be so highly regarded as that of husband and wife. The relation of parent and child may seem very close, but there is one closer still: "A man will leave his father and mother and be united to his wife" (verse 5). He then backs up the quotation by his own solemn words, "What God has joined together, let man not separate" (verse 6). And finally he brings in the grave charge of breaking the seventh commandment, against marriage contracted after a divorce for light and frivolous causes: "Anyone who divorces his wife, except for marital unfaithfulness, and marries another woman commits adultery" (verse 9).

It is clear from the whole tenor of the passage that the relation of marriage ought to be highly honored among Christians. It is a relation which was instituted in paradise, in the time of man's innocence, and is chosen as an image of the mystical union between Christ and his church. It is a relationship which nothing but death ought to terminate. It is a relationship which is sure to have the greatest influence on those it brings together, for happiness or for misery, for good or for evil. Such a relationship should never be entered into unadvisedly, lightly or wantonly, but soberly, discreetly and with due consideration. It is only too true that inconsiderate marriages are one of the most fertile causes of unhappiness, and too often, it may be feared, of sin.

Christ's tenderness to little children *(19:13–15)*

With respect to little children, we find our Lord instructing us in these verses both by word and deed, both by precept and example. "Little children were brought to Jesus for him to place his hands on them and pray for them" (verse 13). They were evidently tender infants, too young to receive instruction, but not too young to derive benefit from prayer. The disciples seem to have thought them beneath their Master's notice, and rebuked those who brought them. But this drew forth a solemn declaration from the great head of the church: "Jesus said, 'Let the little children come to me, and do not hinder them, for the kingdom of heaven belongs to such as these'" (verse 14).

There is something deeply interesting both in the language and action of our Lord on this occasion. We know the weakness and feebleness, both in mind and body, of a little infant: of all creatures born into the world none is so helpless and dependent. We know who took such notice of these infants here, and found time in his busy ministry among grown men and women to "place his hands on them and pray for them." It was the eternal Son of God, the great High Priest, the King of kings, through whom all things exist, "the radiance of God's glory and the exact representation of his being" (Hebrews 1:3). What an instructive picture is set before our eyes! No wonder the great majority of the church of Christ have always seen in this passage a strong, though indirect, argument in favor of infant baptism.

1. Jesus cares for little children

First, let us learn from these verses that the Lord Jesus cares tenderly for the souls of little children. It is probable that Satan specially hates them: it is certain that Jesus specially loves them. Young as they are, they are not beneath his thoughts and attention. That mighty heart of his has room for the baby in its cradle, as well as for the king on his throne. He regards each infant as possessing within its little body an undying principle that will outlive the pyramids of Egypt, and see sun and moon quenched at the last day. With such a passage as this before us we may surely have confident hope about the salvation of all who die in infancy. "The kingdom of heaven belongs to such as these" (verse 14).

2. Encouragement to attempt great things in instructing children

Second, let us draw encouragement from these verses to attempt great things in the religious instruction of children. Let us begin from their very earliest years to deal with them as having souls to be lost or saved, and let us strive to bring them to Christ; let us make them acquainted with the Bible as soon as they can understand anything; let us pray with them, and pray for them, and teach them to pray for themselves. We may rest assured that Jesus looks with pleasure on such endeavors, and is ready to bless them. We may rest assured that such endeavors are not in vain. The seed sown in infancy is often found after many days.

Happy is the church whose infant members are cared for as much as the oldest communicants! The blessing of him who was crucified will surely be on that church! He placed his hands on little children; he prayed for them.

The rich young man (19:16–22)

These verses detail a conversation between our Lord Jesus Christ and a young man who came to him to inquire about the way to eternal life. Like every conversation recorded in the Gospels between our Lord and an individual, it deserves special attention. Salvation is an individual business: every one who wishes to be saved must have private personal dealings with Christ about his own soul.

1. One may desire salvation without being saved

First, we see from the case of this young man that a person may desire salvation, and yet not be saved. Here is one who in a day of abounding unbelief comes of his own accord to Christ. He does not come to have a sickness healed; he does not come to plead about a child: he comes about his own soul. He opens the discussion with the frank question, "Teacher, what good thing must I do to get eternal life?" (verse 16). Surely we might have thought, "This is a promising start: this is no prejudiced ruler or Pharisee: this is a hopeful inquirer." Yet, by and by, this young man "went away sad" (verse 22), and we never read a word to show that he was converted!

We must never forget that good feelings alone in religion are not the grace of God. We may know the truth intellectually; we may often feel pricked in conscience; we may have religious affections awakened within us, have many anxieties about our souls and shed many tears; but all this is not conversion. It is not the genuine saving work of the Holy Spirit.

Unhappily this is not all that must be said on this point. Not only are good feelings alone not grace, but they are even positively dangerous if we content ourselves with them, and do not act as well as feel. It is a profound remark of that mighty master on moral questions, Bishop Butler, that passive impressions, often repeated, produce a habit in a person's mind; feelings often indulged in, without leading to corresponding actions, will finally exercise no influence at all.

Let us apply this lesson to our own state. Perhaps we know what it is to feel religious fears, wishes and desires. Let us beware that we do not rest in them. Let us never be satisfied till we have the witness of the Spirit in our hearts that we are actually born again and new creatures; let us never rest till we know that we have really repented, and laid hold on the hope set before us in the Gospel. It is good to feel; but it is far better to be converted.

2. An unconverted person is often spiritually ignorant

Second, we see from this young man's case that an unconverted person is often profoundly ignorant about spiritual subjects. Our Lord refers this inquirer to the eternal standard of right and wrong, the moral law. Seeing that he speaks so boldly about "doing," he tries him by a command well calculated to draw out the real state of his heart: "If you want to enter life, obey the commandments" (verse 17). He even repeats to him the second tablet of the law; and at once the young man confidently replies, "All these I have kept. What do I still lack?" (verse 20). So utterly ignorant is he of the spirituality of God's commands that he never doubts that he has perfectly fulfilled them. He seems completely unaware that the commandments apply to the thoughts and words as well as to the deeds, and that if God were to enter into judgment with him, he could "not answer him one time out of a thousand" (Job 9:3). How dark must his mind have been about the nature of God's law! How low must his ideas have been about the holiness which God requires!

It is a melancholy fact that ignorance like that of this young man is only too common in the church of Christ. There are thousands of baptized people who know no more of the leading doctrines of Christianity than the heathen. Tens of thousands fill churches and chapels weekly, who are utterly in the dark as to the full extent of man's sinfulness. They cling obstinately to the old notion that in some way or other their own actions can save them; and when ministers visit them on their death-beds, they prove as blind as if they had never heard truth at all. It is so true that the "man without the Spirit does not accept the things that come from the Spirit of God, for they are foolishness to him" (1 Corinthians 2:14).

3. One cherished idol may ruin a soul forever

Third, we know from this young man's case that one idol cherished in the heart may ruin a soul forever. Our Lord, who knew what was in man, at last shows his inquirer his besetting sin. The same searching voice which said to the Samaritan woman, "Go, call your husband" (John 4:16) says to the young man, "Go, sell your possessions and give to the poor" (verse 21). At once the weak point in his character is detected. It turns out that, with all his wishes and desires after eternal life, there was one thing he loved better than his soul, and that was his money. He cannot stand the test. He is weighed in the balance, and found wanting. And the story ends with the melancholy words, "He went away sad, because he had great wealth" (verse 22).

We have in this story one more proof of the truth, "The love of money is a root of all kinds of evil" (1 Timothy 6:10). We must place this young man in our memories by the side of Judas, Ananias and Sapphira, and learn to beware of covetousness. Alas, it is a rock on which thousands are continually being shipwrecked. There is hardly a minister of the Gospel who could not point to many in his congregation who, humanly speaking, are "not far from the kingdom of God," but they never seem to make progress. They wish, they feel, they mean well, they hope, but there they stick fast! And why? Because they are fond of money.

Let us test our own selves, as we leave the passage. Let us see how it touches our own souls. Are we honest and sincere in our professed desire to be true Christians? Have we cast away all our idols? Is there no secret sin that we are silently clinging to, and refusing to give up? Is there no thing or person that we are privately loving more than Christ and our souls? These are questions that ought to be answered. The true explanation of the unsatisfactory state of many hearers of the Gospel is spiritual idolatry. We need not wonder that St. John says, "keep yourselves from idols" (1 John 5:21).

The danger of riches; leaving everything for Christ (19:23–30)

1. The danger riches bring to the soul

First, we learn in these verses the immense danger which riches bring on the souls of those who possess them. The Lord Jesus declares that "it is hard for a rich man to enter the kingdom of heaven" (verse 23). He goes even further. He uses a proverbial saying to strengthen his assertion: "It is easier for a camel to go through the eye of a needle than for a rich man to enter into the kingdom of God" (verse 24).

Few of our Lord's sayings sound more startling than this; few run more counter to the opinions and prejudices of mankind; few are so little believed; yet this saying is true, and deserves to be accepted by everyone. Riches, which all desire to obtain – riches, for which people labor and toil and become gray before their time – riches are the most perilous possession. They often inflict great injury on the soul; they lead people into many temptations; they engross people's thoughts and affections; they bind heavy burdens on the heart, and make the way to heaven even more difficult than it naturally is.

Let us beware of the love of money. It is possible to use it well, and do good with it; but for one who makes a right use of money, there are thousands who make a wrong use of it, and do harm both to themselves and others. Let the worldly, if they want, make an idol of money, and count them happiest who have most of it. But let Christians, who profess to have "treasure in heaven" (verse 21), set their face, like a flint, against the spirit of the world in this matter. Let them not worship gold. The best in God's eyes are not those who have the most money, but those who have the most grace.

Let us pray daily for rich people's souls. They are not to be envied, they are deeply to be pitied. They carry heavy weights in the Christian course; they are the least likely of anyone to "run in such a way as to get the prize" (1 Corinthians 9:24). Their prosperity in this world is often their destruction in the world to come. Well may the Litany of the Church of England contain the words, "In all time of our wealth, good Lord, deliver us."

2. The power of God's grace in the soul

Second, we learn in this passage the almighty power of God's grace in the soul. The disciples were amazed when they heard our Lord's language about rich people. It was language so entirely contrary to all their thoughts about the advantages of wealth that they cried out with surprise, "Who then can be saved?" (verse 25). They drew from our Lord a gracious answer: "With man this is impossible, but with God all things are possible" (verse 26). The Holy Spirit can incline even the richest to seek treasure in heaven. He can dispose even kings to cast their crowns at the feet of Jesus, and to count all things loss for the sake of the kingdom of God. Proof upon proof of this is given to us in the Bible. Abraham was very rich, yet he was the father of the faithful; Moses might have been a prince or king in Egypt, but he left all his brilliant prospects for the sake of him who is invisible; Job was the wealthiest man in the East, yet he was a chosen servant of God; David, Jehoshaphat, Josiah, Hezekiah were all wealthy monarchs, but they loved God's favor more than their earthly greatness. They all show us that "nothing is too hard for the Lord," and that faith can grow even in the most unlikely soil.

Let us hold this doctrine fast, and never let it go. No man's place or circumstances shut him out from the kingdom of God; let us never despair of anyone's salvation. No doubt rich people require special grace, and are exposed to special temptations. But the Lord God of Abraham, Moses, Job and David has not changed. He who saved them in spite of their riches can save other people as well. When he acts, who can reverse it (Isaiah 43:13)?

3. Encouragement to those who give up everything for Christ

Third, we learn in these verses the immense encouragement the Gospel offers to those who give up everything for Christ's sake. We are told that Peter asked our Lord what he and the other apostles, who had forsaken their little all for his sake, should receive in return. He received a most gracious reply. A full recompense shall be made to all who make sacrifices for Christ's sake: they "will receive a hundred times as much and will inherit eternal life" (verse 29).

There is something very cheering in this promise. Few in the present day, except converts among the heathen, are ever required to leave homes, relatives and lands on account of their religion; yet there are few true Christians who do not have to do this in one way or another if they are really faithful to their Lord. The stumbling-block of the cross is not yet over: laughter, ridicule, mockery and family persecution often hit a believer. The favor of the world is frequently forfeited by a conscientious adherence to the demands of the Gospel of Christ. All who are exposed to trials of this kind may take comfort in the promise of these verses. Jesus foresaw their need, and intended these words to be their consolation.

We may rest assured that no one will ever be a real loser by following Christ. The believer may seem to suffer loss for a time when he first begins the life of a committed Christian; he may be cast down by the afflictions that besiege him on account of his religion. Let him rest assured that he will never find himself a loser in the long run. Christ can raise up friends for us who will more than compensate for those we lose; Christ can open hearts and homes to us far more warm and hospitable than those that are closed against us; above all, Christ can give us peace of conscience, inward joy, bright hopes and happy feelings, which will far outweigh every pleasant earthly thing that we have cast away for his sake. He has pledged his royal word that it will be so. No one ever found that word to fail: let us trust it and not be afraid.

Matthew
Chapter 20

The parable of the workers in the vineyard *(20:1–16)*

There are undeniable difficulties in the parable contained in these verses. The key to the right explanation of them must be sought in the passage which concludes the last chapter. There we find the apostle Peter asking our Lord a remarkable question: "We have left everything to follow you! What then will there be for us?" (Matthew 19:27). There we find Jesus giving a remarkable answer. He makes a special promise to Peter and his fellow disciples: they would one day sit on twelve thrones, judging the twelve tribes of Israel (Matthew 19:28). He makes a general promise to all who suffer loss for his sake: they "will receive a hundred times as much and will inherit eternal life" (Matthew 19:29).

Now we must bear in mind that Peter was a Jew, and like most Jews he had probably been brought up in much ignorance about God's purposes respecting the salvation of the Gentiles. In fact we know from Acts that it required a vision from heaven to remove that ignorance (Acts 10:28). Furthermore, we must bear in mind that Peter and his fellow-disciples were weak in faith and knowledge. They were probably apt to attach great importance to their own sacrifices for Christ's sake, and inclined to self-righteousness and conceit. Both these points our Lord knew well. He therefore tells this parable for the special benefit of Peter and his companions. He read their hearts. He saw what spiritual medicine those hearts required, and supplied it without delay. In a word, he checked their rising pride, and taught them humility.

In expounding this parable, we need not inquire closely into the meaning of the "denarius," the "marketplace," the "foreman" or the "hours." Such inquiries often darken counsel by words without knowledge. As a great divine so well says, "the theology of parables is not argumentative." The hint of Chrysostom deserves notice. He says, "It is not right to search curiously, and word by word, into all things in a parable; but when we have learned the object for which it was composed, we are to reap this, and not to busy ourselves about anything further." Two main lessons appear to stand out on the face of the parable, and to embrace the general scope of its meaning. Let us content ourselves with these two.

1. God exercises grace in the calling of nations

First, we learn that in the calling of nations to the professed knowledge of himself, God exercises free, sovereign and unconditional grace. He calls the families of the earth into the visible church in his own time, and in his own way.

We see this truth wonderfully brought out in the history of God's dealings with the world. We see the children of Israel called and chosen to be God's people in the very beginning of "the day" (verse 2). We see some of the Gentiles called at a later period, by the preaching of the apostles; we see others being called in the present age, by the labors of missionaries; we see others, like the millions of Chinese and Hindus, still "standing around," because "no one has hired" them (verses 6–7). And why is all this? We cannot tell. We only know that God loves to hide pride from churches, and to take away all opportunity for boasting. He will never allow the older branches of his church to look contemptuously on the younger. His Gospel holds out pardon and peace with God through Christ to the heathen of our own times, as fully as it did to St. Paul. The converted inhabitants of Tinnevelly and New Zealand will be as fully admitted to heaven as the holiest patriarch who died 3500 years ago. The old wall between Jews and Gentiles is removed. There is nothing to prevent the believing heathen from being "a fellow-heir and partaker of the same hope" with the believing Israelite. The Gentiles converted at "the eleventh hour" of the world (verse 9) will be as really and truly heirs of glory as the Jews; they will sit down with Abraham, Isaac and Jacob in the kingdom of heaven, while many of the children of the kingdom are forever cast out. "The last will" indeed "be first" (verse 16).

2. God acts as a sovereign in saving individuals

Second, we learn that in the saving of individuals, as well as in the calling of nations, God acts as a sovereign, and gives no account of his matters. He will have mercy on whom he has mercy, and that too in his own time (Romans 9:15).

This is a truth which we see illustrated on every side in the church of Christ, as a matter of experience. We see one person called to repentance and faith in childhood, like Timothy, and working in the Lord's vineyard for forty or fifty years; we see another called "at the eleventh hour," like the thief on the cross, and snatched like a burning stick from the fire – one day a hardened impenitent sinner, and the next day in paradise. And yet the whole tenor of the Gospel leads us to believe that both are equally forgiven before God. Both are equally washed in Christ's blood, and clothed in Christ's righteousness; both are equally justified, both accepted, and both will be found at Christ's right hand at the last day.

There can be no doubt that this doctrine sounds strange to the ignorant and inexperienced Christian. It confounds the pride of human nature; it leaves the self-righteous no room to boast; it is a leveling, humbling doctrine, and gives rise to many a grumble: but it is impossible to reject it, unless we reject the whole Bible. True faith in Christ, even if it is only a day old, justifies a person before God as completely as the faith of someone who has followed Christ for fifty years. The righteousness in which Timothy will stand at the day of judgment is the same as that of the penitent thief. Both will be saved by grace alone; both will owe all to Christ. We may not like this, but it is the doctrine of this parable, and not of this parable only, but of the whole New Testament. Happy is he who can receive the doctrine with humility! As Bishop Hall says so well, "If some have cause to magnify God's bounty, none have cause to complain."

Before we leave this parable let us arm our minds with some necessary cautions. It is a portion of Scripture that is frequently perverted and misapplied. People have often drawn from it not milk, but poison.

1. Salvation does not come by good deeds

Let us beware of supposing from anything in this parable that salvation is in the slightest degree to be obtained by performing good deeds. To suppose this is to overthrow the whole teaching of the Bible. Whatever a believer receives in the next world is a matter of grace, and not of debt. God is never a debtor to us in any sense whatever; when we have done everything, we are unworthy servants (Luke 17:10).

2. Jews and Gentiles remain distinct

Let us beware of supposing from this parable that the distinction between Jews and Gentiles is entirely done away by the Gospel. To suppose this is to contradict many plain prophecies, both of the Old Testament and New. In the matter of justification, there is no distinction between the believing Jew and the Greek; but in the matter of national privileges, Israel is still a special people. God has many purposes concerning the Jews which are yet to be fulfilled.

3. Saved souls will not all have the same glory

Let us beware of supposing from this parable that all saved souls will have the same degree of glory. To suppose this is to contradict many plain texts of Scripture. The title of all believers no doubt is the same – a place in heaven. "Each will be rewarded according to his own labor" (1 Corinthians 3:8).

4. It is not safe to delay repentance

Finally, let us beware of supposing from this parable that it is safe for anyone to put off repentance until the end of his days. To suppose this is a most dangerous delusion. The longer people refuse to obey Christ's voice, the less likely they are to be saved. "Now is the time of God's favor, now is the day of salvation" (2 Corinthians 6:2). Few are ever saved on their death-beds. One thief on the cross was saved, that none should despair; but only one, that no one should presume. A false confidence in those words, "the eleventh hour," has ruined thousands of souls.

Christ's coming death; ignorance and faith (20:17–23)

1. Christ announces his coming death

The first thing that we should notice in these verses is the clear announcement which the Lord Jesus Christ makes of his own approaching death. For the third time we find him telling his disciples the astounding truth that he, their wonder-working Master, must soon suffer and die.

The Lord Jesus knew from the beginning all that was ahead of him. The treachery of Judas Iscariot, the fierce persecution of chief priests and teachers of the law, the unjust judgment, the handing over to Pontius Pilate, the mocking, the scourging, the crown of thorns, the cross, the hanging between two thieves, the nails, the spear – all were spread before his mind like a picture.

Foreknowledge is a great aggravation of suffering, as those who have lived with the prospect of some fearful surgical operation know only too well! Yet none of these things moved our Lord. He says, "I have not been rebellious; I have not drawn back. I offered my back to those who beat me, my cheeks to those who pulled out my beard; I did not hide my face from mocking and spitting" (Isaiah 50:5–6). He saw Calvary in the distance all his life, and yet walked calmly up to it without turning to the right hand or to the left. Surely there never was sorrow like unto his sorrow, or love like his love.

The Lord Jesus was a voluntary sufferer. When he died on the cross, it was not because he had no power to prevent it. He suffered intentionally, deliberately, and of his own free will (John 10:18). He knew that without shedding his blood there could be no remission of human sin; he knew that he was the Lamb of God, who must die to take away the sin of the world; he knew that his death was the appointed sacrifice which must be offered up to make reconciliation for iniquity. Knowing all this, he went willingly to the cross: his heart was set on finishing the mighty work he came into the world to do. He was well aware that all hinged on his own death, and that without that death his miracles and preaching would have done comparatively nothing for the world. No wonder he brought it to the attention of his disciples three times that he must die. Blessed and happy are they who know the real meaning and importance of the sufferings of Christ!

2. Ignorance and faith mixed even in true Christians
The next thing that we should notice in these verses is the mixture of

ignorance and faith that may be found even in true-hearted Christians. We see the mother of James and John coming to our Lord with her two sons, and asking on their behalf a strange request. She asks that they "may sit at your right hand and the other at your left, in your kingdom" (verse 21). She seems to have forgotten all he had just been saying about his suffering. Her eager mind can think of nothing but his glory. His plain warnings about the crucifixion appear to have been thrown away on her sons. Their thoughts were full of nothing but his throne, and the day of his power. There was much faith in their request, but there was much more infirmity. There was something to be commended, in that they could see in Jesus of Nazareth a coming king; but there was also much to blame, in that they did not remember that he was to be crucified before he could reign. Truly "the sinful nature desires what is contrary to the Spirit" (Galatians 5:17) in all God's children, and Luther well remarks, "the sinful nature always seeks to be glorified before it is crucified."

There are many Christians who are very like this woman and her sons. They see in part, and know in part, the things of God; they have faith enough to follow Christ; they have knowledge enough to hate sin, and come out from the world, and yet there are many truths of Christianity about which they are deplorably ignorant. They talk ignorantly, they act ignorantly and commit many sad mistakes. Their acquaintance with the Bible is very scanty: their insight into their own hearts is very small. But we must learn from these verses to deal gently with such people, because the Lord has received them. We must not set them down as graceless and godless because of their ignorance. We must remember that true faith may lie at the bottom of their hearts, though there is much rubbish at the top. We must reflect that the sons of Zebedee, whose knowledge was at one time so imperfect, became at a later period pillars of the church of Christ. In the same way a believer may begin his course in much darkness, and yet prove finally to be someone mighty in the Scriptures, and a worthy follower of James and John.

3. Christ's reproof to the ignorant request
Third, we should notice in these verses the solemn reproof which our

Lord gives to the ignorant request of the mother of Zebedee's children and her two sons. He says to them, "You don't know what you are asking" (verse 22). They had asked to share in the Master's reward, but they had not considered that they must first share their Master's sufferings (1 Peter 4:13). They had forgotten that those who want to stand with Christ in glory must drink from his cup, and be baptized with his baptism; they did not see that those who carry the cross, and only those, will receive the crown. Well might our Lord say, "You don't know what you are asking."

But do we never commit the same mistake that the sons of Zebedee committed? Do we never fall into their error, and make thoughtless, inconsiderate requests? Do we not often say things in prayer without "counting the cost," and ask for things to be granted to us without reflecting how much our supplications involve? These are heart-searching questions: it may well be that many of us cannot give them a satisfactory answer.

We ask that our souls may be saved and go to heaven when we die. It is a good request. But are we prepared to take up the cross, and follow Christ? Are we willing to give up the world for his sake? Are we ready to put off the old man and put on the new, to do what is right, to labor, and to run in such a way that we obtain the prize? Are we ready to withstand a taunting world, and endure hardships for Christ's sake? What shall we say? If we are not ready, our Lord might say to us also, "You don't know what you are asking."

We ask God to make us holy and good. This is a good request. But are we prepared to be sanctified by any process that God in his wisdom may call on us to pass through? Are we ready to be purified by affliction, weaned from the world by bereavements, drawn nearer to God by losses, sicknesses and sorrow? Alas, these are hard questions! But if we are not, our Lord might well say to us, "You don't know what you are asking."

Let us leave these verses with a solemn determination to consider carefully what we are doing when we draw near to God in prayer. Let us beware of thoughtless, inconsiderate and rash petitions. Well might Solomon say, "Do not be quick with your mouth, do not be hasty in your heart to utter anything before God" (Ecclesiastes 5:2).

The true standard of greatness among Christians *(20:24–28)*

These verses are few in number, but they contain lessons of great importance to all professing Christians. Let us see what they are.

1. Pride among true disciples

First, we learn that there may be pride, jealousy and love of pre-eminence even among true disciples of Christ. What does the Scripture say? When the ten heard what James and John had asked, "they were indignant with the two brothers" (verse 24).

Pride is one of the oldest and most mischievous of sins: by it the angels fell, for they "did not keep their positions of authority" (Jude 6). Through pride Adam and Eve were seduced into eating the forbidden fruit: they were not content with their lot, and thought they would be "like God" (Genesis 3:5). From pride the saints of God receive their greatest injuries after their conversion. As Hooker so well says, "Pride is a vice which cleaveth so fast unto the hearts of men that if we were to strip ourselves of all faults one by one, we should undoubtedly find it the very last and hardest to put off." It is a quaint but true saying of Bishop Hall, that "pride is the inmost coat, which we put off last, and which we put on first."

2. Self-denying kindness the secret of greatness in the kingdom

Second, we learn that a life of self-denying kindness to others is the true secret of greatness in the kingdom of Christ. What does the Scripture say? "Whoever wants to become great among you must be your servant, and whoever wants to be first must be your slave" (verses 26–27).

The standard of the world and the standard of the Lord Jesus are completely different. They are more than different: they are totally contradictory to each other. Among the children of this world a person is thought the greatest if he has the most land, most money, most servants, most rank and most earthly power; among the children of God a person is reckoned the greatest who does most to promote the spiritual and temporal happiness of his fellow-creatures. True greatness consists not in receiving but in giving; not in selfish absorption of good things but in imparting good to others; not in being served but in serving; not in sitting still and being served but in going about and serving others.

The angels of God see far more beauty in the work of the missionary than in the work of the Australian gold-digger. They take far more interest in the labors of men like Howard and Judson than in the victories of generals, the political speeches of statesmen, or the council-chambers of kings. Let us remember these things. Let us beware of seeking false greatness; let us aim at that greatness which alone is true. There is a mine of profound wisdom in that saying of our Lord's, "It is more blessed to give than to receive" (Acts 20:35).

3. Christ the example

Third, we learn that the Lord Jesus Christ is meant to be the example for all true Christians. What does the Scripture say? We ought to serve one another "just as the Son of Man did not come to be served, but to serve" (verse 28).

The Lord God has mercifully provided his people with everything necessary for their sanctification. He has given those who follow after holiness the clearest of teaching, the best of motives, and the most encouraging of promises. But this is not all. He has furthermore supplied them with the most perfect pattern and example, the life of his own Son. By that life he calls us to frame our own; he tells us to walk in the steps of that life (1 Peter 2:21). It is the model to which we must strive to mold our tempers, our words and our works in this evil world. "Would my Master have spoken in this manner? Would my Master have behaved in this way?" These are the questions against which we should test ourselves each day.

How humbling this truth is! What searchings of heart it ought to raise within us! What a loud call it is to "throw off everything that hinders and the sin that so easily entangles" (Hebrews 12:1). What kind of people should they be who claim to copy Christ! What poor unprofitable religion is that which makes people content with talk and empty claims, while their life is unholy and unclean! Alas, those who know nothing of Christ as an example will find at last that he knows nothing of them as his saved people. "Whoever claims to live in him must walk as Jesus did" (1 John 2:6).

4. Christ's death an atonement for sin

Fourth, let us learn from these verses that Christ's death was an atonement for sin. What does the Scripture say? "The Son of Man" came "to give his life as a ransom for many" (verse 28).

This is the mightiest truth in the Bible. Let us take care that we grasp it firmly, and never let it go. Our Lord Jesus Christ did not die merely as a martyr, or as a splendid example of self-sacrifice and self-denial. Those who can see no more than *that* in his death fall infinitely short of the truth; they lose sight of the very foundation-stone of Christianity, and miss the whole comfort of the Gospel. Christ died as a sacrifice for human sin; he died to make reconciliation for human iniquity; he died to redeem us from the curse which we all deserved, and to satisfy the justice of God, which would have otherwise condemned us. Never let us forget this!

We are all by nature debtors. We owe to our holy Maker ten thousand talents, and are not able to pay. We cannot atone for our own transgressions, for we are weak and frail, and only adding to our debts every day. But, blessed be God, what we could not do, Christ came into the world to do for us; what we could not pay, he undertook to pay for us. To pay it, he died for us upon the cross. He "offered himself unblemished to God" (Hebrews 9:14). He "died for sins once for all, the righteous for the unrighteous, to bring you to God" (1 Peter 3:18). Once more, never let us forget this!

Let us not leave these verses without asking ourselves, where is our humility? What is our idea of true greatness? What is our example? What is our hope? Life, eternal life, depends on the answer we give to these questions. Happy is the person who is truly humble, strives to do good, walks in the steps of Jesus, and sets all his hopes on the ransom paid for him by Christ's blood. Such a person is a true Christian!

The healing of two blind men (20:29-34)

In these verses we have a touching picture of an event in our Lord's story. He heals two blind men sitting by the wayside, near Jericho. The circumstances of the event contain several deeply interesting lessons, which all professing Christians would do well to remember.

1. Strong faith found where least expected

For one thing, let us note that strong faith may sometimes be found where it might be least expected. Blind as these two men were, they believed that Jesus was able to help them. They never saw any of our Lord's miracles; they knew him only by hearsay, and not face to face. Yet, as soon as they heard that he was passing by, they "shouted, 'Lord, Son of David, have mercy on us!'" (verse 30).

Such faith may well put us to shame. With all our books of evidence, lives of saints and libraries of divinity, how few know anything of simple, child-like confidence in Christ's mercy and Christ's power. Even among believers, the degree of faith is often strangely disproportionate to the privileges enjoyed. Many an unlearned man who can only read his New Testament with difficulty possesses the spirit of unhesitating trust in Christ's advocacy, while deeply-read divines are harassed by questionings and doubts. Those who, humanly speaking, ought to be first, are often last, and the last first.

2. Wisdom in using every opportunity for our souls' good

Second, let us note what wisdom there is in using every opportunity for getting good for our souls. These blind men "were sitting by the road-side" (verse 30): had they not done so, they might never have been healed. Jesus never returned to Jericho, and they might never have met with him again.

Let us see, in this simple fact, the great importance of diligence in the use of means of grace. Let us never neglect the house of God, never give up meeting together with God's people, never omit the reading of our Bibles, never let drop the practice of private prayer. These things, no doubt, will not save us without the grace of the Holy Ghost: thousands make use of them, and remain dead in their transgressions and sins. But it is just in the use of these things that souls are converted and saved: they are the ways in which Jesus walks. It is those who "sit by the roadside" who are likely to be healed. Do we know the disease of our souls? Do we feel any desire to see the Great Physician? If we do we must not wait in idleness, saying, "If I am to be saved, I shall be saved." We must get up and go to the road where Jesus walks. Who can tell, he may soon pass by for the last time! Let us sit "by the roadside" daily.

3. The value of perseverance in seeking Christ

Third, let us note the value of pains and perseverance in seeking Christ. These blind men were "rebuked" by the multitude that accompanied our Lord: people told them to "be quiet" (verse 31). But they were not to be silenced in this way: they felt their need of help, and did not care about the check which they received. "They shouted all the louder, 'Lord, Son of David, have mercy on us!'" (verse 31).

In this part of their conduct we have a most important example. We are not to be deterred by opposition or discouraged by difficulties when we begin to seek the salvation of our souls. We must "always pray and not give up" (Luke 18:1); we must remember the parable of the persistent widow, and of the friend who came to borrow bread at midnight. Like them we must press our petitions at the throne of grace, and say, "I will not let you go unless you bless me" (Genesis 32:26). Friends, relatives and neighbors may say unkind things and reprove our earnestness; we may meet with coldness and lack of sympathy where we might have expected help; but let none of these things move us. If we feel our diseases, and want to find Jesus, the Great Physician – if we know our sins, and desire to have them pardoned – let us press on. "Forceful men lay hold of" the kingdom of heaven (Matthew 11:12).

4. Jesus is gracious to those who seek him

Fourth, let us note how gracious the Lord Jesus is to those who seek him. "Jesus stopped and called" the blind men (verse 32); he kindly asked them what it was that they desired; he heard their request and did what they asked. He "had compassion on them and touched their eyes. Immediately they received their sight" (verse 34).

We see here an illustration of that old truth which we can never know too well – the mercifulness of Christ's heart towards mankind. The Lord Jesus is not only a mighty Saviour, but merciful, kind and gracious to a degree that our minds cannot conceive. Well might the apostle Paul write of "this love that surpasses knowledge" (Ephesians 3:19). Like him, let us pray that we may "know" more of that love. We need it when we first begin our Christian course, poor trembling penitents, and babes in grace; we need it afterwards, as we travel along the narrow way, often straying, often stumbling and often cast down; we shall need it in the evening of our days, when we "walk through the valley of the shadow of death" (Psalm 23:4). Let us then grasp the love of Christ firmly, and keep it daily before our minds. We shall never know, till we wake up in the next world, how much we are indebted to it.

Matthew
Chapter 21

Christ's public entry into Jerusalem *(21:1–11)*

These verses contain a very remarkable passage in our Lord Jesus Christ's life. They describe his public entry into Jerusalem when he came there for the last time, before he was crucified.

There is something particularly striking in this incident in the story of our Lord's earthly life. The narrative reads like the account of some royal conqueror's return to his own city: "A very large crowd" (verse 8) accompanies him in a kind of triumphal procession. Loud cries and expressions of praise are heard around him: "The whole city was stirred" (verse 10). The whole incident is singularly at variance with the past tenor of our Lord's life; it is curiously unlike the ways of him who did not "quarrel or cry out" or let his voice be heard "in the streets" (Matthew 12:19) – who withdrew himself from the multitude on other occasions, and sometimes said to those he healed, "See that you don't tell this to anyone" (Mark 1:44). And yet the whole incident can be explained. The reasons of this public entry are not hard to find out. Let us see what they were.

The plain truth is that our Lord knew well that the time of his earthly ministry was drawing to a close; he knew that the hour was approaching when he must finish the mighty work he came to do, by dying for our sins upon the cross. He knew that his last journey had been accomplished, and that there remained nothing now in his earthly ministry except to be offered as a sacrifice on Calvary. Knowing all this, he no longer, as in times past, sought secrecy; knowing all this, he thought it good to enter the place where he was to be delivered to death, with particular solemnity and publicity. It was not fitting that the Lamb of God should come to be slain on Calvary privately and silently. Before the great sacrifice for the sin of the world was offered up, it was right that every eye should be fixed on the victim. It was suitable that the crowning act of our Lord's life should be done with as much notoriety as possible. That was why he made this public entry; that was why he attracted to himself the eyes of the wondering multitude; that was why "the whole city was stirred" (verse 10). The atoning blood of the Lamb of God was about to be shed; this deed was not to be "done in a corner" (Acts 26:26).

It is good to remember these things. The real meaning of our Lord's conduct at this period is not sufficiently considered by many readers of this passage. It remains for us to consider the practical lessons which these verses appear to point out.

1. An example of Christ's perfect knowledge
First, let us notice in these verses an example of our Lord Jesus Christ's perfect knowledge. He sends his two disciples into a village; he tells them that they will there find the ass on which he is to ride; he provides them with an answer to the inquiry of those to whom the ass belonged; he tells them that on giving the answer the ass will be sent. Everything happens exactly as he foretells.

There is nothing hidden from the Lord's eyes; there are no secrets with him. Alone or in company, by night or by day, in private or in public, he is acquainted with all our ways. He saw Nathaniel under the fig-tree, and he has not changed. Go where we will, and retire from the world as we may, we are never out of sight of Christ.

This is a thought that ought to exercise a restraining and sanctifying effect on our souls. We all know the influence which the presence of the rulers of this world has upon their subjects: nature itself teaches us to put a check on our tongues, demeanor and behavior when we are under the eye of a King. The sense of our Lord's Jesus Christ's perfect knowledge of all our ways ought to have the same effect upon our hearts. Let us do nothing we would not like Christ to see, and say nothing we would not like Christ to hear; let us seek to live and move and have our being under a continual recollection of Christ's presence; let us behave as we would have done had we walked beside him in the company of James and John, by Lake Galilee. This is the way to be trained for heaven. In heaven, "we will be *with the Lord* forever" (1 Thessalonians 4:17).

2. An example of how prophecies were fulfilled

Second, let us notice in these verses an example of the manner in which prophecies concerning our Lord's first coming were fulfilled. We are told that his public entry fulfilled the words of Zechariah: "Your king comes to you, gentle and riding on a donkey" (verse 5).

It appears that this prediction was literally and exactly fulfilled. The words which the prophet spoke through the Holy Spirit were not accomplished in a merely figurative way: as he said, so it came to pass; as he foretold, so it was done. Five hundred and fifty years had passed away since the prediction was made – and then, when the appointed time arrived, the long-promised Messiah did literally ride into Zion "on a donkey." No doubt the vast majority of the inhabitants of Jerusalem saw nothing in the circumstance; the veil was upon their hearts. But we are not left in doubt as to the fulfillment of the prophecy. We are told plainly, "This took place to fulfill what was spoken through the prophet" (verse 4).

From the fulfillment of God's word in time past we are surely intended to gather something as to the manner of its fulfillment in time to come. We have a right to expect that prophecies respecting the second advent of Christ will be as literally fulfilled as those respecting his first advent. He came to this earth literally in person the first time; he will come to this earth literally in person the second time; he came in humiliation once literally to suffer; he will come again in glory literally to reign. Every prediction respecting things accompanying his first advent was literally accomplished: it will be just the same when he returns. All that is foretold about the restoration of the Jews – the judgments on the ungodly, the unbelief of the world, the gathering of the elect – shall be made good to the letter. Let us not forget this. In the study of unfulfilled prophecy, a fixed principle of interpretation is of the first importance.

3. An example of the worthlessness of human favor

Third, let us notice in these verses a striking example of the worthlessness of human favor. Of all the admiring crowds who thronged round our Lord as he entered Jerusalem, none stood by him when he was delivered into the hands of wicked men. Many cried, "Hosanna" (verse 9) who four days afterwards cried, "Take him away! Crucify him!" (John 19:15).

But this is a faithful picture of human nature: this is a proof of the utter folly of thinking more of human praise than the praise of God. Nothing in truth is so fickle and uncertain as popularity: it is here today and gone tomorrow; it is a sandy foundation, and sure to fail those who build upon it. Let us not care for it. Let us seek the favor of him who is "the same yesterday and today and forever" (Hebrews 13:8). Christ never changes: those whom he loves, he loves to the end. His favor endures forever.

Christ at the temple; the barren fig-tree *(21:12–22)*

We have in these verses an account of two remarkable events in our Lord's history. In both, there was something eminently figurative and symbolic: each was a picture of spiritual things. Beneath the surface of each lie lessons of solemn instruction.

1. Jesus' visit to the temple

The first event that demands our attention is our Lord's visit to the temple. He found his Father's house in a state which too truly shadowed the general condition of the whole Jewish church: everything out of order and out of course. He found the courts of that holy building disgracefully profaned by worldly transactions. Trading, buying and selling were actually going on within its walls; there stood dealers ready to supply the Jew who came from some distant country with any sacrifice he wanted; there sat the money-changer, ready to change foreign money for the current coin of the land. Bullocks, sheep, goats and pigeons were displayed for sale as if the place were a market. The jingling of money could be heard there as if those holy courts were a bank or an exchange. Such were the scenes that met our Lord's eyes. He saw it all with holy indignation. He "drove out all who were buying and selling there. He overturned the tables of the money changers" (verse 12). There was no resistance, for people knew that he was right. There was no objection, for everyone felt that he was only reforming a notorious abuse which had been basely permitted for the sake of gain. Well might he sound in the ears of the astonished traders, as they fled from the temple, those solemn words of Isaiah, "It is written, 'My house shall be called a house of prayer,' but you are making it a 'den of robbers'" (verse 13).

Let us see in our Lord's conduct on this occasion a striking picture of what he will do when he comes again the second time. He will purify his visible church as he purified the temple; he will cleanse it from everything that defiles and works iniquity, and drive out everyone who claims to be a Christian but is still of the world; he will allow no worshiper of money or lover of gain to have a place in that glorious temple which he will finally exhibit before the world. May we all strive to live in the daily expectation of that coming! May we judge ourselves so that we are not condemned and driven out in that searching and sifting day! We should often study those words of Malachi: "Who can endure the day of his coming? Who can stand when he appears? For he will be like a refiner's fire or a launderer's soap" (Malachi 3:2).

2. Jesus' curse on the fruitless fig-tree

The second event that demands our attention in these verses is our Lord's curse on the fruitless fig-tree. We are told that, being hungry, he came to a fig-tree on the way and "found nothing on it except leaves. Then he said to it, 'May you never bear fruit again!' Immediately the tree withered" (verse 19). This is an instance almost without parallel in all our Lord's ministry: it is almost the only occasion on which we find him making one of his creatures suffer, in order to teach a spiritual truth. There was a heart-searching lesson in that withered fig-tree: it preaches a sermon we shall do well to hear.

That fig-tree, full of leaves, but barren of fruit, was a striking picture of the Jewish church when our Lord was upon earth. The Jewish church had everything to make an outward show: it had the temple, the priesthood, the daily service, the yearly feasts, the Old Testament Scriptures, the courses of the Levites, the morning and evening sacrifice. But beneath these good leaves, the Jewish church was utterly destitute of fruit. It had no grace, no faith, no love, no humility, no spirituality, no real holiness, no willingness to receive its Messiah (John 1:11). And hence, like the fig-tree, the Jewish church was soon to wither away. It was to be stripped of all its outward ornaments, and its members scattered over the face of the earth; Jerusalem was to be destroyed; the temple was to be burned; the daily sacrifice was to be taken away; the tree was to wither down to the very ground. And so it happened: never was there a symbol so literally fulfilled. In every wandering Jew we see a branch of the fig-tree that was cursed.

But we must not stop here. We may find even more instruction in the event we are now considering. These things were written for our sakes, as well as for the Jews.

Is not every fruitless branch of Christ's visible church in awful danger of becoming a withered fig-tree? Beyond doubt it is. High profession of Christianity, without holiness among a people – overweening confidence in councils, bishops, liturgies, and ceremonies, while repentance and faith have been neglected – have ruined many a visible church in time past, and may yet ruin many more. Where are the once-famous churches of Ephesus, Sardis, Carthage and Hippo? They are all gone. They had leaves, but no fruit. Our Lord's curse came upon them: they became withered fig-trees. The decree went out, "Cut down the tree and destroy it" (Daniel 4:23). Let us remember this. Let us beware of church pride: let us not be high-minded, but fear (Romans 11:20).

Finally, is not everyone who claims to be a Christian but does not bear fruit, in awful danger of becoming a withered fig-tree? There can be no doubt of it. So long as a person is content with the mere leaves of religion – with a reputation for being alive while he is dead, and a form of godliness without the power – so long his soul is in great peril. So long as he is satisfied with going to church or chapel, or receiving the Lord's Supper, and being called a Christian, while his heart is not changed, and his sins not forsaken – so long he is daily provoking God to cut him off without remedy. Fruit, fruit – the fruit of the Spirit is the only sure proof that we are savingly united to Christ, and on the way to heaven. May this sink down into our hearts, and never be forgotten!

Christ's reply to the Pharisees; the two sons *(21:23–32)*

These verses contain a conversation between our Lord Jesus Christ and the chief priests and elders of the people. Those bitter enemies of all righteousness saw the sensation which the public entry into Jerusalem, and the cleansing of the temple, had produced. At once they came about our Lord, like bees, and endeavored to find occasion for an accusation against him.

1. The authority of Jesus questioned

First, let us observe how ready the enemies of truth are to question the authority of all who do more good than themselves. The chief priests have not a word to say about our Lord's teaching: they make no charge against the lives or conduct of himself or his followers. The point on which they fasten is his commission: "By what authority are you doing these things? And who gave you this authority?" (verse 23).

The same charge has often been made against the servants of God when they have tried to check the progress of ecclesiastical corruption. It is the old device by which the children of this world have often labored to stop the progress of revivals and reformations. It is the weapon which was often brandished in the face of the Reformers, the Puritans, and the Methodists of the eighteenth century. It is the poisoned arrow which is often shot at city missionaries and lay agents at the present day. Too many care nothing for the clear blessing of God on a person's work, if they are not sent out by their own sect or party. It matters nothing to them that some humble laborer in God's harvest can point to numerous conversions of souls through his instrumentality; they still cry, "By what authority are you doing these things?" His success is nothing: they demand his commission. His cures are nothing: they want his diploma. Let us neither be surprised nor moved when we hear such things. It is an old charge which was brought against Christ himself. "There is nothing new under the sun" (Ecclesiastes 1:9).

2. The wisdom of Christ's reply

Second, let us observe the consummate wisdom with which our Lord replied to the question. His enemies asked him for his authority for doing what he did. They doubtless intended to make his answer a handle for accusing him. He knew the drift of their inquiry, and said, "I will also ask you one question. If you answer me, I will tell you by what authority I am doing these things. John's baptism – where did it come from? Was it from heaven, or from men?" (verses 24–25).

We must clearly understand that in this answer of our Lord's there was no evasion: to suppose this is a great mistake. The counter-question which he asked was in reality an answer to his enemies' inquiry. He knew they dared not deny that John the Baptist was "a man sent from God"; he knew that, this being granted, he needed only to remind them of John's testimony to himself – had not John declared him to be "the Lamb of God, who takes away the sin of the world" (John 1:29)? Had not John pronounced him to be the Mighty One, who was to "baptize with the Holy Spirit" (John 1:33)? In short, our Lord's question was a home-thrust to the conscience of his enemies. If they once conceded the divine authority of John the Baptist's mission, they must also concede the divinity of his own; if they acknowledged that John came from heaven, they must acknowledge that he himself was the Christ.

Let us pray that in this difficult world, we may be supplied with the same kind of wisdom which was here displayed by our Lord. No doubt we ought to act on the injunction of St. Peter: "be prepared to give an answer to everyone who asks you the reason for the hope that you have. But do this with gentleness and respect" (1 Peter 3:15). We ought to shrink from no inquiry into the principles of our holy religion, and to be ready at any time to defend and explain our practice; but for all this we must never forget that "wisdom is profitable to direct" (Ecclesiastes 10:10, KJV), and that we should strive to speak wisely in defense of a good cause. The words of Solomon deserve consideration: "Do not answer a fool according to his folly, or you will be like him yourself" (Proverbs 26:4).

3. Christ encourages those who repent

Third, let us observe in these verses what immense encouragement our Lord holds out to those who repent. We see this strikingly brought out in the parable of the "two sons." Both were told to go and work in their father's vineyard: one son, like the profligate tax collectors, for some time flatly refused obedience, but "later" changed his mind and went (verse 29); the other, like the formal Pharisees, pretended willingness to go, but after all did not go. "Which of the two," says our Lord, "did what his father wanted?" (verse 31). Even his enemies were obliged to reply, "The first."

Let it be a settled principle in our Christianity that the God and Father of our Lord Jesus Christ is infinitely willing to receive penitent sinners. It matters nothing what a man has been in time past. Does he repent, and come to Christ? Then old things are passed away, and all things are become new. It matters nothing how high and self-confident a man's profession of religion may be. Does he really give up his sins? If not, his profession is abominable in God's sight, and he himself is still under the curse. Let us take courage ourselves if we have been great sinners hitherto: only let us repent and believe in Christ, and there is hope. Let us encourage others to repent; let us hold the door wide open to the very chief of sinners. Never will that word fail, "If we confess our sins, he is faithful and just and will forgive us our sins and purify us from all unrighteousness" (1 John 1:9).

The parable of the tenants *(21:33–46)*

The parable contained in these verses was spoken with special reference to the Jews. They are the farmers described: their sins are set before us here as in a picture. Of this there can be no doubt: it is written that "he was talking about them" (verse 45).

But we must not flatter ourselves that this parable contains nothing for the Gentiles. There are lessons laid down for us, as well as for the Jews. Let us see what they are.

1. Special privileges bestowed by God on some nations
First, we see what special privileges God chooses to give to some nations.

He chose Israel to be a people special to himself. He separated them from the other nations of the earth, and bestowed on them countless blessings; he gave them revelations of himself, while all the rest of the earth was in darkness; he gave them the law, and the covenants, and the oracles of God, while all the world beside was let alone. In short, God dealt with the Jews as a man deals with a piece of land which he fences out and cultivates, while all the country around is left untilled and waste. The vineyard of the Lord was the house of Israel (Isaiah 5:7).

And have we no privileges? Beyond doubt we have many. We have the Bible, and liberty for everyone to read it; we have the Gospel, and permission to everyone to hear it; we have spiritual mercies in abundance of which five hundred millions of our fellow-men know nothing at all. How thankful we ought to be! The poorest person in our country may say every morning, "There are five hundred millions of immortal souls worse off than I am. Who am I, that I should differ? Bless the Lord, O my soul."

2. Bad use made of national privileges
Second, we see what a bad use nations sometimes make of their privileges.

When the Lord separated the Jews from other people, he had a right to expect that they would serve him, and obey his laws. When a man has taken pains with a vineyard, he has a right to expect fruit. But Israel did not give a proper return for all God's mercies. "They mingled with the nations, and adopted their customs" (Psalm 106:35). They hardened themselves in sin and unbelief. They turned aside to idols. They did not keep God's commands. They despised God's temple. They refused to listen to his prophets; they ill-used those whom he sent to call them to repentance; and finally they brought their wickedness to a height by killing the Son of God himself, namely Christ the Lord.

And what we are doing ourselves with our privileges? Truly this is a serious question, and one that ought to make us think. It may well be feared that we are not, as a nation, living up to our light, or walking worthy of our many mercies. Must we not confess with shame that millions amongst us seem utterly without God in the world? Must we not acknowledge that in many a town and in many a village Christ seems hardly to have any disciple, and the Bible seems hardly to be believed? It is vain to shut our eyes to these facts. The fruit that the Lord receives from his vineyard in our own country, compared with what it ought to be, is disgracefully small. It may well be doubted whether we are not just as provoking to him as the Jews were.

3. God's reckoning with nations who abuse their privileges

Third, we see what an awful reckoning God sometimes has with nations and churches which make a bad use of their privileges.

A time came when the long-suffering of God towards the Jews had an end. Forty years after our Lord's death, the cup of their inquity was at length full, and they received a heavy chastisement for their many sins. Their holy city, Jerusalem, was destroyed; their temple was burned; they themselves were scattered over the face of the earth. "The kingdom of God" was "taken away" from them and "given to a people who will produce its fruit" (verse 43).

And will the same thing ever happen to us? Will the judgments of God ever come down on this nation because of her unfruitfulness under so many mercies? Who can tell? We may well cry with the prophet, "O Soveriegn LORD, you alone know" (Ezekiel 37:3). We only know that judgments have come on many a church and nation in the last 1900 years. The kingdom of God has been taken from the African churches; the Muslim power has overwhelmed most of the churches of the East. At all events, it becomes all believers to intercede much on behalf of our country. Nothing offends God so much as neglect of privileges. Much has been given to us, and much will be demanded.

3. The power of conscience

Third, we see the power of conscience even in the wicked.

The chief priests and elders at last discovered that our Lord's parable was specially meant for themselves: the point of its closing words was too sharp to be escaped. "They knew he was talking about them."

There are many hearers of the Gospel in every congregation who are exactly in the condition of these unhappy men. They know that what they hear Sunday after Sunday is all true; they know that they are wrong themselves, and that every sermon condemns them: but they have neither will nor courage to acknowledge this. They are too proud or too fond of the world to confess their past mistakes, and to take up the cross and follow Christ. Let us all beware of this awful state of mind. The last day will prove that there was more going on in the consciences of hearers than was at all known to preachers. Thousands and ten thousands will be found, like the chief priests, to have been convicted by their own consciences, and yet to have died unconverted.

Matthew
Chapter 22

The parable of the great supper *(22:1–14)*

The parable related in these verses is one of very wide signification. In its first application it unquestionably points to the Jews. But we must not confine it to them. It contains heart-searching lessons for all among whom the Gospel is preached: it is a spiritual picture which speaks to us today, if we have an ear to hear. The remark of a learned divine is wise and true: "Parables are like many-sided precious stones, cut so as to cast luster in more than one direction."

1. Salvation compared to a weedding banquet
First, let us observe in the first place that the salvation of the Gospel is compared to a wedding banquet. The Lord Jesus tells us that a king "prepared a wedding banquet for his son" (verse 2).

There is in the Gospel a complete provision for all the needs of the human soul: there is a supply of everything that can be required to relieve spiritual hunger and spiritual thirst. Pardon, peace with God, living hope in this world, glory in the world to come are set before us in rich abundance. It is "a feast of rich food" (Isaiah 25:6). All this provision is owing to the love of the Son of God, Jesus Christ our Lord. He offers to take us into union with himself, to restore us to the family of God as dear children, to clothe us with his own righteousness, to give us a place in his kingdom, and to present us faultless before his Father's throne at the last day. The Gospel, in short, is an offer of food to the hungry, of joy to the mourner, of a home to the outcast, of a loving friend to the lost. It is glad tidings. God offers, through his dear Son, to be at one with sinful people. Let us not forget this. "This is love:

202

not that we loved God, but that he loved us and sent his Son as an atoning sacrifice for our sins" (1 John 4:10).

2. Unlimited invitations

Second, let us observe that the invitations of the Gospel are wide, full,
broad and unlimited. The Lord Jesus tells us in the parable that the
king's servants said to those who were invited, "Everything is ready.
Come to the wedding banquet" (verse 4).

There is nothing lacking on God's part for the salvation of sinners'
souls: no one will ever be able to say at last that it was God's fault, if
he is not saved. The Father is ready to love and receive; the Son is ready
to pardon and cleanse guilt away; the Spirit is ready to sanctify and
renew; angels are ready to rejoice over the returning sinner; grace is
ready to assist him; the Bible is ready to instruct him; heaven is ready
to be his everlasting home. One thing only is needed, and that is, the
sinner must be ready and willing himself. Let this also never be forgotten: let us not quibble and split hairs upon the point. God will be found
clear of the blood of all lost souls. The Gospel always speaks of sinners
as *responsible* and accountable beings; the Gospel places an open door
before all mankind: no one is excluded from the range of its offers.
Though efficient only to believers, those offers are sufficient for all the
world: though few enter the narrow gate, all are invited to come in.

3. Salvation rejected by many

Third, let us observe that the salvation of the Gospel is rejected by
many to whom it is offered. The Lord Jesus tells us that the people
invited to the wedding by the king's servants "paid no attention and
went off" (verse 5).

There are thousands of hearers of the Gospel who derive from it no
benefit whatever. They listen to it Sunday after Sunday, and year after
year, and do not believe so that their souls are saved. They feel no
special need of the Gospel; they see no special beauty in it; they do not
perhaps hate it, or oppose it, or scoff at it, but they do not receive it into
their hearts. They like other things far better. Their money, their land,
their business, or their pleasures, are all far more interesting subjects to
them than their souls. It is an awful state of mind to be in, but awfully
common. Let us search our own hearts, and take heed that it is not our

own. Open sin may kill its thousands; but indifference and neglect of the Gospel kill their tens of thousands. Crowds will find themselves in hell not so much because they openly broke the Ten Commandments as because they paid no attention to the truth. Christ died for them on the cross, but they neglected him.

4. Spurious believers will be exposed and condemned

Fourth, let us observe that all who claim to be Christians but are not Christ's will be detected, exposed and eternally condemned at the last day. The Lord Jesus tells us that when the wedding was at last furnished with guests, the king came in to see them, and "noticed a man there who was not wearing wedding clothes" (verse 11). He asked him how he came in there without them, and he received no reply; and he then commanded the servants to "tie him hand and foot, and throw him outside" (verse 13).

There will always be some in the church of Christ who are not true believers, as long as the world stands. "In this parable," it has been truly remarked, "one single castaway represents all the rest." It is impossible to read the human heart: deceivers and hypocrites will never be entirely excluded from the ranks of those who call themselves Christians. So long as a man claims to submit to the Gospel, and lives an outwardly correct life, we dare not say positively that he is not clothed in the righteousness of Christ. But there will be no deception at the last day: the unerring eye of God will discern who are his own people, and who are not. Only true faith will endure the fire of his judgment; all spurious Christianity will be weighed on the scales and found wanting: only true believers will sit down at the wedding banquet of the Lamb. It will avail the hypocrite nothing that he has been a loud talker about religion, and had the human reputation of being an eminent Christian. His triumphing will last only a moment: he will be stripped of his borrowed plumage, and stand naked and shivering before the bar of God, speechless, self-condemned, hopeless and helpless. He will be cast into outer darkness with shame, and reap according to what he has sown. Well may our Lord say, "There will be weeping and gnashing of teeth" (verse 13).

Let us learn wisdom from the solemn pictures of this parable, and work hard to make our calling and election sure. We ourselves are among those to whom the word is spoken: "Everything is ready. Come to the wedding banquet" (verse 4). Let us see that we do not refuse the one who speaks. Do not let us sleep as others do, but watch and be sober. Time hastens on. The king will soon come in to see the guests: have we or have we not got on the wedding garment? Have we put on Christ? That is the grand question that arises out of this parable. May we never rest till we can give a satisfactory answer! May those heart-searching words daily ring in our ears, "Many are invited, but few are chosen" (verse 14).

The Pharisees' question about paying taxes *(22:15–22)*

We see in this passage the first of a series of subtle attacks which were made on our Lord during the last days of his earthly ministry. His deadly foes, the Pharisees, saw the influence which he was obtaining, both by his miracles and by his preaching. They were determined by some means to silence him, or put him to death; they therefore tried to "trap him in his words" (verse 15). They sent out "their disciples . . . along with the Herodians" (verse 16), to test him with hard questions: they wanted to entice him into saying something which might serve as a handle for an accusation against him. Their scheme, we are told in these verses, entirely failed: they took nothing by their aggressive movement, and retreated in confusion.

1. Flattering language
The first thing which demands our attention in these verses is the flattering language with which our Lord was accosted by his enemies. " 'Teacher,' they said, 'we know that you are a man of integrity and that you teach the way of God in accordance with the truth. You aren't swayed by men, because you pay no attention to who they are'" (verse 16). How well the Pharisees and Herodians talked! What smooth and honeyed words were these! They thought, no doubt, that by good words and fair speeches they would throw our Lord off his guard. It might truly be said of them that their "speech is smooth as butter, yet war is in [their] heart; [their] words are more soothing than oil, yet they are drawn swords" (Psalm 55:21).

It suits all practicing Christians to be much on their guard against flattery. We make a great mistake if we suppose that persecution and harsh treatment are the only weapons in Satan's armory: that crafty foe has other devices for doing us mischief, and he knows full well how to work them. He knows how to poison souls by the world's seductive kindness, when he cannot frighten them by the "flaming arrows" or the sword. Let us not be ignorant of his devices. "When they feel secure, he will destroy many" (Daniel 8:25).

We are only too apt to forget this truth: we overlook the many examples which God has given us in Scripture for our learning. What brought about the ruin of Samson? Not the armies of the Philistines, but the pretended love of a Philistine woman. What led to Solomon's backsliding? Not the strength of outward enemies, but the blandishment of his numerous wives. What was the cause of King Hezekiah's greatest mistake? Not the sword of Sennacherib, or the threats of the field commander, but the flattery of the Babylonian ambassadors. Let us remember these things, and be on our guard. Peace often ruins nations more than war; sweet things occasion far more sickness than bitter; the sun makes the traveler cast off his protective garments far sooner than the north wind. Let us beware of the flatterer. Satan is never so dangerous as when he appears as an angel of light: the world is never so dangerous to the Christian as when it smiles. When Judas betrayed his Lord, it was with a kiss. The believer that is proof against the world's frown is doing well; but the one who is proof against its flattery is doing better.

2. Christ's wise reply

The second thing that demands our attention in these verses is the marvelous wisdom of the reply which our Lord made to his enemies. The Pharisees and Herodians asked whether it was right to pay taxes to Caesar or not. They doubtless thought that they had put a question which our Lord could not answer without giving them an advantage. Had he simply replied that it was right to pay taxes, they would have denounced him to the people as one who dishonored the privileges of Israel and considered the children of Abraham no longer free, but subject to a foreign power. Had he, on the other hand, replied that it was not right to pay taxes, they would have denounced him to the Romans as a mover of sedition and a rebel against Caesar, who refused to pay his taxes. But our Lord's conduct completely baffled them. He demanded to see the coin used for paying the tax. He asks them whose head is on the coin. They reply, "Caesar's" (verse 21). They acknowledge that the Roman Emperor Caesar has some authority over them, by using money bearing his portrait and inscription, since the person who coins the current money is ruler of the land where that money is current. And at once they receive an irresistibly conclusive answer to their question: "Give to Caesar what is Caesar's, and to God what is God's" (verse 21).

The principle laid down in these well-known words is one of deep importance. There is *one* obedience owed by every Christian to the civil government under which he lives, in all matters which are temporal, and not purely spiritual. He may not approve of every requirement of that civil government; but he must submit to the laws of the community, so long as those laws are unrepealed. He must "give to Caesar what is Caesar's." There is *another* obedience which the Christian owes to the God of the Bible in all matters which are purely spiritual. No temporal loss, no civil disability, no displeasure of the powers that be must ever tempt him to do things which the Scripture plainly forbids. His position may be very trying; he may have to suffer much for his conscience' sake: but he must never fly in the face of unmistakable requirements of Scripture. If Caesar coins a new Gospel, he is not to be obeyed. We must "give to God what is God's."

The subject unquestionably is one of great difficulty and delicacy. It is certain that the church must not swallow up the state; it is no less certain that the state must not swallow up the church. On no point, perhaps, have conscientious people been so much tried; on no point have good people disagreed so much as in solving the problem where the things of Caesar end, and where the things of God begin. The *civil* power, on the one side, has often encroached terribly on the rights of conscience – as the English Puritans found to their cost in the unhappy times of the Stuarts; the *spiritual* power, on the other side, has often pushed its claims to an extravagant extent, so as to take Caesar's scepter out of his hands – as it did when the church of Rome trampled on King John of England. In order to have a right judgment in all questions of this kind, every true Christian should constantly pray for "wisdom that comes from heaven" (James 3:17). The person whose eye is single, and who daily seeks for grace and practical common sense, will never be allowed greatly to err.

The Sadducees' question about the resurrection (22:23–33)

This passage describes a conversation between our Lord Jesus Christ and the Sadducees. These unhappy men, who said that there was "no resurrection" (verse 23), attempted, like the Pharisees and Herodians, to perplex our Lord with hard questions. Like them, they hoped "to trap him in his words" (verse 15), and to injure his reputation among the people. Like them, they were completely baffled.

1. Skeptical objections to the Bible are not new
First, let us observe that absurd skeptical objections to Bible truths are ancient things. The Sadducees wished to show the absurdity of the doctrine of the resurrection and the life to come; they therefore came to our Lord with a story which was probably invented for the occasion. They told him that a certain woman had married seven brothers in succession, who had all died and left no children. They then asked, "whose wife" this woman would be in the next world, when all rose again (verse 28). The object of the question was plain and transparent. They meant, in reality, to bring the whole doctrine of a resurrection into contempt; they meant to insinuate that there must be confusion, strife and unseemly disorder if after death men and women were to live again.

It must never surprise us if we meet with similar objections against the doctrines of Scripture, and especially against those doctrines which concern another world. There will probably never lack unreasonable people who will intrude into things unseen and make imaginary difficulties their excuse for unbelief. *Supposed cases* are one of the favorite strongholds in which an unbelieving mind loves to entrench itself. Such a mind will often set up a shadow of its own imagining, and fight with it as if it were a truth; such a mind will often refuse to look at the overwhelming mass of plain evidence by which Christianity is supported, and will fasten on a single difficulty which it fancies is unanswerable. The talk and arguments of people of this sort should never shake our faith for a moment. For one thing, we should remember that there must be deep and dark things in a religion which comes from God, and that a child may put forth questions which the greatest philosopher cannot answer. Again, we should remember that there are countless truths in the Bible which are clear and unmistakable. Let us first attend to them, believe them and obey them. In so doing, we need not doubt that many a thing now unintelligible to us will yet be made plain; in so doing, we may be sure that what we do not know now we shall know in the future.

2. Christ's proof of the reality of a life to come

Second, let us observe what a remarkable text our Lord brings forward in proof of the reality of a life to come. He places before the Sadducees the words which God spoke to Moses in the bush: "I am . . . the God of Abraham, the God of Isaac and the God of Jacob" (Exodus 3:6). He adds the comment, God "is not the God of the dead, but of the living" (verse 32). At the time when Moses heard these words, Abraham, Isaac, and Jacob had been dead and buried many years; two centuries had passed away since Jacob, the last of the three, was carried to his tomb: and yet God spoke of them as being still his people, and of himself as being still their God. He did not say, "I was their God," but "I am."

Perhaps we are not often tempted to doubt the truth of a resurrection and a life to come, but, unhappily, it is easy to hold truths theoretically, and yet not realize them practically. There are few of us who would not find it good to meditate on the mighty truth which our Lord here unfolds, and to give it a prominent place in our thoughts. Let us settle it in our minds that the dead are in one sense still alive. From our eyes they have passed away and their place knows them no more, but in the eyes of God they live and will one day come out of their graves to receive an everlasting sentence. There is no such thing as annihilation; the idea is a miserable delusion. The sun, moon and stars, the solid mountains and deep sea, will one day come to nothing; but the weakest baby of the poorest man will live forevermore in another world. May we never forget this! Happy is the person who can say from the heart the words of the Nicene Creed: "I look for the resurrection of the dead, and the life of the world to come."

3. Christ's account of people's state after the resurrection

Third, let us observe the account which our Lord gives of the state of men and women after the resurrection. He silences the fancied objections of the Sadducees by showing that they entirely mistook the true character of the resurrection state. They took it for granted that it must be a gross, bodily existence like that of mankind upon earth. Our Lord tells them that in the next world we may have a real material body, and yet a body of very different constitution and different requirements from what we have now. He speaks only of the saved, be it remembered: he omits all mention of the lost. He says, "At the resurrection people will neither marry nor be given in marriage; they will be like the angels in heaven" (verse 30).

We know little of the life to come in heaven. Perhaps our clearest ideas of it are drawn from considering what it will *not* be, rather than what it will be. It is a state in which we will no longer be hungry or thirsty; sickness, pain and disease will not be known; wasting old age and death will have no place. Marriages, births and a constant succession of inhabitants will no more be needed: those who are once admitted into heaven will dwell there forevermore. And, to pass from negatives to positives, one thing we are told plainly: we shall be "like the angels in heaven." Like them, we shall serve God perfectly, unhesitatingly and unwearyingly; like them, we shall always be in God's presence; like them, we shall always delight to do his will; like them, we shall give all glory to the Lamb. These are deep things, but they are all true.

Are we ready for this life? Would we enjoy it, if admitted to take part in it? Is the company of God and the service of God pleasant to us now? Is the occupation of angels one in which we would delight? These are solemn questions. Our hearts must be heavenly on earth, while we live, if we hope to go to heaven when we rise again in another world (Colossians 3:1–4).

The great commandment; Christ's question *(22:34–46)*

In the beginning of this passage we find our Lord replying to the question of a certain lawyer, who asked him which was "the greatest commandment in the Law" (verse 36). That question was asked in no friendly spirit, but we have reason to be thankful that it was asked at all as it drew from our Lord an answer full of precious instruction. Thus we see how good may come out of evil.

An admirable summary

Let us note what an admirable summary these verses contain of our duty towards God and our neighbor. Jesus says, "Love the Lord your God with all your heart and with all your soul and with all your mind" (verse 37). He says again, "Love your neighbor as yourself" (verse 39), and he adds, "All the Law and the Prophets hang on these two commandments" (verse 40).

How simple are these two rules, and yet how comprehensive! How soon the words are repeated, and yet how much they contain! How humbling and condemning they are! How much they prove our daily need of mercy and the precious blood of atonement! It would be happy for the world if these rules were more known and more practiced.

Love is the grand secret of true obedience to God. When we feel towards him as children feel towards a dear father, we shall delight to do his will; we shall not find his commandments grievous, or work for him like slaves under fear of the lash; we shall take pleasure in trying to keep his laws, and mourn when we transgress them. No one works so well as those who work for love: the fear of punishment or the desire of reward are principles of far less power. They do the will of God best who do it from the heart. Would we train children right? Let us teach them to *love* God.

Love is the grand secret of the right behavior towards our fellows. Those who love their neighbors will scorn to do them any willful injury, either in person, property or character. But they will not rest there: they will desire in every way to do them good; they will try to promote their comfort and happiness in every way; they will endeavor to lighten their sorrows, and increase their joys. When someone loves us, we feel confidence in them: we know that they will never intentionally do us harm, and that in every time of need they will be our friend. Do we want to teach children to behave properly towards others? Let us teach them to "love everybody as themselves, and do to others as they would have others do to them."

But how shall we obtain this love towards God? It is no natural feeling. We are "born to sin," and, as sinners, are afraid of him. How then can we love him? We can never really love him till we are at peace with him through Christ. When we feel our sins forgiven, and ourselves reconciled to our holy Maker, then, and not till then, we shall love him and have the Spirit of adoption. Faith in Christ is the true spring of love to God: they love most who feel most forgiven. "We love because he first loved us" (1 John 4:19).

And how shall we obtain this love towards our neighbor? This also is no natural feeling. We are born selfish, hateful, and hating one another (Titus 3:3). We shall never love our fellows properly till our hearts are changed by the Holy Spirit: we must be born again; we must put off the old man, and put on the new, and receive the mind that was in Christ Jesus. Then, and not till then, our cold hearts will know true God-like love towards all. "The fruit of the Spirit is love" (Galatians 5:22).

Let these things sink down into our hearts. There is much vague talk these days about "love" and "charity": people claim to admire them and desire to see them increased, and yet hate the principles which alone can produce them. Let us stand fast in the old paths. We cannot have fruits and flowers without roots: we cannot have love of God and man without faith in Christ, and without regeneration. The way to spread true love in the world is to teach the atonement of Christ, and the work of the Holy Spirit.

A question put to the Pharisees

The concluding portion of the passage contains a question put to the Pharisees by our Lord. After answering with perfect wisdom the inquiries of his adversaries, he at last asks them, "What do you think about the Christ? Whose son is he?" (verse 42). They reply at once, "The son of David." He then asks them to explain why David in the book of Psalms calls him "Lord" (Psalm 110:1). "How is it then that David, speaking by the Spirit, calls him 'Lord'?" (verse 43). At once his enemies were put to silence: "No one could say a word in reply" (verse 46). The teachers of the law and Pharisees no doubt were familiar with the Psalm he quoted, but they could not explain its application: it could only be explained by conceding the pre-existence and divinity of the Messiah. This the Pharisees would not concede: their only idea of

Messiah was that he was to be a man like one of themselves: their ignorance of the Scriptures, of which they pretended to know more than others, and their low, material view of the true nature of Christ, were thus exposed at one and the same time. Well may Matthew say, by the Holy Spirit, "from that day on no one dared to ask him any more questions" (verse 46).

Let us not leave these verses without making practical use of our Lord's solemn question, "What do you think about the Christ?" What do we think of his person, and his offices? What do we think of his life, and what of his death for us on the cross? What do we think of his resurrection, ascension, and intercession at the right hand of God? Have we tasted that he is gracious? Have we laid hold on him by faith? Have we found by experience that he is precious to our souls? Can we truly say, "He is my Redeemer and my Saviour, my Shepherd and my Friend"?

These are serious inquiries. May we never rest till we can give a satisfactory answer to them! It will not profit us to read about Christ if we are not joined to him by living faith. Once more then let us test our religion by this question: "What do we think about the Christ?"

Matthew
Chapter 23

**Warnings against the teachers of the law and the Pharisees
(23:1–12)**

We are now beginning a chapter which in one respect is the most
remarkable in the four Gospels: it contains the last words which the
Lord Jesus ever spoke within the walls of the temple. Those last words
consist of a withering exposure of the teachers of the law and the
Pharisees, and a sharp rebuke of their doctrines and practices. Knowing full well that his time on earth was drawing to a close, our Lord no
longer keeps back his opinion of the leading teachers of the Jews.
Knowing that he would soon leave his followers alone, like sheep
among wolves, he warns them plainly against the false shepherds by
whom they were surrounded.

The whole chapter is a signal example of boldness and faithfulness in
denouncing error. It is a striking proof that it is possible for the most
loving heart to use the language of stern reproof: above all, it is an awful
evidence of the guilt of unfaithful teachers. So long as the world stands,
this chapter ought to be a warning and a beacon to all ministers of religion: no sins are so sinful as theirs in the sight of Christ.

1. False teachers and their example
First, we see the duty of distinguishing between the job a false teacher
does and the example he sets. "The teachers of the law and the Pharisees
sit in Moses' seat" (verse 2): rightly or wrongly, they occupied the position of the chief public teachers of religion among the Jews; however
unworthily they filled the place of authority, their position entitled
them to respect. But while their position was respected, their bad lives

were not to be copied. Although their teaching was to be followed so long as it was scriptural, it was not to be observed when it contradicted the Word of God. To use the words of a great divine, "They were to be heard when they taught what Moses taught," but no longer. The whole of this chapter shows that this was our Lord's meaning; false doctrine is denounced as well as false practice.

The duty here placed before us is one of great importance. There is a constant tendency in the human mind to go to extremes: if we do not regard the position of a minister with idolatrous veneration, we are apt to treat it with indecent contempt. We need to be on our guard against both these extremes. However much we may disapprove of a minister's practice, or dissent from his teaching, we must never forget to respect his position: we must show that we can honor the commission, whatever we may think of the officer that holds it. The example of St. Paul on a certain occasion is worth noticing: "Brothers, I did not realize that he was the high priest; for it is written: 'Do not speak evil about the ruler of your people'" (Acts 23:5).

2. Inconsistency and ostentation displeasing to Christ

Second, we see in these verses that inconsistency, ostentation and love of preeminence among people who claim to be Christians are specially displeasing to Christ. With regard to *inconsistency*, note that the very first thing our Lord says of the Pharisees is that "they do not practice what they preach" (verse 3). They required from others what they did not practice themselves. With regard to *ostentation*, our Lord declares that they did all their works "for men to see" (verse 5): they had their phylacteries, or strips of parchment with texts written on them, which many Jews wore on their clothes, made of an excessive size; they had the "tassels" of their garments, which Moses told the Israelites to wear as a remembrance of God (Numbers 15:38), made very large; and all this was done to attract notice and make people think how holy they were. With regard to *love of preeminence*, our Lord tells us that the Pharisees loved to have "the most important seats" given them in public places (verse 6), and have flattering titles addressed to them (verse 7). All these things our Lord condemns. He wants us to watch and pray against them all. They are soul-ruining sins: "How can you believe if you accept praise from one another?" (John 5:44). It would have been happy for the church of Christ if this passage had been more deeply pondered and the spirit of it more implicitly obeyed. The Pharisees are not the only people who have imposed burdens on others and worn "holy" clothes, and loved human praise. The annals of church history show that too many Christians have walked closely in their steps. May we remember this and be wise! It is perfectly possible for a baptized Englishman to be in spirit a thorough Pharisee.

3. Titles and honors due only to God

Third, we see from these verses that Christians must never give to humans the titles and honors which are due to God alone and to his Christ. "Do not call anyone on earth 'father'" (verse 9).

The rule here laid down must be interpreted with proper scriptural qualification. We are not forbidden to esteem ministers very highly in love for their work's sake (1 Thessalonians 5:13). Even St. Paul, one of the humblest saints, called Titus his "true son in our common faith" (Titus 1:4), and says to the Corinthians, "I became your father through the gospel" (1 Corinthians 4:15). But still we must be very careful that we do not give to ministers, unawares, a place and an honor which do not belong to them. We must never allow them to come between ourselves and Christ. The very best are not infallible. They are not priests who can atone for us; they are not mediators who can undertake to manage our soul's affairs with God: they are human just like us, needing the same cleansing blood and the same renewing Spirit; they are set apart to a high and holy calling, but still after all only human. Let us never forget these things. Such cautions are always useful: human nature would always rather lean on a visible minister than an invisible Christ.

4. Humility

Fourth, we see that there is no grace which should distinguish the Christian so much as humility. If you want to be great in the eyes of Christ, you must aim at a totally different mark from that of the Pharisees: your aim must be not so much to rule as to serve the church. As Baxter said so well, "Church greatness consisteth in being greatly serviceable." The desire of the Pharisee was to receive honor, and to be called "teacher" (verse 10); the desire of Christians must be to do good, and to give themselves and all that they have to the service of others. Truly this is a high standard, but a lower one must never content us. The example of our blessed Lord and the direct command of the apostles' letters both alike require us to be clothed with humility (1 Peter 5:5). Let us seek that blessed grace day by day. There is no grace so beautiful, however much despised by the world; none is such an evidence of saving faith and true conversion to God; none is so often commended by our Lord. Of all his sayings, hardly any is so often repeated as that which concludes the passage we have now read. "Whoever humbles himself will be exalted" (verse 12).

Eight charges against the teachers of the law and Pharisees (23:13–33)

We have in these verses the charges of our Lord against the Jewish teachers, ranged under eight heads. Standing in the middle of the temple, with a listening crowd around him, he publicly denounces the main errors of the teachers of the law and the Pharisees, in unsparing terms. Eight times he uses the solemn expression, "Woe to you;" seven times he calls them "hypocrites;" twice he speaks of them as "blind guides" – twice as "blind fools" – once as "You snakes! You brood of vipers!" (verse 33). Let us mark that language well. It teaches a solemn lesson. It shows how utterly abominable the spirit of the teachers of the law and the Pharisees is in God's sight, in whatever form it may be found.

Let us glance briefly at the eight charges which our Lord brings forward, and then seek to draw from the whole passage some general instruction.

1. Opposition to the Gospel
The first "woe" in the list is directed against the systematic opposition of the teachers of the law and Pharisees to the progress of the Gospel. They "shut the kingdom of heaven" (verse 13); they would neither go in themselves, nor let others go in. They rejected the warning voice of John the Baptist; they refused to acknowledge Jesus when he appeared among them as the Messiah; they tried to keep back Jewish inquirers.

They would not believe the Gospel themselves, and they did all in their power to prevent others believing it: this was a great sin.

2. Covetousness

The second "woe" in the list is directed against the covetousness and self-aggrandizing spirit of the teachers of the law and Pharisees. They "devour widows' houses and for a show make lengthy prayers" (verse 14, footnote). They imposed on the credulity of weak and unprotected women by pretending to be very devout, until they were regarded as their spiritual directors. They did not scruple to abuse the influence which they obtained in this unjust way to their own temporal advantage, and, in a word, to make money by their religion: this, again, was a great sin.

3. Zeal for conversion

The third "woe" in the list is directed against the zeal of the teachers of the law and the Pharisees for making converts. They "travel over land and sea to win a single convert" (verse 15). They worked unceasingly to make people join their party and adopt their opinions. They did this from no desire to benefit people's souls in the least, or to bring them to God; they only did it to swell the ranks of their sect, and to increase the number of their adherents and their own importance. Their religious zeal arose from sectarianism, and not from the love of God: this also was a great sin.

4. Swearing

The fourth "woe" in the list is directed against the doctrines of the teachers of the law and Pharisees about swearing. They drew subtle distinctions between one kind of oath and another; they taught that some oaths were binding while others were not; they attached greater importance to oaths sworn "by the gold" offered to the temple, than to oaths sworn "by the temple" itself (verse 16). By so doing they brought the third commandment into contempt – and by making men overrate the value of charitable giving and offerings advanced their own interests: this again was a great sin.

[This practice with oaths was well known among the heathen as a feature in the Jewish character. It is a striking fact that Martial, the Roman poet, specifically refers to it.]

5. Priorities

The fifth "woe" in the list is directed against the practice of the teachers of the law and Pharisees of exalting trifles in religion above serious things – of putting the last things first, and the first last. They made great ado about tithing "mint" and other garden herbs, as if they could not be too strict in their obedience to God's law (verse 23); and yet at the same time they neglected great plain duties, such as justice, mercy and faithfulness: this again was a great sin.

6. External appearances

The sixth and seventh "woes" in the list possess too much in common to be divided. They are directed against a general characteristic of the religion of the teachers of the law. They set outward purity and decency above inward sanctification and purity of heart; they made it a religious duty to clean the "outside" of their cup and dishes (verse 25), while they neglected their own inner being; they were like "whitewashed tombs" (verse 27), clean and beautiful externally, but full of all corruption inside. "In the same way, on the outside you appear to people as righteous but on the inside you are full of hypocrisy and wickedness" (verse 28): this also was a great sin.

7. Veneration of the dead

The last "woe" in the list is directed against the affected veneration of the teachers of the law and the Pharisees for the memory of dead saints. They built the "tombs for the prophets" and decorated "the graves of the righteous" (verse 29), and yet their own lives proved that they were of one mind with those who "murdered the prophets" (verse 31): their own conduct was a daily evidence that they liked dead saints better than living ones. The very men who pretended to honor dead prophets could see no beauty in a living Christ: this also was a great sin.

[A passage from the Berlenberger Bible on this subject is striking enough to reproduce here: "Ask in Moses' time who were the good people: they will be Abraham, Isaac and Jacob, but not Moses – he should be stoned. Ask in Samuel's time who were the good people: they will be Moses and Joshua, but not Samuel. Ask in the times of

Christ who they were: they will be all the former prophets, with Samuel, but not Christ and his apostles."]

This is the sad picture which our Lord gives of Jewish teachers. Let us turn from the contemplation of it with sorrow and humiliation. It is a fearful exhibition of the morbid anatomy of human nature: it is a picture which unhappily has been reproduced over and over again in the history of the church of Christ. There is much in the character of the teachers of the law and the Pharisees in which it might be easily shown that persons calling themselves Christians have often walked in their steps.

[I cannot resist the opportunity of here expressing my firm conviction that our Lord's sayings in this chapter were meant to be taken prophetically, as applying to corruptions which he foresaw would spring up in his church. Beyond doubt there is a most unhappy similarity between the teachings and practices of the teachers of the law and Pharisees and many of the leading corruptions of the church of Rome.]

1. Deplorable state of the Jewish nation

Let us learn from the whole passage how deplorable was the condition of the Jewish nation when our Lord was upon earth. When the teachers were like this, what must have been the miserable darkness of the taught! Truly the wickedness of Israel had come to the full. It was high time, indeed, for the Sun of Righteousness to arise, and for the Gospel to be preached.

2. How abominable is hypocrisy

Let us learn, too, how abominable is hypocrisy in the sight of God. These teachers of the law and Pharisees are not charged with being thieves or murderers, but with being hypocrites to the very core. Whatever we are in our religion, let us resolve never to wear a cloak: let us by all means be honest and real.

3. Danger of unfaithful ministers

Let us learn, too, how awfully dangerous is the position of an unfaithful minister. It is bad enough to be blind ourselves; it is a thousand times worse to be a blind guide. Of all people none is so culpably wicked as an unconverted minister, and none will be judged so severely. It is a solemn saying about such a person that "he resembles an unskillful ship captain: he does not perish alone."

4. Danger of not being committed

Finally, let us beware of supposing from this passage that the safest course in religion is to make no profession at all. This is to run into a dangerous extreme. It does not follow that there is no such thing as true profession because some people are hypocrites. It does not follow that all money is bad because there is much counterfeit coin. Let not hypocrisy stop us confessing Christ, or move us from our firm intention, if we have confessed him. Let us press on, looking to Jesus and resting on him, praying daily to be kept from error, and saying with David, "May my heart be blameless towards your decrees" (Psalm 119:80).

Christ's last public words to the Jews (23:34–39)

These verses form the conclusion of our Lord Jesus Christ's speech about the teachers of the law and Pharisees. They are the last words which he ever spoke as a public teacher in the hearing of the people. The characteristic tenderness and compassion of our Lord shine strikingly at the close of his ministry. Though he left his enemies in unbelief, he shows that he loved and pitied them to the last.

1. God takes pains with the ungodly

First, we learn from these verses that God often takes great pains with ungodly people. He sent the Jews "prophets and wise men and teachers" (verse 34). He gave them repeated warnings; he sent them message after message. He did not allow them to go on sinning without rebuke. They could never say they were not told when they did wrong.

This is the way in which God generally deals with unconverted Christians. He does not cut them off in their sins without a call to repentance: he knocks at the door of their hearts by sicknesses and afflictions; he assails their consciences by sermons, or by the advice of friends; he calls them to consider their ways by opening the grave under their eyes, and taking away from them their idols. They often do not know what it all means; they are often blind and deaf to all his gracious messages. But they will see his hand at last, though perhaps too late. They will find that "God does speak – now one way, now another – though man may not perceive it" (Job 33:14). They will discover that they too, like the Jews, had prophets, wise men and teachers sent to them. There was a voice in every providence, "Turn! Turn from your evil ways! Why will you die?" (Ezekiel 33:11).

2. God notices how his messengers are treated

Second, we learn from these verses that God takes notice of the treatment which his messengers and ministers receive, and will one day reckon for it. The Jews, as a nation, had often treated the servants of God most shamefully: they had often dealt with them as enemies because they told them the truth. Some they had persecuted, some they had scourged and some they had even killed. They thought, perhaps, that no account would be required of their conduct, but our Lord tells them they were mistaken. There was an eye that saw all they did, a hand that registered all the innocent blood they shed, in books of everlasting remembrance. The dying words of Zechariah, who was "murdered between the temple and the altar" (verse 35), would be found, after 850 years, not to have fallen to the ground. He said, as he died, "May the LORD see this and call you to account" (2 Chronicles 24:22). A few years more, and there would be such an inquisition for blood at Jerusalem as the world had never seen. The holy city would be destroyed. The nation which had murdered so many prophets would itself be wasted by famine, pestilence, and the sword; and even those who escaped would be scattered to the four winds and become, like Cain the murderer, restless wanderers on earth (Genesis 4:12). We all know how literally these sayings were fulfilled. Well might our Lord say, "I tell you the truth, all this will come upon this generation" (verse 36).

[It is remarkable that the Zechariah spoken of in verse 35 is described in Chronicles as the son of Jehoiada. Our Lord speaks of him as the son of Berakiah. This discrepancy has led some to suppose that the Zechariah here spoken of could not be the one who was murdered in the days of Joash, but an entirely different person. But there does not seem to be a good enough reason for this. By far the most satisfactory explanation appears to be that Zechariah's father had two names, Jehoiada and Berekiah. It was not at all uncommon among the Jews to have two names. Matthew was called Levi; and Jude, Thaddeus.]

It is good for us all to mark this lesson well. We are too apt to think that "bygones are bygones," and that things which to us are past and done and old will never be raked up again. But we forget that with God "a day is like a thousand years" (2 Peter 3:8), and that the events of a thousand years ago are as fresh in his sight as the events of this very hour. God "will call the past to account" (Ecclesiastes 3:15) and, above all, will require an account of the treatment of his saints. The blood of the early Christians shed by the Roman Emperors; the blood of the Vallenses and Albigenses, and the sufferers at the St. Batholomew's Day massacre; the blood of the martyrs who were burned at the Reformation, and of those put to death by the Inquisition – all, all will yet be accounted for. It is an old saying that "the mill-stones of God's justice grind slowly, but they grind very fine." The world will yet see that "there is a God who judges the earth" (Psalm 58:11).

Let those who persecute God's people in the present take care what they are doing. Let them know that all who injure, ridicule, mock or slander others on account of their religion commit a great sin. Let them know that Christ takes notice of everyone who persecutes his neighbor because he is better than himself, or because he prays, reads his Bible, and thinks about his soul. "Whoever touches you touches the apple of his eye" (Zechariah 2:8). The judgment-day will prove that the King of kings will reckon with all who insult his servants.

3. Lost by their own fault

Third, we learn from these verses that those who are lost forever are lost through their own fault.

The words of our Lord Jesus Christ are very remarkable. He says, "I have longed to gather your children together . . . but you were not willing" (verse 37).

There is something specially worth noticing in this expression: it throws light on a mysterious subject, and one which is often darkened by human explanations. It shows that Christ has feelings of pity and mercy for many who are not saved, and that the grand secret of people's ruin is their lack of will. Impotent as people are by nature, unable by themselves to think any good, without power to turn in faith and call on God, they still appear to have a great ability to ruin their own souls. Powerless as they are to do good, they are still able to do evil. We say rightly that a person can do nothing by himself, but we must always remember that the seat of impotence is the will. No one can give themselves the will to repent and believe, but everyone by nature has the will to reject Christ and have their own way; if they are not saved at last, that will may prove to have been their destruction. "You refuse to come to me to have life," says Christ (John 5:40).

Let us leave the subject with the comforting reflection that with Christ nothing is impossible. The hardest heart can be made willing in the day of his power. Grace beyond doubt is irresistible; but never let us forget that the Bible speaks of people as responsible beings and that it says of some, "You always resist the Holy Spirit!" (Acts 7:51). Let us understand that the ruin of those who are lost is not because Christ was not willing to save them, nor because they wanted to be saved but could not, but because they would not come to Christ. Christ wants to gather people, but they do not want to be gathered; Christ wants to save people, but they do not want to be saved. Let it be a settled principle in our religion, that people's ruin, if they are lost, is wholly their own. The evil that is in us is all our own: the good, if we have any, is all of God. The saved in the next world will give God all the glory: the lost in the next world will find that they have destroyed themselves (Hosea 13:9).

Matthew
Chapter 24

Christ's prophecy on the Mount of Olives *(24:1–14)*

These verses begin a chapter full of prophecy: prophecy of which a large portion is unfulfilled; prophecy which ought to be deeply interesting to all true Christians. It is a subject to which, the Holy Spirit says, we "do well to pay attention" (2 Peter 1:19).

All portions of Scripture like this ought to be approached with deep humility and earnest prayer for the teaching of the Spirit. On no point have good people so entirely disagreed as on the interpretation of prophecy; on no point have the prejudices of one group, the dogmatism of a second and the extravagance of a third done so much to rob the church of truths which God intended to be a blessing. A minister put it well when he wrote, "What does not man see, or fail to see, when it serves to establish his own favorite opinions?"

To understand the drift of the whole chapter we must carefully keep in view the question which gave rise to our Lord's discourse. On leaving the temple for the last time, the disciples, with the natural feeling of Jews, had called their Master's attention to the splendid buildings of which it was composed. To their surprise and amazement, he tells them that the whole was about to be destroyed. These words appear to have sunk deeply into the minds of the disciples. They came to him as he was sitting on the Mount of Olives and asked him with evident anxiety, "Tell us, when will this happen, and what will be the sign of your coming and of the end of the age?" (verse 3). In these words we see the clue to the subject of the prophecy now before us. It embraces three points: one, the destruction of Jerusalem; another, the second personal coming of Christ; and a third, the end of the world. These three points are undoubtedly in some parts of the chapter so entwined together that it is difficult to separate and disentangle them: but all these points appear distinctly in the chapter and without them it cannot be explained properly.

The first fourteen verses of the prophecy are taken up with general lessons of wide range and application. They seem to apply with equal force to the close of both Jewish and Christian dispensations, the one being a striking pattern of the other. They certainly demand special notice from us, "on whom the fulfillment of the ages has come" (1 Corinthians 10:11). Let us now see what those lessons are.

1. A warning against deception
The first general lesson here is a warning against deception: "Watch out that no one deceives you" (verse 4).

A more merciful warning than this cannot be conceived. Satan knows well the value of prophecy, and has always labored to bring the subject into contempt. The works of Josephus prove repeatedly how many false Christs and false prophets arose before the destruction of Jerusalem. It might easily be shown that human eyes today are continually blinded to things to come, in many ways. Irvingism and Mormonism have been only too successfully used as arguments for rejecting the whole doctrine of the second coming of Christ. Let us watch, and be on our guard.

Let no one deceive us as to the leading *facts* of unfulfilled prophecy, by telling us they are impossible; or as to the *manner* in which they will be brought to pass, by telling us it is improbable, and contrary to past experience. Let no one deceive us as to the *time* when unfulfilled prophecies will be accomplished, either by fixing dates on the one hand or telling us to wait for the conversion of the world on the other. On all these points let the plain meaning of Scripture be our only guide, and not traditional human interpretations. Let us not be ashamed to say that we expect a literal fulfillment of unfulfilled prophecy. Let us frankly admit that there are many things we do not understand, but still hold our ground tenaciously – believe much, wait long – and not doubt that one day everything will be made clear. Above all, let us remember that when the Messiah first came to *suffer* it was the most improbable event that could have been conceived, and let us not doubt that as he literally came in person to suffer, so he will literally come again in person to *reign*.

2. A warning against expectations of events

The second grand lesson before us is a warning against over-sanguine and extravagant expectations as to things which are to happen before the end comes. It is a warning as deeply important as the preceding one. It would have been happy for the church if it had not been so much neglected.

We are not to expect a reign of universal peace, happiness and prosperity before the end comes: if we do, we shall be greatly deceived. Our Lord tells us to look for wars, famines and persecution (verses 7, 9). It is vain to expect peace until the Prince of peace returns: then, and not till then, swords will be beaten into plowshares, and nations train for war no more (Isaiah 2:4); then, and not till then, "the land will yield its harvest" (Psalm 67:6).

We are not to expect a time of universal purity of doctrine and practice in the church of Christ before the end comes: if we do, we shall be greatly mistaken. Our Lord tells us to look for the rising of "false prophets" (verse 11) and the "increase of wickedness," and "the love of most will grow cold" (verse 12). The truth will never be received by all who claim to be Christians, and holiness will never be the rule among men, until the great head of the church returns, and Satan is bound: then, and not till then, will there be a glorious church without stain or wrinkle of any other blemish (Ephesians 5:27).

We are not to expect that all the world will be converted before the end comes: if we do, we shall be greatly mistaken. "This gospel of the kingdom will be preached in the whole world as a testimony to all nations" (verse 14), but we must not think that we shall see it universally believed. It will take from the Gentiles, wherever it is faithfully preached, a people as witnesses to Christ (Acts 15:14), but the full gathering of the nations will never take place until Christ comes: then, and not till then, the earth will be filled with the knowledge of the glory of the LORD, as the waters cover the sea (Habakkuk 2:14).

Let us lay these things to heart and remember them well. They are eminently truths for the present times. Let us learn to be moderate in our expectations from any existing machinery in the church of Christ, and we shall be spared much disappointment: let us make haste to spread the Gospel in the world, for the time is short, not long. "Night is coming, when no one can work" (John 9:4). Troubled times are ahead. Heresies and persecutions may soon weaken and distract the churches; a fierce war of principles may soon convulse the nations. Doors now open to do good may soon be shut forever. Our eyes may yet see the sun of Christianity go down like the sun of Judaism, in clouds and storm. Above all, let us long for our Lord's return. May we all have a heart to pray daily, "Come, Lord Jesus" (Revelation 22:20).

Miseries to come in Jerusalem *(24:15–28)*

One main subject of this part of our Lord's prophecy is the taking of Jerusalem by the Romans. That great event took place about forty years after the words we have now read were spoken. A full account of it is to be found in the writings of the historian Josephus.

[These are the words of Josephus. They are the more remarkable when we remember that he was not a Christian. "No other city ever suffered such things. All the calamities which have ever happened to any from the beginning, seem not comparable to those which befell the Jews."]

Josephus' writings are the best comment on our Lord's words; they are a striking proof of the accuracy of every detail of his predictions. The horrors and miseries which the Jews endured throughout the siege of their city exceed anything on record: it was truly a time of great distress, unequalled from the beginning of the world (verse 21).

It surprises some people to find so much importance attached to the taking of Jerusalem: they would rather regard the whole chapter as unfulfilled. Such persons forget that Jerusalem and the temple were the heart of the old Jewish dispensation. When they were destroyed, the old Mosaic system came to an end. The daily sacrifice, the yearly feasts, the altar, the holy of holies and the priesthood were all essential parts of revealed religion, till Christ came – but no longer. When he died on the cross, their work was done: they were dead, and it only remained that they should be buried. But it was not fitting that this thing should be done quietly. The ending of a dispensation given with so much solemnity at Mount Sinai might well be expected to be marked with particular solemnity; the destruction of the holy temple, where so many old saints had seen "shadows of good things to come," might well be expected to form a subject of prophecy: and so it was. The Lord Jesus specially predicts the desolation of "the holy place" (verse 15). The great High Priest describes the end of the dispensation which had been put in charge to lead people to himself.

But we must not suppose that this part of our Lord's prophecy is exhausted by the first taking of Jerusalem. It is more than probable that our Lord's words have a further and deeper application still. It is more than probable that they apply to a second siege of Jerusalem, which is to take place when Israel has returned to their own land; and to further great distress for its its inhabitants, which will only be stopped by the coming of our Lord Jesus Christ. Such a view of this passage may sound startling to some. But those who doubt its correctness would do well to study the last chapter of the prophet Zechariah, and the last chapter of Daniel. These two chapters contain solemn things: they throw great light on these verses we are now reading and their connection with the verses which immediately follow.

[Irenaeus and Hilary among the Fathers, and Ferus in the 16th century, all refer the fulfillment of this part of our Lord's prophecy to the end of the world, when a personal Antichrist appears. Hilary considers that verse 15, which speaks of "the abomination that causes desolation" in the holy place, will be fulfilled by the rise of a mighty personal Antichrist who will be worshiped by unbelievers. In connection with this verse, 2 Thessalonians 2:4 deserves attentive study.]

It now remains for us to consider the lessons which this passage contains for our own personal edification. These lessons are plain and unmistakable: in them at least there is no darkness at all.

1. It may be our duty to flee from danger
First, we see that flight from danger may sometimes be the positive duty of a Christian. Our Lord himself commanded his people under certain circumstances to "flee" (verse 16).

The servant of Christ undoubtedly is not to be a coward. He is to confess his Master publicly; he is to be willing to die, if necessary, for the truth. But the servant of Christ is not required to run into danger unless it comes in the line of duty. He is not to be ashamed to use reasonable means to provide for his personal safety, when no good is to be done by dying at his post. There is deep wisdom in this lesson. The true martyrs are not always those who court death and are in a hurry to be beheaded or burned. There are times when it shows more grace to be quiet, wait, pray and watch for opportunities, than to defy our adversaries and rush into the battle. May we have wisdom to know how to act in time of persecution! It is possible to be rash as well as to be a coward; and to stop our own usefulness by being too hot as well as by being too cold.

2. Christ specially mentions the Sabbath

Second, we see that in delivering this prophecy our Lord makes special mention of the Sabbath. "Pray," he says, "that your flight will not take place . . . on the Sabbath" (verse 20).

This is a fact that deserves special notice. We live in times when the obligation of the Sabbath upon Christians is frequently denied by good men. They tell us that it is no more binding on us than the ceremonial law. It is difficult to see how such a view can be reconciled with our Lord's words on this solemn occasion. He seems intentionally to mention the Sabbath when he is foretelling the final destruction of the temple and the Mosaic ceremonies, as if to mark the day with honor. He seems to hint that although his people would be absolved from the yoke of sacrifices and ordinances, there would remain a Sabbath for them (Hebrews 4:9). The friends of a holy Sunday ought carefully to remember this text. It is one which will bear much weight.

3. God cares specially for his chosen people

Third, we see that God's chosen people are always special objects of God's care. Twice in this passage our Lord mentions them. "For the sake of the elect those days will be shortened" (verse 22). It will not be possible to deceive the "elect."

Those whom God has chosen to salvation by Christ are those he specially loves in this world: they are the jewels among mankind. He cares more for them than for kings on their thrones, if kings are not converted; he hears their prayers; he orders all the events of nations and the results of wars for their good and their sanctification; he keeps them by his Spirit; he allows neither other people nor the devil to snatch them out of his hand. Whatever distress comes on the world, God's elect are safe. May we never rest till we know that we are of this blessed number! There is no man or woman living who can prove that they are not among them. The promises of the Gospel are open to all. May we work hard to make our calling and election sure! God's elect are a people who cry to him night and day. When Paul saw the faith, hope and love of the Thessalonians, then he knew that God had chosen them (1 Thessalonians 1:4; see also Luke 18:7).

4. A sudden event

Fouurth, we see from these verses that whenever the second coming of Christ takes place it will be a very sudden event. It will be "as lightning that comes from the east" which is "visible even in the west" (verse 27).

This is a practical truth that we should always keep in mind. We know from Scripture that our Lord Jesus will come again in person to this world; we also know that he will come in a time of great distress; but the precise period, year, month, day and hour are all hidden. We only know that it will be a very sudden event. Our plain duty then is to live always prepared for his return. Let us walk by faith and not by sight; let us believe in Christ, serve Christ, follow Christ, and love Christ. By living like that, we shall be ready to meet Christ whenever he may return.

The second coming of Christ described (24:29–35)

In this part of our Lord's prophecy he describes his own second coming to judge the world. This, at all events, seems the natural meaning of the passage: to take any lower view appears to be a violent straining of Scripture language. If the solemn words used here mean nothing more than the coming of the Roman armies to Jerusalem, we may explain away anything in the Bible. The event here described is one of far greater moment than the march of an earthly army; it is nothing less than the closing act of the present dispensation – the second personal advent of Jesus Christ.

1. Christ will come with glory and majesty

First, these verses teach us that when the Lord Jesus returns to this world he will come with special glory and majesty. He will come "on the clouds of the sky, with power and great glory" (verse 30). Before his presence the very sun, moon and stars will be darkened, and "the heavenly bodies will be shaken" (verse 29).

The second personal coming of Christ will be as different as possible from the first. He came the first time as "a man of sorrows, and familiar with suffering" (Isaiah 53:3): he was born in the manger of Bethlehem, in lowliness and humiliation; he took the very nature of a servant, and was despised and not esteemed; he was betrayed into the hands of wicked men, condemned by an unjust judgment, mocked, flogged, crowned with thorns and at last crucified between two thieves. He will come the second time as the King of all the earth, with royal majesty: the princes and great men of this world will themselves stand before his throne to receive an eternal sentence: before him every mouth shall be silenced, and every knee bow, and every tongue shall confess that Jesus Christ is Lord. May we all remember this! Whatever ungodly men may do now, there will be no scoffing, no jesting at Christ, no unbelief at the last day. The servants of Jesus may well wait patiently: their Master will one day be acknowledged King of kings by all the world.

2. He will take care of his believing people

Second, these verses teach us that when Christ returns to this world he will first take care of his believing people. He will "send his angels . . and they will gather his elect" (verse 31).

When Christ returns in glory and the judgment begins, true Christians will be perfectly safe. Not a hair of their heads will fall to the ground: not one bone of Christ's mystical body will be broken. There was an ark for Noah at the time of the flood; there was a Zoar for Lot, when Sodom was destroyed; there will be a hiding place for all believers in Jesus, when the wrath of God at last bursts on this wicked world. Those mighty angels who rejoiced in heaven when each sinner repented, will gladly catch up the people of Christ to meet their Lord in the air. The day of Christ's second coming no doubt will be an awful day, but believers may look forward to it without fear.

When Christ returns in glory, true Christians will at length be gathered together. The saints of every age and every language will be assembled out of every country: everyone will be there from righteous Abel down to the last soul that is converted to God, from the oldest patriarch down to a little infant that just breathed and died. Let us think what a happy gathering that will be, when all the family of God are at length together. If it has been pleasant to meet one or two saints occasionally on earth, how much more pleasant will it be to meet a "multitude that no one could count"! Surely we may be content to carry the cross, and to put up with partings for a few years. We travel on towards a day when we will meet to part no more.

3. The Jews will remain separate

Third, these verses teach us that until Christ returns the Jews will remain a separate people. Our Lord tells us, "This generation will certainly not pass away until all these things have happened" (verse 34).

[I see no other interpretation of these much controverted words, "this generation," which is in the least satisfactory and not open to very serious objections. The word "generation" admits of the sense in which I have taken it, and seems to me to be used in that sense in Matthew 12:45, 17:17 and 23:36; Luke 16:8 ["this world" NIV, ed. note] and 17:25; and Philippians 2:15. The view that I have propounded is not new. It is adopted by Mede, Pareus, Flacius, Illyricus, Calorius, Jansenius, Du Veil, Adam Clarke and Steir. Chrysostom, Origen and Theophylact consider "this generation" to mean "true believers."]

The continued existence of the Jews as a distinct nation is undeniably a great miracle: it is one of those evidences of the truth of the Bible which the unbeliever can never overthrow. Without a land, without a king, without a government, scattered and dispersed over the world for 1900 years, the Jews are never absorbed among the people of the countries where they live, like the French, English and Germans, but "live apart" (Number 23:9). Nothing can account for this but the finger of God. The Jewish nation stands before the world a crushing answer to unbelief, and a living book of evidence that the Bible is true. But we ought not to regard the Jews only as witnesses of the truth of Scripture; we should see in them a continual pledge that the Lord Jesus is coming again one day. Like the sacrament of the Lord's Supper, they witness to the reality of the second coming as well as of the first. Let us remember this. Let us see in every wandering Jew a proof that the Bible is true, and that Christ will one day return.

4. Christ's predictions will be fulfilled

Fourth, our Lord's predictions will certainly be fulfilled: "Heaven and earth will pass away, but my words will never pass away" (verse 35).

Our Lord knew well the natural unbelief of human nature. He knew that "in the last days scoffers will come. . . . They will say, 'Where is this "coming" he promised?'" (2 Peter 3:4). He knew that when he came, faith would be rare on the earth. He foresaw how many would contemptuously reject the solemn predictions he had just been delivering, as improbable, unlikely and absurd. He warns us against such skeptical thoughts, with a caution of particular solemnity: he tells us that, whatever man may say or think, his words will be fulfilled in due time, and will not "pass away" unfulfilled. May we all lay to heart his warning! We live in an unbelieving age. Few believed the report of our Lord's first coming (Isaiah 53:1), and few believe the report of his second. Let us beware of this infection, and believe so that our souls are saved. We are not reading "cleverly invented stories" (2 Peter 1:16), but deep and momentous truths: may God give us a heart to believe them!

The time just before the second coming (24:36–51)

There are verses in this passage which are often much misapplied. "The coming of the Son of Man" (verse 37) is frequently spoken of as being the same thing as death; the texts which describe the uncertainty of his coming are used in epitaphs, and thought suitable to the tomb. But there is no solid ground for such an application of this passage. Death is one thing, and the coming of the Son of Man is quite another. The subject of these verses is not death, but the second coming of Jesus Christ. Let us remember this. It is a serious thing to wrest Scripture and use it in any but its true meaning.

1. The state of the world when Christ comes again

The first thing that demands our attention in these verses is the awful account that they give of the state of the world when the Lord Jesus comes again.

The world will not be converted when Christ returns: it will be found in the same condition as it was in the day of the flood. When the flood came, men were found "eating and drinking, marrying and giving in marriage" (verse 38), absorbed in their worldly pursuits and utterly regardless of Noah's repeated warnings. They saw no likelihood of a flood; they would not believe there was any danger. But at last the flood came suddenly and took them all away. All that were not with Noah in the ark were drowned: they were all swept away to their last account, unpardoned, unconverted and unprepared to meet God. And our Lord says, "That is how it will be at the coming of the Son of Man" (verse 39).

Let us note this text, and store it up in our minds. There are many strange opinions current on this subject, even among good people. Let us not flatter ourselves that the heathen will all be converted and the earth filled with the knowledge of God before the Lord comes; let us not dream that the end of all things cannot be at hand because there is still much wickedness both in the church and in the world. Such views receive a flat contradiction in the passage now before us: the days of Noah are the true picture of the days when Christ returns. Millions of people who claim to be Christians will be found thoughtless, unbelieving, godless, Christless, worldly and unfit to meet their Judge. Let us take care that we are not found amongst them.

2. Awful separation

The second thing that demands our attention is the awful separation that will take place when the Lord Jesus comes again. We read twice over that "one will be taken and the other left" (verses 40, 41).

The godly and the ungodly at present are mingled together; in the congregation and in the place of worship, in the city and in the field, the children of God and the children of the world are all side by side; but it will not always be like this. When our Lord returns, there will at length be a complete division. In a flash, in the twinkling of an eye, at the last trumpet, each party will be separated from the other forevermore. Wives will be separated from husbands, parents from children, brothers from sisters, masters from servants, preachers from hearers.

There will be no time for repentance or a change of mind when the Lord appears: everyone will be taken as they are, and reap according as they have sown. Believers will be caught up to glory, honor and eternal life; unbelievers will be left behind to shame and everlasting contempt. Happy are those who are of one heart in following Christ! Their union alone will never be broken: it will last forevermore. Who can describe their happiness when the Lord returns? Who can imagine the misery of those who are left behind? May we think on these things, and consider our ways!

3. The duty of watchfulness

The last thing that demands our attention in these verses is the practical duty of watchfulness in view of Christ's second coming. "Keep watch," says our Lord, "because you do not know on what day your Lord will come" (verse 42). "Be ready, because the Son of Man will come at an hour when you do not expect him" (verse 44).

This is a point which our blessed Master frequently presses: we hardly ever find him dwelling on the second coming without adding a warning to "watch." He knows the sleepiness of our nature; he knows how soon we forget the most solemn subjects in religion; he knows how unceasingly Satan labors to obscure the glorious doctrine of his second coming. He exhorts us to keep awake, if we do not want to be ruined forevermore. May we all have an ear to hear his words!

True Christians ought to live like watchmen. The day of the Lord is coming like a thief in the night: they should try always to be on their guard; they should behave like the sentinel of an army in an enemy's land, resolving by God's grace not to sleep at their post. That text of St. Paul's deserves many a thought: "Let us not be like others, who are asleep, but let us be alert and self-controlled" (1 Thessalonians 5:6).

True Christians ought to live like good servants whose master is not at home. They should try always to be ready for their Master's return: they should never give way to the feeling, "My master is staying away a long time" (verse 48); they should seek to keep their hearts in such a frame that whenever Christ appears they can at once give him a warm and loving reception. There is a vast depth in the saying, "It will be good for that servant whose master finds him doing so when he returns" (verse 46). We may well doubt whether we are true believers in Jesus if we are not ready at any time to have our faith changed into sight.

Let us close the chapter with solemn feelings. What we have just been reading calls for great heart-searching. Let us make sure that we are in Christ, and will have an ark of safety when the day of wrath breaks on the world; let us try so to live that we may be pronounced "blessed" at the last, and not cast off forevermore. Not least, let us dismiss from our minds the common idea that unfulfilled prophecy is speculative and not practical: if the things we have been considering are not practical, there is no such thing as practical religion at all. "Everyone who has this hope in him purifies himself, just as he is pure" (1 John 3:3).

Matthew
Chapter 25

The chapter we have now begun is a continuation of our Lord's prophetic discourse on the Mount of Olives. The time to which it refers is plain and unmistakable: from first to last, there is a continual reference to the second coming of Christ and the end of the world. The whole chapter contains three great divisions. In the first, our Lord uses his own second coming as an argument for watchfulness and heart-religion: this he does by the parable of the ten virgins. In the second, he uses his own second coming as an argument for diligence and faithfulness: this he does by the parable of the talents. In the third, he winds up all by a description of the great day of judgment: a passage which for majesty and beauty stands unequalled in the New Testament.

The parable of the ten virgins (25:1–13)

The parable of the ten virgins contains lessons peculiarly solemn and awakening. Let us see what they are.

1. The church will contain evil as well as good at the second coming
First, we see that the second coming of Christ will find his church a mixed body, containing evil as well as good.

The professing church is compared to "ten virgins who took their lamps and went out to meet the bridegroom" (verse 1): all of them had lamps, but only five had oil in their vessels to feed the flame; all of them professed to have one object in view, but only five were truly "wise," and the rest were foolish (verse 2). The visible church of Christ is in just the same condition: all its members are baptized in the name of Christ, but not all really hear his voice and follow him; all are called Christians, and profess to be of the Christian religion, but not all have the grace of

238

the Spirit in their hearts, and are really what they profess to be. Our own eyes tell us that it is so now: the Lord Jesus tells us that it will be so when he comes again.

[I think it is fair to say that a different view of this parable is held by some interpreters. They consider that all the ten virgins represent true believers, and that the five foolish ones are believers who fall away, or believers who are only shut out from certain privileges at the Lord's return, and are finally saved.

I cannot admit the correctness of this view. It appears to me to do great violence to the plain meaning of the conclusion of the parable, to be out of keeping with the general tenor of our Lord's discourse in this place, and to contradict many texts of Scripture.

I believe that the ten virgins represent the two great classes which compose the visible church of Christ: the converted and the unconverted – the spurious believers and the real Christians – the hypocrites and the true believers – the foolish builders and the wise builders – the good fish and the bad – the living and the dead – the wheat and the weeds.

This view is neither new nor uncommon. It is held in the main by the following commentators: Bullinger, Brentius, Gualter, Pellican, Beza, Ferus, Pareus, Piscator, Musculus, Leigh, Baxter, Quesnel, Poole, Manton, Henry, Burkitt, Doddridge, Gill and Scott.]

Let us note this description well. It is a humbling picture. After all our preaching and praying, after all our visiting and teaching, after all our missionary exertions abroad, and means of grace at home, many will be found at last dead in trespasses and sins! The wickedness and unbelief of human nature is a subject about which we all have much to learn.

2. Christ's second coming will take people by surprise

Second, we see that Christ's second coming, whenever it may be, will take people by surprise.

This is a truth which is set before us in the parable in a very striking manner. "At midnight," when the virgins were slumbering and sleeping, there was a cry, "Here's the bridegroom! Come out to meet him!" (verses 5–6). It will be just the same when Jesus returns to the world. He will find the vast majority of mankind utterly unbelieving and unprepared; he will find the bulk of his believing people in a sleepy and indolent state of soul. Business will be going on in town and country just as it does now; politics, trade, farming, buying, selling, pleasure-seeking will be taking up men's atttention just as they do now; rich men will still be faring sumptuously, and poor men grumblng and complaining; churches will still be full of divisions, or wrangling about trifles; theological controversies will be still raging; ministers will still be calling men to repent, and the vast majority in all congregations will still be putting off the day of decision. In the midst of all this, the Lord Jesus himself will suddenly appear. At an hour it is not aware of, the startled world will be summoned to break off what it is doing and stand before its rightful King. There is something unspeakably awesome in the idea: but that is what is written, and that is how it will be. Well might a dying minister say, "We are none of us more than half-awake."

3. Many people will find the value of religion too late

Third, we see that when the Lord comes again many will find the value of saving religion too late.

The parable tells us that when the bridegroom came, the foolish virgins said to the wise, "Give us some of your oil; our lamps are going out" (verse 8). It tells us, further, that as the wise had no oil to spare, the foolish went to "buy the oil" (verse 10). It tells us, finally, that they came when the door was shut, and asked in vain for admission: "Sir! Sir!" they said, "Open the door for us!" (verse 11). All these expressions are striking pictures of things to come. Let us take care that we do not find them true by experience, to our own eternal ruin.

We may settle it in our minds that there will be an entire change of opinion one day as to the necessity of Christian commitment. At present, we must all be aware that the vast majority of professing Christians care nothing at all about it: they have no sense of sin; they have no love towards Christ; they know nothing of being born again. Repentance, faith, grace and holiness are mere words to them; they are subjects which they either dislike, or about which they feel no concern. But this state of things will one day come to an end. Knowledge, conviction, the value of the soul, the need of a Saviour, will all burst on people's minds one day like a flash of lightning. But it will be too late! It will be too late to be buying oil when the Lord returns. The mistakes that are not found out till that day are irretrievable.

Are we ever mocked, and persecuted, and thought foolish because of our religion? Let us bear it patiently and pray for those who persecute us: they do not know what they are doing; they will certainly alter their minds one day. We may yet hear them confessing that we were "wise" and they were "foolish." One day the whole world will acknowledge that the saints of God made a wise decision.

4. True Christians will receive a rich reward

Fourth, we see in this parable that when Christ returns, true Christians will receive a rich reward for all they have suffered for their Master's sake. We are told that when the bridegroom came, "the virgins who were ready went in with him to the wedding banquet. And the door was shut" (verse 10).

Only true Christians will be found ready at the second coming. Washed in the blood of atonement, clothed in Christ's righteousness, renewed by the Spirit, they will meet their Lord with boldness and sit down at the wedding banquet of the lamb, to go out no more. Surely this is a blessed prospect.

They will be with their Lord: with him who loved them and gave himself for them; with him who bore with them and carried them through their earthly pilgrimage: with him whom they loved truly and followed faithfully on earth, though with much weakness, and many a tear. Surely this is also a blessed prospect.

The door will be shut at last, shut on all pain and sorrow; shut on an ill-natured and wicked world; shut on a tempting devil; shut on all doubts and fear; shut to be opened again no more. Surely we may again say, this is a blessed prospect.

Let us remember these things: they will bear meditation; they are all true. The believer may have much distress, but he has before him abounding consolations. "Weeping may remain for a night, but rejoicing comes in the morning" (Psalm 30:5). The day of Christ's return will surely make amends for all.

Let us leave this parable determined never to be content with anything short of indwelling grace in our hearts. The lamp and the name of Christian, the profession and the ordinances of Christianity, are all very well in their way, but they are not the "one thing needed." Let us never rest till we know that we have the oil of the Spirit in our hearts.

The parable of the talents (25:14–30)

The parable of the talents is very like that of the ten virgins. Both direct our minds to the same important event: the second coming of Jesus Christ. Both bring before us the same people: the members of the professing church of Christ. The virgins and the servants are one and the same people – but the same people regarded from a different point, and viewed on different sides. The practical lesson of each parable is the main point of difference: vigilance is the keynote of the first parable, diligence that of the second. The story of the virgins calls on the church to watch; the story of the talents calls on the church to work.

1. All Christians have received something from God

First, we learn from this parable that all professing Christians have received something from God. We are all God's "servants": we all have "talents" entrusted to our charge.

The word "talents" is an expression that has been curiously turned aside from its original meaning. It is generally applied only to people of remarkable ability or gifts: they are called "talented" people. Such a use of the expression is a mere modern invention. In the sense in which our Lord used the word in this parable, it applies to all baptized persons without distinction. We have all "talents" in God's sight: we are all talented people.

Anything whereby we may glorify God is a "talent." Our gifts, our influence, our money, our knowledge, our health, our strength, our time, our senses, our reason, our intellect, our memory, our affections, our privileges as members of Christ's church, our advantages as possessors of the Bible – all, all are talents. Where did these things come from? Whose hand bestowed them? Why are we what we are? Why are we not the worms that crawl on the earth? There is only one answer to these questions: all that we have is a loan from God: we are God's stewards; we are God's debtors. Let this thought sink deeply into our hearts.

2. Many make bad use of their talents

Second, we learn that many make a bad use of the privileges and mercies they receive from God. We are told in the parable of one who "dug a hole in the ground and hid his master's money" (verse 18). That man represents a large class of mankind.

To hide our talent is to neglect opportunities of glorifying God, when we have them. The baptized Bible-despiser, the prayer-neglecter and the Sabbath-breaker; the unbelieving, the sensual and the earthly-minded; the trifler, the thoughtless and the pleasure-seeker; the money-lover, the covetous and the self-indulgent – all, all are alike burying their Lord's money in the ground. They all have light that they do not use: they might all be better than they are. But they are all daily robbing God: he has lent them much, and they bring him no return. The words of Daniel to Belshazzar are strictly applicable to every unconverted person: "You did not honor the God who holds in his hand your life and all your ways" (Daniel 5:23).

3. All Christians must face a reckoning with God

Third, we learn that all professing Christians must one day have a reckoning with God. The parable tells us that "after a long time the master of those servants returned and settled accounts with them" (verse 19).

There is a judgment before us all. If there is not, words have no meaning in the Bible: it is mere trifling with Scripture to deny it. There is a judgment before us according to our works – certain, strict and unavoidable. High or low, rich or poor, learned or unlearned, we will all have to stand at the bar of God and receive our eternal sentence. There will be no escape: concealment will be impossible. We and God must at last meet face to face. We shall have to render an account of every privilege that was granted to us, and of every ray of light that we enjoyed; we will find that we are dealt with as accountable and responsible creatures, and whoever is given much, of them much will be demanded. Let us remember this every day we live: let us judge ourselves so that we do not come under judgment (1 Corinthians 11:31).

4. True Christians will receive a reward

Fourth, we learn that true Christians will receive an abundant reward on the great day of reckoning. The parable tells us that the servants who had used their Lord's money well were commended as "good and faithful," and told to "share your master's happiness!" (verse 23).

These words are full of comfort to all believers, and may well fill us with wonder and surprise. The best of Christians is a poor frail creature, and needs the blood of atonement every day that he lives; but the least and lowest of believers will find that he is counted among Christ's servants, and that his labor has not been in vain in the Lord. He will discover to his amazement that his Master's eye saw more beauty in his efforts to please him, than he ever saw himself; he will find that every hour spent in Christ's service, and every word spoken on Christ's behalf, has been written in a book of remembrance. Let believers remember these things and take courage. The cross may be heavy now, but the glorious reward will make up for everything. As Leighton so well says, "Here some drops of joy enter into us, but there we shall enter into joy."

5. Unfruitful Christians will be condemned

Fifth, we learn that all unfruitful members of Christ's church will be condemned and thrown out on the day of judgment. The parable tells us that the servant who buried his master's money was reminded that he "knew" his master's character and requirements, and was therefore without excuse (verse 26). It tells us that he was condemned as "wicked," "lazy" and "worthless" (verses 26, 30), and thrown "outside, into the darkness." Our Lord adds the solemn words, "There will be weeping and gnashing of teeth."

There will be no excuse for an unconverted Christian on the last day. The reasons with which he now pretends to satisfy himself will prove useless and vain: the judge of all the earth will be found to have done right; the ruin of the lost soul will be found to be his own fault. Those words of our Lord, "you knew," are words that ought to ring loudly in many people's ears, and prick them to the heart. Thousands today are living "without Christ" and without conversion, and yet pretending that they cannot help it! And all this time they "know," in their own conscience, that they are guilty. They are burying their talent: they are not doing what they can. Happy are those who find this out quickly! It will all come out at the last day.

Let us leave this parable with a solemn determination, by God's grace, never to be content with a profession of Christianity without practice. Let us not only talk about religion, but act; let us not only feel the importance of religion, but do something too. We are not told that the unprofitable servant was a murderer, or a thief, or even a waster of his Lord's money: but he did nothing – and this was his ruin! Let us beware of a do-nothing Christianity: such Christianity does not come from the Spirit of God. "To do no harm," says Baxter, "is the praise of a stone, not of a man."

The last judgment *(25:31–46)*

In these verses our Lord Jesus Christ describes the judgment day, and some of its leading circumstances. There are few passages in the whole Bible more solemn and heart-seaching than this. May we read it with the deep and serious attention which it deserves.

1. Who will be the judge?

First, let us note who will be the judge on the last day. We read that it will be "the Son of Man" (verse 31): Jesus Christ himself.

That same Jesus who was born in the manger of Bethlehem and took the very nature of a servant; who was despised and rejected by men and often had no place to lay his head; who was condemned by the princes of this world, beaten, flogged and nailed to the cross – that same Jesus will himself judge the world when he comes in his glory. The Father entrusts all judgment to him (John 5:22). To him at last every knee shall bow, and every tongue confess that he is Lord (Philippians 2:10–11).

Let believers think of this and take comfort. The one who sits on the throne on that great and dreadful day will be their Saviour, their Shepherd, their High Priest, their elder Brother, their Friend. When they see him they will have no cause to be alarmed.

Let unconverted people think of this and be afraid. Their judge will be that very Christ whose Gospel they now despise, and whose gracious invitations they refuse to hear. How great will be their confusion at last if they go on in unbelief and die in their sins! To be condemned on the day of judgment by anyone would be awful; but to be condemned by the one who would have saved them will be awful indeed. Well may the psalmist say, "Kiss the Son, lest he be angry" (Psalm 2:12).

2. Who will be judged?

Second, let us note who will be judged on the last day. We read that before Christ "all the nations will be gathered" (verse 32).

Everyone who has ever lived will one day give account of themselves at the bar of Christ: they must all obey the summons of the great King and come forward to receive their sentence. Those who would not come to worship Christ on earth will find they must come to his great assize when he returns to judge the world.

All who are judged will be divided into two great classes. There will no longer be any distinction between kings and subjects, or masters and servants, or dissenters and churchmen; there will be no mention of ranks and denominations, for the old order of things will have passed away. Grace or no grace, conversion or unconversion, faith or no faith will be the only distinction on the last day. All who are found in Christ will be placed among the sheep "on his right;" all who are not found in Christ will be placed among the goats "on his left" (verse 33). As Sherlock puts it: "Our separations will avail us nothing, unless we take care to be found in the number of Christ's sheep, when he comes to judgment."

3. The manner of judgment

Third, let us mark the manner in which the judgment will be conducted on the last day. We read of several striking details on this point: let us see what they are.

The last judgment will be a judgment *according to evidence*. People's deeds are the witnesses which will be brought forward, and above all their works of charity. The question will not merely be what we said, but what we did: not merely what we professed, but what we practiced. Our works unquestionably will not justify us: no one will be declared righteous by observing the law; but the truth of our faith will be tested by our lives. "Faith by itself, if it is not accompanied by action, is dead" (James 2:17).

The last judgment will be a judgment that *will bring joy to all true believers.* They will hear those precious words, "Come, you who are blessed by my Father; take your inheritance" (verse 34); they will be owned and acknowledged by their Master before his Father and the holy angels; they will find that the wages he gives to his faithful servants are nothing less than a "kingdom." The least, lowest and poorest of the family of God will have a crown of glory and be a king!

The last judgment will be a judgment that will bring confusion on all unconverted people. They will hear those awful words, "Depart from me, you who are cursed, into the eternal fire" (verse 41). They will be disowned by the great head of the church in front of the assembled world: they will find that they "sow to please their sinful nature," so from that nature they must "reap destruction" (Galatians 6:8). They would not hear Christ when he said, "Come to me . . . and I will give you rest" (Matthew 11:28), and now they must hear him say, "Depart from me . . . into the eternal fire": they would not carry his cross, and so they can have no place in his kingdom.

The last judgment will be a judgment that will strikingly bring out the characters both of the lost and saved. Those on the right, who are Christ's sheep, will still be "clothed with humility" (1 Peter 5:5): they will marvel to hear any work of theirs brought forward and commended. Those on the left, who are not Christ's, will still be blind and self-righteous. They will not feel they have neglected Christ: "Lord," they say, "when did we see you hungry . . . and did not help you?" (verse 44). Let this thought sink down into our hearts. Character on earth will prove an everlasting possession in the world to come: with the same heart that men die, with that heart they will rise again.

4. The final results
Fourth, let us mark the final results of the judgment day. We are told this in words that ought never to be forgotten: the wicked "will go away to eternal punishment, but the righteous to eternal life" (verse 46).

The state of things after the judgment is changeless and without end. The misery of the lost and the blessedness of the saved are both alike forever: let no man deceive us on this point. It is clearly revealed in Scripture: the eternity of God, heaven and hell all stand on the same foundation. As surely as God is eternal, so surely is heaven an endless day without night, and hell an endless night without day.

Who can describe the blessedness of eternal life? It passes human power to conceive: it can only be measured by contrast and comparison. An eternal rest, after warfare and conflict; the eternal company of saints, after buffeting with an evil world; an eternally glorious and painless body, after struggling with weakness and infirmity; an eternal sight of Jesus face to face, after only hearing and believing – all this is blessedness indeed. And yet the half of it remains untold.

Who can describe the misery of eternal punishment? It is something utterly indescribable and inconceivable. The eternal pain of body; the eternal sting of an accusing conscience; the eternal society of none but the wicked, the devil and his angels; the eternal remembrance of opportunities neglected and Christ despised; this is misery indeed. It is enough to make our ears tingle, and our blood run cold. And yet this picture is nothing compared to the reality.

Let us close these verses with serious self-inquiry. Let us ask ourselves on which side of Christ we are likely to be on the last day. Will we be on the right, or will we be on the left? Happy is he who never rests till he can give a satisfactory answer to this question.

Matthew
Chapter 26

The woman who anointed our Lord's head *(26:1–13)*

We now approach the closing scene of our Lord Jesus Christ's earthly ministry. Hitherto we have read of his sayings and doings: we are now about to read of his sufferings and death. Hitherto we have seen him as the Great Prophet; we are now about to see him as the great High Priest.

It is a portion of Scripture which ought to be read with particular reverence and attention. The place we stand on is holy ground. Here we see how the seed of the woman crushed the serpent's head; here we see the great sacrifice to which all the sacrifices of the Old Testament had long pointed; here we see how the blood was shed which "purifies us from all sin" (1 John 1:7), and the Lamb slain who "takes away the sin of the world" (John 1:29). We see in the death of Christ the great mystery revealed, how God can be just, and yet declare the ungodly to be righteous. No wonder all four Gospels contain a full account of this wonderful event: on other points in our Lord's history, we often find that when one evangelist speaks the other three are silent; but when we come to the crucifixion, we find it minutely described by all four.

1. Christ calls the disciples' attention to his death
First, let us observe how careful our Lord is to call the attention of his disciples to his own death. He said to them, "As you know, the Passover is two days away – and the Son of Man will be handed over to be crucified" (verse 2).

The connection of these words with the preceding chapter is very striking. Our Lord had just been dwelling on his own second coming in power and glory at the end of the world; he had been describing the last judgment and all its awful accompaniments; he had been speaking of himself as the judge before whose throne all nations would be gathered. Then at once, without pause or interval, he goes on to speak of his crucifixion. While the marvelous predictions of his final glory were still ringing in the ears of his disciples, he tells them once and again of his coming sufferings: he reminds them that he must die as a sin-offering before he reigns as a King; that he must make atonement on the cross before he takes the crown.

We can never attach too much importance to the atoning death of Christ: it is the leading fact in the Word of God, on which the eyes of our soul ought always to be fixed. Without the shedding of his blood, there is no remission of sin. It is the cardinal truth on which the whole system of Christianity hinges. Without it the Gospel is an arch without a keystone, a beautiful building without a foundation, a solar system without a sun. Let us make much of our Lord's incarnation and example, his miracles and his parables, his works and his words, but above all let us make much of his death. Let us delight in the hope of his second personal coming and millennial reign, but let us not think more even of these blessed truths than of the atonement on the cross. This after all is the master-truth of Scripture; on this let us daily feed our souls. Some, like the Greeks of old, may sneer at the doctrine and call it "foolishness"; but let us never be ashamed to say with Paul, "May I never boast except in the cross of our Lord Jesus Christ" (Galatians 6:14).

2. Christ loves to honor those who honor him

Second, let us observe in these verses what honor Christ loves to put on those who honor him.

We are told that when he was in "the home of a man known as Simon the Leper" (verse 6), a woman came while he sat at meat and poured a jar of very expensive perfume on his head. She did it, no doubt, out of reverence and affection: she had received soul-benefit from him, and she thought no mark of honor too costly to be bestowed on him in return. But this act of hers earned the disapproval of some who saw it: they called it "waste" (verse 8); they said it might have been better to sell the ointment and give the money to the poor. At once our Lord rebuked these cold-hearted fault-finders. He tells them that the woman "has done a beautiful thing to me" (verse 10), and one that he accepts and approves; and he goes on to make a striking prediction: "Wherever this gospel is preached throughout the world, what she has done will also be told, in memory of her" (verse 13).

We see in this little incident how perfectly our Lord knew things to come, and how easy it is for him to confer honor. This prophecy of his about this woman is receiving a fulfilment every day before our eyes: wherever the Gospel of St. Matthew is read, her action is known. The deeds and titles of many a king and emperor and general are as completely forgotten as if written in the sand; but the grateful act of one humble Christian woman is recorded in 150 different languages, and is known all over the globe. Human praise lasts only a few days: the praise of Christ endures forever. The pathway to lasting honor is to honor Christ.

3. A foretaste of things to come

Third, we see in this incident a blessed foretaste of things that will take place in the day of judgment. On that great day no honor done to Christ on earth will be found to have been forgotten. The speeches of parliamentary orators, the exploits of warriors, the works of poets and painters, will not be mentioned on that day; but the least work that the weakest Christian woman has done for Christ, or his members, will be found written in a book of everlasting remembrance. Not a single kind word or deed, not a cup of cold water, or a jar of perfume, will be omitted from the record. Silver and gold she may not have had; rank, power and influence she may not have possessed; but if she loved Christ, confessed Christ and worked for Christ her memorial will be found on high: she will be commended before assembled worlds.

Do we know what it is to work for Christ? If we do, let us take courage, and work on. What greater encouragement can we desire than we see here? We may be laughed at and ridiculed by the world. Our motives may be misunderstood; our conduct may be misrepresented; our sacrifices for Christ's sake may be called "waste" – waste of time, waste of money, waste of strength. Let none of these things move us. The eye of him who sat in Simon's house at Bethany is upon us: he notes all we do, and is well pleased. Therefore, "stand firm. Let nothing move you. Always give yourselves fully to the work of the Lord, because you know that your labor in the Lord is not in vain" (1 Corinthians 15:58).

The false apostle and his besetting sin *(26:14–25)*

We read, in the beginning of this passage, how our Lord Jesus Christ was betrayed into the hands of his deadly enemies. The priests and teachers of the law, however anxious to put him to death, were at a loss how to do what they wanted, fearing an uproar among the people. At this juncture a suitable instrument for carrying out their plans offered himself to them in the person of Judas Iscariot. That false apostle undertook to deliver his Master into their hands for thirty pieces of silver.

There are few blacker pages in all history than the character and conduct of Judas Iscariot: there is no more awful evidence of the wickedness of man. A poet of our own has said that "sharper than a serpent's tooth is a thankless child"; but what shall we say of a disciple who would betray his own Master: an apostle who could sell Christ? Surely this was not the least bitter part of the cup of suffering which our Lord drank.

1. *Great privileges do not make a heart right with God*
First, let us learn from these verses that someone may enjoy great privileges, and make a great religious profession, and yet their heart all the time may not be right before God.

Judas Iscariot had the highest possible religious privileges. He was a chosen apostle and companion of Christ; he was an eyewitness of our Lord's miracles and a hearer of his sermons; he saw what Abraham and Moses never saw, and heard what David and Isaiah never heard; he lived in the society of the eleven apostles; he was a fellow-laborer with Peter, James and John: but for all this his heart was never changed. He clung to one darling sin.

Judas Iscariot made a reputable profession of religion: there was nothing but what was right and proper and becoming in his outward conduct. Like the other apostles, he appeared to believe and to give up all for Christ's sake: like them, he was sent out to preach and work miracles. No one of the eleven seems to have suspected him of hypocrisy. When our Lord said, "One of you will betray me," no one said, "Is it Judas?" Yet all this time his heart was never changed.

We ought to observe these things: they are deeply humbling and instructive. Like Lot's wife, Judas is intended to be a beacon to the whole church. Let us often think about him, and say, as we think, "Search me, O God, and know my heart; . . . See if there is any offensive way in me" (Psalm 139:23–24). Let us resolve, by God's grace, that we will never be content with anything short of sound and thorough heart conversion.

2. Love of money a great snare

Second, let us learn from these verses that the love of money is one of the greatest snares to the soul. We cannot conceive a clearer proof of this, than the case of Judas. That wretched question, "What are you willing to give me?" (verse 15) reveals the secret sin which was his ruin. He had given up much for Christ's sake, but he had not given up his covetousness.

The words of the apostle Paul should often ring in our ears: "the love of money is a root of all kinds of evil" (1 Timothy 6:10). The history of the church abounds in illustrations of this truth. For money Joseph was sold by his brothers; for money Samson was betrayed to the Philistines; for money Gehazi deceived Naaman and lied to Elisha; for money Ananias and Sapphira tried to deceive Peter; for money the son of God was delivered into the hands of wicked men. It does indeed seem incredible that the cause of so much evil should be loved so much.

Let us all be on our guard against the love of money. The world is full of it in our days: the plague is about. Thousands who would abhor the idea of worshiping Juggernaut are not ashamed to make an idol of gold. We are all liable to the infection, from the least to the greatest. We may love money without having it, just as we may have money without loving it: it is an evil that works very deceitfully: it carries us captives before we are aware of our chains. Once let it get the mastery, and it will harden, paralyze, sear, freeze, blight and wither our souls. It overthrew an apostle of Christ: let us take care that it does not overthrow us. One leak may sink a ship: one unmortified sin may ruin a soul.

We ought frequently to call to mind the solemn words, "What good is it for a man to gain the whole world, yet forfeit his soul?" (Mark 8:36). "We brought nothing into the world" (1 Timothy 6:7). Our daily prayer should be "Give me neither poverty nor riches, but give me only my daily bread" (Proverbs 30:8). Our constant aim should be to be rich in grace. "People who want to get rich" in worldly possessions often find at last that they have made the worst of bargains (1 Timothy 6:9). Like Esau, they have bartered an eternal portion for a little temporary gratification; like Judas Iscariot, they have sold themselves to everlasting perdition.

3. The hopeless condition of those who die unconverted

Third, let us learn from these verses the hopeless condition of all who die unconverted. The words of our Lord on this subject are particularly solemn: he says of Judas, "It would be better for him if he had not been born" (verse 24).

This saying admits of only one interpretation. It teaches plainly that it is better never to live at all than to live without faith and die without grace. To die in this state is to be ruined forevermore: it is a fall from which there is no rising, a loss which is utterly irretrievable. There is no change in hell: the gulf between hell and heaven is one that no one can cross.

This saying could never have been used if there were any truth in the doctrine of universal salvation. If it really were true that all would sooner or later reach heaven, and hell sooner or later be emptied of inhabitants, it could never be said that it would have been "better for him if he had not been born." Hell itself would lose its terrors if it had an end: hell itself would be endurable if after millions of ages there were a hope of freedom and of heaven. But universal salvation will find no foothold in Scripture: the teaching of the Word of God is plain and express on the subject. There is a worm that never dies, and a fire that is not quenched (Mark 9:44 [NIV footnote, ed. note]). "Unless a man is born again," he will wish one day he had never been born at all. "Better," says Burkett, "have no being, than not have a being in Christ."

Let us grasp this truth firmly, and not let it go. There are always people who deny the reality and eternity of hell. We live in a time when a morbid charity induces many to exaggerate God's mercy at the expense of his justice, and when false teachers are daring to talk of a "love of God lower even than hell." Let us resist such teaching with a holy jealousy, and abide by the doctrine of Holy Scripture: let us not be ashamed to walk in the old paths, and to believe that there is an eternal God, and an eternal heaven and an eternal hell. Once depart from this belief, and we admit the thin end of the wedge of skepticism, and may at last deny any doctrine of the Gospel. We may rest assured that there is no firm standing ground between a belief in the eternity of hell, and downright unbelief.

The Lord's Supper and the first communicants *(26:26–35)*

These verses describe the institution of the sacrament of the Lord's Supper. Our Lord knew well the things that were before him, and graciously chose the last quiet evening that he could have before his crucifixion as an occasion for bestowing a parting gift on his church. How precious must this ordinance have appeared to his disciples afterwards when they remembered the events of the night! How sad is the thought that no ordinance has led to such fierce controversy, and been so grievously misunderstood, as the ordinance of the Lord's Supper! It ought to have united the church, but our sins have made it a cause of division. The thing which should have been for our welfare has been too often made an occasion of falling.

1. The meaning of the words Jesus used
The first thing that demands our notice in these verses is the right meaning of our Lord's words, "This is my body . . . this is my blood" (verses 26, 28).

Needless to say, this question has divided the visible church of Christ. It has caused volumes of controversial theology to be written: but we must not shrink from having decided opinions upon it because theologians have disputed and differed. Unsoundness on this point has given rise to many deplorable superstitions.

The plain meaning of our Lord's words appears to be this: "This bread *represents* my body. This wine *represents* my blood." He did not mean that the bread he gave to his disciples was really and literally his body; he did not mean that the wine he gave to his disciples was really and literally his blood. Let us lay firm hold on this interpretation: it may be supported by several serious reasons.

[Watson in his commentary on Matthew (p. 386) writes:

"Bishop Law has remarked that there is no term in the Hebrew language, which expresses *to signify* or *denote*; and that the Greek here naturally takes the impress of the Hebrew or Syriac idiom, *it is* being used for *it signifies*. Hence the similar use of the verb in various passages. 'The three branches *are* days' (Genesis 40:12); 'the seven good cows *are* seven years' (Genesis 41:26); 'the ten horns *are* ten kings' (Daniel 7:24); 'the field *is* the world' (Matthew 13:38); 'the seven stars *are* the angels of the seven churches, and the seven lampstands *are* the seven churches' (Revelation 1:20).]

The conduct of the disciples at the Lord's Supper forbids us to believe that the bread they received was Christ's body, and the wine they received was Christ's blood. They were all Jews, taught from their infancy to believe that it was sinful to eat flesh with the blood (Deuteronomy 12:23–25); yet there is nothing in the narrative to show that they were startled by our Lord's words. They evidently perceived no change in the bread and wine.

Our own senses at the present day forbid us to believe that there is any change in the bread and wine in the Lord's Supper; our own taste tells us that they are really and literally what they appear to be. Things above our reason the Bible requires us to believe; but we are never asked to believe anything that contradicts our senses.

The true doctrine about our Lord's human nature forbids us to believe that the bread in the Lord's Supper can be his body, or the wine his blood; the natural body of Christ cannot be at one time in more places than once. If our Lord's body could sit at table, and at the same time be eaten by the disciples, it is perfectly clear that it was not a human body like our own. But this we must never allow for one moment. It is the glory of Christianity that our Redeemer is perfect man as well as perfect God.

Finally, the genius of the language in which our Lord spoke at the

Lord's Supper makes it entirely unnecessary to interpret his words literally. The Bible is full of expressions of a similar kind, to which no one thinks of giving any but a figurative meaning. Our Lord speaks of himself as the "door" and the "vine," and we know that he is using imagery when he speaks like this; there is therefore no inconsistency in supposing that he used figurative language when he instituted the Lord' Supper. We have the more right to say so when we remember the grave objections which stand in the way of a literal view of his words.

Let us lay up these things in our minds, and not forget them. In a day of abounding heresy, it is good to be well armed. Ignorant and confused views of the meaning of Scripture language are one great cause of religious error.

2. The purpose of the Lord's Supper

The second thing which demands our notice in these verses is the purpose and object for which the Lord's Supper was instituted.

This is a subject again on which great darkness prevails. The ordinance of the Lord's Supper has been regarded as something mysterious and past understanding. Immense harm has been done to Christianity by the vague and highflown language in which many writers have indulged in treating of the sacrament. There is certainly nothing to warrant such language in the account of its original institution. The more simple our views of its purpose, the more scriptural they are likely to be.

The Lord's Supper is not a sacrifice. There is no oblation in it, no offering up of anything but our prayers, praises and thanksgivings. From the day that Jesus died there needed no more offering for sin: "by one sacrifice he has made perfect forever those who are being made holy" (Hebrews 10:14). Priests, altars and sacrifices all ceased to be necessary when the Lamb of God offered up himself. Their role came to an end; their work was done.

The Lord's Supper has no power to confer benefit on those who come to it if they do not come to it with faith. The mere formal act of eating the bread and drinking the wine is utterly unprofitable unless it is done with a right heart. It is eminently an ordinance for the living soul, not for the dead; for the converted, not for the unconverted.

The Lord's Supper was ordained as a continual remembrance of the sacrifice of Christ's death, until he comes again. The benefits it confers are spiritual, not physical: its effects must be looked for in our inner being. It was intended to remind us, by the visible, tangible emblems of bread and wine, that the offering of Christ's body and blood for us on the cross is the only atonement for sin, and the life of a believer's soul; it was meant to help our poor weak faith to closer fellowship with our crucified Saviour, and to assist us in spiritually feeding on Christ's body and blood. It is an ordinance for redeemed sinners, and not for unfallen angels. By receiving it we publicly declare our sense of guilt, and our need of a Saviour – our trust in Jesus, and our love to him, our desire to live upon him, and our hope to live with him. Using it in this spirit, we shall find our repentance deepened, our faith increased, our hope brightened, our love enlarged, our besetting sins weakened and our graces strengthened. It will draw us nearer to Christ.

Let us bear these things in mind: they need to be remembered these days. There is nothing in our religion which we are so ready to pervert and misunderstand as those parts which approach our senses. Whatever we can touch with our hand and see with our eyes, we are apt to exalt into an idol, or to expect good from it as a mere charm: let us specially beware of this tendency in the matter of the Lord's Supper. Above all, "let us take heed," in the words of the Church of England Homily, "lest of the memory it be made a sacrifice."

3. The character of the first communicants

The last thing which deserves a brief notice in this passage is the character of the first communicants. It is a point full of comfort and instruction.

The little company to which the bread and wine were first administered by our Lord was composed of the apostles whom he had chosen to accompany him during his earthly ministry. They were poor and unlearned men, who loved Christ, but were weak alike in faith and knowledge: they knew but little of the full meaning of their Master's sayings and doings; they knew but little of the frailty of their own hearts. They thought they were ready to die with Jesus, and yet that very night they all forsook him and fled. All this our Lord knew perfectly well. The state of their hearts was not hidden from him, and yet he did not keep back from them the Lord's Supper!

There is something very instructive in this. It shows us plainly that we must not make great knowledge and great strength of grace an indispensable qualification for communicants. People may know but little, and be no better than children in spiritual strength, but they are not on that account to be excluded from the Lord's table. Do they really feel their sins? Do they really love Christ? Do they really desire to serve him? If so, we ought to encourage and receive them. Doubtless we must do all we can to exclude unworthy communicants: no graceless person ought to come to the Lord's Supper. But we must take care that we do not reject those whom Christ has not rejected. There is no wisdom in being more strict than our Lord and his disciples.

Let us leave the passage with serious self-inquiry as to our own conduct with respect to the Lord's Supper. Do we turn away from it when it is administered? If so, how can we justify our conduct? It will not do to say it is not a necessary ordinance: to say so is to pour contempt on Christ himself and declare that we are unfit to die, and unprepared to meet God. These are solemn considerations: all non-communicants should ponder them well.

Are we in the habit of coming to the Lord's table? If so, in what frame of mind do we come? Do we draw near intelligently, humbly and with faith? Do we understand what we are about? Do we really feel our sinfulness and our need of Christ? Do we really desire to live a Christian life, as well as profess the Christian faith? Happy is that soul who can give a satisfactory answer to these questions! Let him go forward, and persevere.

The agony in the garden *(26:36–46)*

The verses we have now read describe what is commonly called Christ's agony at Gethsemane. It is a passage which undoubtedly contains deep and mysterious things. We ought to read it with reverence and wonder, for there is much in it which we cannot fully comprehend.

Why do we find our Lord so "sorrowful and troubled," as he is here described (verse 37)? What are we to make of his words, "My soul is overwhelmed with sorrow to the point of death" (verse 38)? Why do we see him going apart from his disciples, and falling on his face, and crying to his Father with strong cries, and his prayer repeated three times? Why is the almighty Son of God, who had worked so many miracles, so heavy and disquieted? Why is Jesus, who came into the world to die, so ready to faint at the approach of death? Why is all this?

There is but one reasonable answer to these questions: the weight that pressed down our Lord's soul was not the fear of death and its pains. Thousands have endured the most agonizing sufferings of body, and died without a groan, and so, no doubt, might our Lord. But the real weight that bowed down the heart of Jesus was the weight of the sin of the world, which seems to have now pressed down upon him with unique force: it was the burden of our guilt imputed to him, which was now laid on him, as on the head of the scapegoat. How great that burden must have been no human heart can conceive! It is known only to God. Well may the Greek Litany speak of the "unknown sufferings of Christ." The words of Scott on this subject are probably correct: "Christ at this time endured as much misery of the same kind with that of condemned spirits, as could possibly consist with a pure conscience, perfect love of God and man, and an assured confidence of a glorious event."

[I believe that this view is the only reasonable solution that can be given of our Lord's agony. I am totally at a loss to conceive what explanation can be given for it by any Socinian, or any theologian who denies that humanity's sin was imputed to Christ, and denies the vicarious nature of Christ's sufferings.

The Socinian utterly denies the doctrine of atonement and says that our Lord was only a man, and not God. Yet on his view Jesus showed less firmness in suffering than many men have shown! Some modern theologians say that our Lord's death was not a propitiation and expiation for sin, but only a great example of self-sacrifice. On this view, the intense agony of body and mind here described is equally unaccountable. Both views appear to me alike dishonoring to our Lord Jesus Christ, and utterly unscriptural and unsatisfactory. I believe the agony in the garden to be a knot that nothing can untie except the old doctrine of our sin being really imputed to Christ, and Christ being made sin and a curse for us.

There are deep things in this passage of Scripture containing the account of the agony, which I purposely leave untouched. They are too deep for the human mind to fathom. The extent to which Satan was allowed to tempt our Lord at this time; the degree of suffering, both mental and bodily, which an entirely sinless person like our Lord would endure in bearing the sin of all mankind; the manner in which the human and divine wills both operated in our Lord's experience, since he was at all times as really man as God – all these are points which I prefer to leave alone. It is easy on such questions to "darken counsel with words without knowledge."]

But however mysterious this part of our Lord's history may seem to us, we must not fail to observe the precious lessons of practical instruction which it contains. Let us now see what those lessons are.

1. Prayer the best remedy in time of trouble

First, let us learn that prayer is the best practical remedy that we can use in time of trouble. We see that Christ himself prayed when his soul was sorrowful: all true Christians ought to do the same.

Trouble is a cup that all must drink in this world of sin: we are "born to trouble as surely as sparks fly upward" (Job 5:7); we cannot avoid it. Of all creatures, none is so vulnerable as mankind: our bodies, our minds, our families, our business, our friends, are all so many doors through which trial will come in. The holiest saints can claim no exemption from it: like their Master, they are often people of sorrow.

But what is the first thing to be done in time of trouble? We must pray. Like Job, we must fall down and worship (Job 1:20); like Hezekiah, we must spread it out before the Lord (2 Kings 19:14). The first person we must turn to for help must be our God. We must tell our Father in heaven all our sorrow; we must believe confidently that nothing is too trivial or minute to be laid before him, so long as we do it with entire submission to his will. It is the mark of faith to keep nothing back from our best Friend: so doing, we may be sure we shall have an answer. "If it is possible" (verse 39), and the thing we ask is for God's glory, it will be done: the thorn in the flesh will either be removed, or grace to endure it will be given to us, as it was to St. Paul (2 Corinthians 12:9). May we all store up this lesson against the day of need. It is a true saying that "prayers are the leeches of care."

2. Submission to God's will should be one of our chief aims

Second, let us learn that entire submission of will to the will of God should be one of our chief aims in this world. The words of our Lord are a beautiful example of the spirit that we should follow after in this matter: he says, "Not as I will, but as you will" (verse 39). He says again, "May your will be done" (verse 42).

A will unsanctified and uncontrolled is one great cause of unhappiness in life. It may be seen in little infants; it is born with us. We all like our own way. We wish and want many things, and forget we are entirely ignorant what is for our good, and unfit to choose for ourselves. Happy the person who has learned to have no "wishes," and in every state to be content! It is a lesson which we are slow to learn and, like St. Paul, we must learn it not in the school of mortals, but of Christ (Philippians 4:11).

Do we want to know whether we are born again and growing in grace? Let us see how it is with us in the matter of our wills. Can we bear disappointment? Can we put up patiently with unexpected trials and vexations? Can we see our favorite plans and darling schemes crossed, without grumbling and complaint? Can we sit still, and suffer calmly, as well as go up and down and work actively? These are the things that prove whether we have the mind of Christ. It ought never to be forgotten that warm feelings and joyful frames are not the truest evidences of grace: a mortified will is a far more valuable possession. Even our Lord himself did not always rejoice; but he could always say, "May your will be done."

3. Christians must watch and pray against weakness

Third, let us learn that there is great weakness even in true disciples of Christ, and that they need to watch and pray against it. We see Peter, James and John, those three chosen apostles, sleeping. We find our Lord addressing them in these solemn words: "Watch and pray so that you will not fall into temptation. The spirit is willing, but the body is weak" (verse 41).

There is a double nature in all believers. Converted, renewed, sanctified as they are, they still carry about with them a mass of indwelling corruption, a body of sin. St. Paul speaks of this, when he says, "I find this law at work: When I want to do good, evil is right there with me. For in my inner being I delight in God's law; but I see another law at work in the members of my body, waging war against the law of my mind" (Romans 7:21–23). The experience of all true Christians in every age confirms this. They find within two contrary principles, and a continual strife between the two; to these two principles our Lord alludes when he addresses his half-awakened disciples: he calls the one "body" and the other "spirit." He says, "the spirit is willing, but the body is weak."

But does our Lord excuse this weakness of his disciples? Far from it: those who draw this conclusion mistake his meaning. He uses that very weakness as an argument for watchfulness and prayer; he teaches us that the very fact that we are hedged about with weakness should stir us up continually to "watch and pray."

If we know anything of true religion, let us never forget this lesson. If we desire a strong walk with God and not to fall like David or Peter, let us never forget to watch and pray. Let us live like men on enemy's ground, and be always on our guard. We cannot walk too carefully; we cannot be too jealous over our souls. The world is very ensnaring; the devil is very busy. Let our Lord's words ring in our ears daily, like a trumpet. Our spirits may sometimes be very willing; but our bodies are also very weak. Then let us always watch and always pray.

The false apostle's kiss; Christ's submission (26:47–56)

We see in these verses the cup of our Lord Jesus Christ's sufferings beginning to be filled. We see him betrayed by one of his disciples, forsaken by the rest, and taken prisoner by his deadly enemies. Never surely was there sorrow like his sorrow. Never may we forget, as we read this part of the Bible, that our sins were the cause of these sorrows! Jesus was "delivered over to death for our sins" (Romans 4:25).

1. Christ's gracious dealing with his disciples
First, let us notice in these verses how graciously our Lord dealt with his disciples.

We have this point proved by a deeply touching circumstance at the moment of our Lord's betrayal. When Judas Iscariot undertook to guide the crowd to the place where his Master was, he gave them a sign by which they might distinguish Jesus in the dim moonlight from his disciples: he said, "The one I kiss is the man" (verse 48). And so, when he came to Jesus, he said, "'Greetings, Rabbi!' and kissed him" (verse 49). That simple fact reveals the affectionate terms on which the disciples associated with our Lord. It is a universal custom in eastern countries, when friend meets friend, to greet one another with a kiss (Exodus 18:7; 1 Samuel 20:41). It would seem therefore, that when Judas kissed our Lord, he only did what all the apostles were accustomed to do when they met their Master after an absence.

Let us draw comfort from this little circumstance for our own souls. Our Lord Jesus Christ is a most gracious Saviour. He is not an "austere man," repelling sinners and keeping them at a distance; he is not a being so different from us in nature that we must regard him with awe rather than affection: he would rather have us regard him as an elder brother, and a beloved friend. His heart in heaven is still the same as it was on earth: he is always meek and merciful and comes down to meet lowly people on their own level. Let us trust him, and not be afraid.

2. Christ's condemnation of force

Second, let us notice how our Lord condemns those who think to use physical weapons in defense of him and his cause. He reproves one of his disciples for striking a servant of the high priest (verse 51). "Put your sword back in its place," he says (verse 52) – and adds a solemn declaration of perpetual significance, "all who draw the sword will die by the sword."

The sword has a legitimate role. It may be used righteously, in the defense of nations against oppression; it may become positively necessary to use it to prevent riots and looting on earth; but the sword is not to be used in the propagation and maintenance of the Gospel. Christianity is not to be enforced by bloodshed, and belief in it extorted by force. It would have been better for the church if this sentence had been remembered more frequently! There are few countries in Christendom where the mistake has not been made of attempting to change people's religious opinions by compulsion, penalties, imprisonment and death. And with what effect? The pages of history supply an answer. No wars have been so bloody as those which have arisen out of the collision of religious opinions: often, sadly often, the very men who have been most forward to promote those wars have themselves been slain. May we never forget this! The weapons of the Christian warfare are not physical, but spiritual (2 Corinthians 10:4).

3. Christ's submission of his own free will

Third, let us notice how our Lord submitted to being made a prisoner of his own free will. He was not taken captive because he could not escape: it would have been easy for him to scatter his enemies to the winds if he had thought fit. "Do you think," he says to a disciple, "I cannot call on my Father, and he will at once put at my disposal more than twelve legions of angels? But how then would the Scriptures be fulfilled that say it must happen in this way?" (verses 53–54).

We see in those words the secret of his voluntary submission to his foes. He came on purpose to fulfill the patterns and promises of Old Testament Scriptures and, by fulfilling them, to provide salvation for the world. He came intentionally to be the true Lamb of God, the Passover Lamb. He came voluntarily to be the scapegoat on whom the iniquities of the people were to be laid. His heart was set on accomplishing this great work. It could not be done without the "hiding of his power," for a time: to do it he became a willing sufferer. He was taken, tried, condemned and crucified entirely of his own free will.

Let us observe this: there is much encouragement in it. The willing sufferer will surely be a willing Saviour. The almighty Son of God, who allowed men to bind him and lead him away captive when he might have prevented them with a word, must surely be full of readiness to save the souls that flee to him. Once more then let us learn to trust him and not be afraid.

4. Christians do not know their weakness until they are tried

Fourth, let us notice how little Christians know the weakness of their own hearts until they are tried. We have a sad illustration of this in the conduct of our Lord's apostles. The verses we have read conclude with the words, "Then all the disciples deserted him and fled" (verse 56). They forgot their confident assertions made a few hours before; they forgot that they had declared their willingness to die with their Master; they forgot everything but the danger that stared them in the face. The fear of death overcame them: they "deserted him and fled."

How many professing Christians have done the same! How many, under the influence of excited feelings, have promised that they would never be ashamed of Christ! They have come away from the communion table, or the striking sermon, or the Christian meeting, full of zeal and love and ready to say to all who caution them against backsliding, "How could your servant, a mere dog, accomplish such a feat?" (2 Kings 8:13). And yet in a few days these feelings have cooled down and passed away: a trial has come and they have fallen before it. They have deserted Christ!

Let us learn, from this passage, lessons of humiliation and self-abasement. Let us resolve, by God's grace, to cultivate a spirit of lowliness, and self-distrust. Let us settle it in our minds that there is nothing too bad for the very best of us to do unless he watches, prays and is held up by the grace of God; and let it be one of our daily prayers. "Uphold me, and I shall be delivered" (Psalm 119:117).

Christ before the Sanhedrin (26:57–68)

We read, in these verses, how our Lord Jesus Christ was brought before Caiaphas, the high priest, and solemnly pronounced guilty. It was fitting that it should be so. The great day of atonement had come: the wonderful type of the scapegoat was about to be completely fulfilled. It was only suitable that the Jewish high priest should do his part, and declare sin to be upon the head of the victim, before he was led out to be crucified (Leviticus 26:21). May we ponder these things and understand them. There was a deep meaning in every step of our Lord's passion.

1. The chief priests were the principal agents
First, let us observe in these verses that the chief priests were the principal agents in bringing about our Lord's death. It was not so much the Jewish people, we must remember, who pushed forward this wicked deed, as Caiaphas and his companions, the chief priests.

This is an instructive fact, and deserves notice. It is a clear proof that high ecclesiastical office exempts no one from gross errors in doctrine, and tremendous sins in practice. The Jewish priests could trace their pedigree back to Aaron, and were his lineal successors; their office was one of special sanctity, and carried special responsibilities. Yet these very men were the murderers of Christ.

Let us beware of regarding ministers of religion as infallible: their position, however correct, is no guarantee that they will not lead us astray, and even ruin our souls. The teaching and conduct of all ministers must be tested against the Word of God: they are to be followed so long as they follow the Bible, but no longer. The maxim laid down in Isaiah must be our guide: "To the law and to the testimony! If they do not speak according to this word, they have no light of dawn" (Isaiah 8:20).

2. Christ declared his own Messiahship and second coming

Second, let us observe how fully our Lord declared to the Jewish council his own Messiahship and his future coming in glory.

The unconverted Jew can never tell us at the present day that his forefathers were left in ignorance that Jesus was the Messiah. Our Lord's answer to the solemn oath of the high priest was sufficient reply: he tells the council plainly that he is "the Christ, the Son of God" (verses 63–64). He goes on to warn them that though he had not yet appeared in glory, as they expected the Messiah to do, a day would come when he would do so. "In the future you will see the Son of man sitting at the right hand of the Mighty One, and coming on the clouds of heaven" (verse 64). They would yet see that very Jesus of Nazareth, whom they had arraigned at their bar, appear in all majesty as King of kings (Revelation 1:7).

It is a striking fact which we should not fail to notice, that almost the last word spoken by our Lord to the Jews was a warning about his own second coming: he tells them plainly that they would yet see him in glory. No doubt he was referring to Daniel 7:13 in the language that he used. But he spoke to deaf ears. Unbelief, prejudice, self-righteousness covered them like a thick cloud: never was there such an instance of spiritual blindness. Well may the Church of England litany contain the prayers, "From all blindness, and from hardness of heart, Good Lord, deliver us."

3. Christ endured false witness and mockery

Third, let us observe how much our Lord endured before the council from false witness and mockery.

Falsehood and ridicule are old and favorite weapons of the devil. "He is a liar, and the father of lies" (John 8:44). All through our Lord's earthly ministry we see these weapons continually employed against him. He was called "a glutton and a drunkard, a friend of tax collectors and 'sinners'" (Matthew 11:19); he was held up to contempt as "a Samaritan" (John 8:48). The closing scene of his life was only in keeping with all the past tenor of it. Satan stirred up his enemies to add insult to injury: no sooner was he pronounced guilty than every sort of mean indignity was heaped upon him: "they spat in his face and struck him with their fists. Others slapped him and said, 'Prophesy to us, Christ. Who hit you?'" (verses 67–68).

How strange it all sounds! How wonderful that the Holy Son of God should have voluntarily submitted to such indignities to redeem such miserable sinners as we are! How wonderful, not least, that every detail of these insults was foretold 700 years before they were inflicted! Seven hundred years before, Isaiah had written down the words, "I did not hide my face from mocking and spitting" (Isaiah 50:6).

Let us draw from this passage one practical conclusion. Let it never surprise us if we have to endure mockery, ridicule and false reports because we belong to Christ. "A student is not above his teacher, nor a servant above his master" (Matthew 10:24). If lies and insults were heaped upon the Saviour, we need not wonder if the same weapons are constantly used against his people. It is one of Satan's great devices to blacken the characters of godly men and bring them into contempt: the lives of Luther, Cranmer, Calvin and Wesley supply abundant examples of this. If we are ever called upon to suffer in this way, let us bear it patiently. We drink the same cup that was drunk by our beloved Lord. But there is one great difference: at the worst, we only drink a few bitter drops; he drank the cup to the very dregs.

Peter's denial of his Master (26:69–75)

These verses relate a remarkable and deeply instructive event: the apostle Peter's denial of Christ. It is one of those events which indirectly prove the truth of the Bible. If the Gospel had been a mere human invention, we should never have been told that one of its principal preachers was once so weak and erring as to deny his Master.

1. The nature of Peter's sin

The first thing that demands our notice is the full nature of the sin of which Peter was guilty.

It was a great sin. We see a man who had followed Christ for three years, and been forward in professing faith and love towards him – a man who had received boundless mercies and loving kindness and had been treated by Christ as a familiar friend. We see this man denying three times that he knows Jesus! This was bad. It was a sin committed under circumstances of great aggravation: Peter had been warned plainly of his danger and had heard the warning; he had just been receiving the bread and wine at our Lord's hands, and declaring loudly that though he died with him, he would not deny him! This also was bad. It was a sin committed under apparently small provocation: two weak women made the remark that he was with Jesus. Those who stood nearby said, "Surely you are one of them" (verse 73). No threat seems to have been used, no violence seems to have been done, but it was enough to overthrow Peter's faith: he denies before all. He denies with an oath: he curses and swears. Truly it is a humbling picture!

Let us mark this story, and treasure it in our minds: it teaches us plainly that the best of saints are only human, and have many weaknesses. A person may be converted to God, have faith, hope and love towards Christ, and yet be overtaken in a fault, and have awful falls. It shows us the necessity of humility: so long as we are in the body, we are in danger. The body is weak, and the devil is active. We must never think, "I cannot fall." It points out to us the duty of charity towards erring saints. We must not write people off as graceless reprobates because they occasionally stumble and err; we must remember Peter and "restore them gently" (Galatians 6:1).

2. The steps by which he was led to sin

The second thing that demands our notice is the series of steps by which Peter was led to deny his Lord.

These steps are mercifully recorded for our learning. The Spirit of God has taken care to have them written down for the perpetual benefit of the church of Christ. Let us trace them one by one.

The first step to Peter's fall was *self-confidence*: he said, "Even if all fall away on account of you, I never will" (verse 33). The second step was *indolence:* his Master told him to watch and pray; instead of doing so he slept. The third step was *cowardly compromising:* instead of keeping close to his Master, he first deserted him, and then "followed him at a distance" (verse 58). The last step was *needless venturing* into evil company: he went into the priest's palace and "sat down with the guards" (verse 58), like one of themselves. And then came the final fall: the cursing, the swearing and the three-fold denial. Startling as it appears, his heart had been preparing it: it was the fruit of seeds which he himself had sown.

Let us remember this part of Peter's story: it is deeply instructive to all who call themselves Christians. Great illnesses seldom attack the body without warning symptoms coming first; great falls seldom happen to a saint without a previous course of secret backsliding. The church and the world are sometimes shocked by the sudden misconduct of some great Christian; believers are discouraged and stumbled by it; the enemies of God rejoice and mock; but if the truth could be known, the explanation of such cases would generally be found to have been private departure from God. People fall in private long before they fall in public. The tree falls with a great crash, but the secret decay which accounts for it is often not discovered till it is down on the ground.

3. The sorrow Peter's sin brought to him

The last thing which demands our notice is the sorrow which Peter's sin brought upon him. We read at the end of the chapter, "He went outside and wept bitterly" (verse 75).

These words deserve more attention than they generally receive. Thousands have read the story of Peter's sin, but have thought little of Peter's tears and repentance. May we have an eye to see, and a heart to understand!

We see in Peter's tears *the close connection between unhappiness and departure from God.* It is a merciful arrangement of God that in one sense holiness always brings its own reward. A heavy heart and an uneasy conscience, a clouded hope and an abundant crop of doubts will always be the consequence of backsliding and inconsistency. The words of Solomon describe the experience of many an inconsistent child of God: "The faithless will be fully repaid for their ways" (Proverbs 14:14). Let it be a settled principle in our religion that if we love inward peace we must walk closely with God.

We see in Peter's bitter tears *the grand mark of difference between the hypocrite and the true believer.* When the hypocrite is overtaken by sin, he generally falls to rise no more: he has no principle of life within him to raise him up. When the child of God is overtaken, he rises again by true repentance, and by the grace of God amends his life. Let no man flatter himself that he may sin with impunity because David committed adultery, and because Peter denied his Lord. No doubt these holy men sinned greatly: but they did not continue in their sins. They repented greatly; they mourned over their falls; they loathed and abhorred their own wickedness. It would be good for many people if they would imitate them in their repentance as well as in their sins! Too many are acquainted with their fall but not with their recovery. Like David and Peter, they have sinned, but they have not, like David and Peter, repented.

The whole passage is full of lessons that ought never to be forgotten. Do we profess to have a hope in Christ? Let us mark the weakness of a believer and the steps that lead to a fall. Have we unhappily backslidden and left our first love? Let us remember that the Saviour of Peter still lives. There is mercy for us as well as for him: but we must repent and seek that mercy if we would find it. Let us turn unto God and he will turn to us: his compassions never fail (Lamentations 3:22).

Matthew
Chapter 27

The end of Judas Iscariot *(27:1–10)*

The opening of this chapter describes the delivery of our Lord Jesus
Christ into the hands of the Gentiles. The chief priests and elders of the
Jews led him away to Pontius Pilate, the Roman governor. We may see
in this incident the finger of God: it was ordered by his providence that
Gentiles as well as Jews should be concerned in the murder of Christ;
it was ordered by his providence that the priests should publicly confess that the "scepter had departed from Judah." They were unable to
put anyone to death without going to the Romans: the words of Jacob
were therefore fulfilled. The Messiah, "to whom it belongs," had
indeed come (Genesis 49:10).

The subject that principally occupies these verses is the sad end of the
false apostle, Judas Iscariot. It is a subject full of instruction: let us
mark well what it contains.

1. Proof of Christ's innocence
First, we see in the end of Judas a plain proof of our Lord's innocence
of every charge laid against him.

If there was any living witness who could give evidence against our
Lord Jesus Christ, Judas Iscariot was the man. A chosen apostle of
Jesus, a constant companion in all his journeyings, a hearer of all his
teaching, both in public and private – he must have known well if our
Lord had done any wrong, either in word or deed. As a deserter from
our Lord's company, a betrayer of him into the hands of his enemies,
it was in his interest for his own character's sake, to prove Jesus guilty.
It would extenuate and excuse his own conduct if he could make out

that his former Master was an offender and an impostor.

Why then did Judas Iscariot not come forward? Why did he not stand before the Jewish council and specify his charges, if he had any to make? Why did he not venture to accompany the chief priests to Pilate, and prove to the Romans that Jesus was a malefactor? There is but one answer to these questions. Judas did not come forward as a witness, because his conscience would not let him. Bad as he was, he knew he could prove nothing against Christ; wicked as he was, he knew well that his Master was holy, harmless, innocent, blameless and true. Let this never be forgotten. The absence of Judas Iscariot at our Lord's trial is one among many proofs that the Lamb of God was without blemish, a sinless man.

2. Repentance can come too late

Second, we see in the end of Judas that there is such a thing as repentance which is too late. We are told plainly that Judas "was seized with remorse" (verse 3); we are even told that he went to the priests and said, "I have sinned" (verse 4). Yet it is clear that his repentance did not lead to salvation.

This is a point which deserves special attention. It is a common saying that "it is never too late to repent." The saying, no doubt, is true, if repentance be true; but unhappily, late repentance is often not genuine. It is possible for a man to feel his sins, and be sorry for them – to be under strong conviction of guilt, and express deep remorse – to be pricked in conscience, and exhibit much distress of mind – and yet, for all this, not repent with his heart. Present danger, or the fear of death, may account for all his feelings, and the Holy Spirit may have done no work whatever on his soul.

Let us beware of trusting to a late repentance. "Now is the time of God's favor, now is the day of salvation" (2 Corinthians 6:2). One penitent thief was saved in the hour of death, that no man might despair; but only one, that no man might presume. Let us put off nothing that concerns our souls, and above all not put off repentance, under the misapprehension that it is in our own power. The words of Solomon on this subject are very fearful: "they will call to me but I will not answer; they will look for me but will not find me" (Proverbs 1:28).

3. Ungodliness brings little comfort in the end

Third, let us see in the end of Judas how little comfort ungodliness brings a man at the last. We are told that he returned the thirty pieces of silver for which he had sold his Master, and went away in bitterness of soul. That money was dearly earned. It brought him no pleasure, even when he had it: "ill-gotten treasures are of no value" (Proverbs 10:2).

[It is a great and undeniable difficulty, that the words quoted as having been used by "Jeremiah the prophet" are not to be found in any writings of Jeremiah that we possess, and that they are found in the prophet Zechariah. The following solutions of the difficulty have been suggested.

1. Some think that the prophecy quoted by Matthew was really delivered by Jeremiah, though not written, and only handed down and recorded by Zechariah. In favor of this view, we must remember that we have a saying of our Lord's in Act 20:35 which is not recorded in the Gospel, and a prophecy of Enoch's in Jude 14.

2. Some think that the name of Jeremiah was applied by the Jews to all that part of the Old Testament containing prophecies, and that Matthew did not really mean that Jeremiah had delivered the prophecy. This is the view of Lightfoot.

3. Some think that Matthew originally wrote the words "The prophet," without quoting the name of any particular one, and that the word "Jeremiah" was inserted by an ignorant transcriber. In favor of this view, it is fair to say that the Syriac version, one of the oldest extant, simply says "the prophet," and omits Jeremiah's name. The Persian version of the Gospels also omits it.

4. Some think that Matthew originally wrote the words "Zechariah the prophet," and that some ignorant transcriber changed the word to Jeremiah. In favor of this view it must be fairly remembered that in manuscripts, names were often written short, and that IOU and ZOU are not very unlike.

I offer no opinion on these solutions of the difficulty. A question of this sort, which has puzzled so many interpreters, is not likely to be settled at this date.

One solution of the difficulty I only mention in order to enter my protest against it. That solution is adopted by many modern theologians.

It is that Matthew simply forgot what he was doing, and made a blunder – that he quoted from memory, inaccurately, putting Jeremiah when he meant Zechariah. I can only say that at this rate we must give up the inspiration of Scripture altogether! If writers of the Bible could make blunders like this, we never know where we are in quoting a text. To use such an argument is giving the Arians and Socinians a weapon which they well know how to use. Once give up the *verbal* inspiration of Scripture, we stand on a quicksand.]

Sin is, in truth, the hardest of all masters. In its service there are plenty of fair promises, but an utter dearth of actual rewards. Its pleasures last only for a while: its wages are sorrow, remorse, self-accusation and, too often, death. Those who sow to please their sinful nature do indeed reap destruction (Galatians 6:8).

Are we tempted to commit sin? Let us remember the words of Scripture, "your sin will find you out" (Numbers 32:23), and resist the temptation. Let us be sure that sooner or later, in this life or in the life to come, in this world or on the judgment day, sin and the sinner will meet face to face, and have a bitter reckoning. Let us be sure that of all trades sin is the most unprofitable. Judas, Achan, Gehazi, Ananias and Sapphira all found it so to their cost. Well might St. Paul say, "What benefit did you reap at that time from the things you are now ashamed of?" (Romans 6:21).

4. The miserable end of someone who does not use privileges

Fourth, let us see in the case of Judas the miserable end a person may come to if he has great privileges and does not use them rightly. We are told that this unhappy man "went away and hanged himself" (verse 5). What an awful death to die. An apostle of Christ, a former preacher of the Gospel, a companion of Peter and John, commits suicide and rushes into God's presence unprepared and unforgiven.

Let us never forget that no sinners are so sinful as sinners against light and knowledge. None are so provoking to God: none, if we look at Scripture, have been so often removed from this world by sudden and fearful visitations. Let us remember Lot's wife, Pharaoh, Korah, Dathan, Abiram and Saul, King of Israel: they are all cases in point. It is a solemn saying of Bunyan that "none fall so deep into the pit, as those who fall backward." It is written in Proverbs, "A man who remains stiff-necked after many rebukes will suddenly be destroyed – without rememdy" (Proverbs 29:1). May we all strive to live up to our light. There is such a thing as sin against the Holy Spirit: clear knowledge of truth in the head, combined with deliberate love of sin in the heart, go a long way towards it.

And now what is the state of our hearts? Are we ever tempted to rest on our knowledge and profession of religion? Let us remember Judas, and beware. Are we disposed to cling to the world, and to give money a prominent place in our minds? Again, let us remember Judas, and beware. Are we trifling with any one sin and flattering ourselves we may repent later? Once more, let us remember Judas, and beware. He is set up before us as a beacon: let us look well at him, and not get shipwrecked.

Christ condemned before Pilate (27:11–26)

These verses describe our Lord's appearance before Pontius Pilate, the Roman governor. That sight must have been wonderful to the angels of God. He who will one day judge the world allowed himself to be judged and condemned, though "he had done no violence, nor was any deceit in his mouth" (Isaiah 53:9). Pilate and Caiaphas will one day receive their eternal sentence from him, yet he was silent as an unjust sentence was passed on him. Those silent sufferings fulfilled the words of Isaiah: "as a sheep before her shearers is silent, so he did not open his mouth" (Isaiah 53:7). To those silent sufferings believers owe all their peace and hope. Through them they will have boldness in the day of judgment, who in themselves would have nothing to say.

1. An unprincipled great man
Let us learn from the conduct of Pilate how pitiful is the condition of an unprincipled great man.

Pilate appears to have been inwardly satisfied that our Lord had done nothing worthy of death: we are told distinctly that "he knew it was out of envy that they had handed Jesus over to him" (verse 18). Left to the exercise of his own unbiased judgment, he would probably have dismissed the charges against our Lord, and let him go free.

But Pilate was the governor of a jealous and turbulent nation; his great desire was to procure favor with them and please them: he cared little how much he sinned against God and conscience so long as he had human praise. Though willing to save our Lord's life, he was afraid to do it if it offended the Jews; and so, after a feeble attempt to divert the fury of the people from Jesus to Barabbas, and a feebler attempt to satisfy his own conscience by washing his hands publicly before the people, he at last condemned one whom he himself called a "just person" (verse 24, KJV)! He rejected the strange and mysterious warning which his wife sent to him after her dream (verse 19); he stifled the remonstrances of his own conscience. He "handed him over to be crucified" (verse 26).

We see in this miserable man a living pattern of many a ruler of this world! How many there are who know well that their public acts are wrong, and yet have not the courage to act up to their knowledge. They fear the people; they dread being laughed at: they cannot bear being unpopular! Like dead fish, they float with the tide. Human praise is the idol before which they bow down, and to that idol they sacrifice conscience, inner peace and an immortal soul.

Whatever our position in life may be, let us seek to be guided by principle, and not by expediency. Human praise is a poor, feeble, uncertain thing: it is here today and gone tomorrow. Let us strive to please God, and then we may care little who else is pleased; let us fear God, and then there is no one else of whom we need to be afraid.

2. The wickedness of human nature

Second, let us learn from the conduct of the Jews described in these verses how desperately wicked is human nature.

The behavior of Pilate gave the chief priests and elders an opportunity to reconsider what they were doing. The difficulties he raised about condemning our Lord gave time for second thoughts. But there were no second thoughts in the minds of our Lord's enemies. They pressed on their wicked deed; they rejected the compromise that Pilate offered: they actually preferred having a wretched felon named Barabbas set at liberty rather than Jesus. They clamored loudly for our Lord's crucifixion; and they wound up by recklessly taking on themselves all the guilt of our Lord's death, in words of portentous meaning: "Let his blood be on us and on our children!" (verse 26).

And what had our Lord done that the Jews should hate him so? He was no robber or murderer: he was no blasphemer of their God, or reviler of their prophets. He was one whose life was love: he was one who "went around doing good and healing all who were under the power of the devil" (Acts 10:38). He was innocent of any transgression against the law of God or man; and yet the Jews hated him, and never rested till he was slain! They hated him because he told them the truth; they hated him because he witnessed that their actions were evil; they hated the light, because it made their own darkness visible. In a word, they hated Christ because he was righteous and they were wicked – because he was holy and they were unholy – because he testified against sin, and they were determined to keep their sins and not let them go.

Let us observe this. There are few things so little believed and realized as the corruption of human nature. People imagine that if they saw a perfect person they would love and admire them; they flatter themselves that it is the inconsistency of people who claim to be Christians that they dislike, and not their religion: they forget that when a really perfect man was on earth, in the person of the Son of God, he was hated and put to death. That single fact goes far to prove the truth of an old saying, that "unconverted men would kill God, if they could get at him."

Let us never be surprised at the wickedness there is in the world. Let us mourn over it, and labor to make it less, but let us never be surprised at its extent. There is nothing which the heart of man is not capable of conceiving, or the hand of man of doing. As long as we live, let us mistrust our own hearts: even when renewed by the Spirit, they are still "deceitful above all things, and beyond cure" (Jeremiah 17:9).

Christ's sufferings and crucifixion (27:27–44)

These verses describe the sufferings of our Lord Jesus Christ after his condemnation by Pilate, his sufferings at the hands of the brutal Roman soldiers, and his final sufferings on the cross. They form a marvelous record. They are marvelous when we remember the sufferer – the eternal Son of God. They are marvelous when we remember the people for whom these sufferings were endured. We and our sins were the cause of all this sorrow! He "died for our sins" (1 Corinthians 15:3).

1. The extent and reality of Christ's sufferings

First, let us observe the extent and reality of our Lord's sufferings.

The catalog of all the pains endured by our Lord's body is indeed a fearful one: seldom has such suffering been inflicted on one body in the last few hours of a life. The most savage tribes, in their refinement of cruelty, could hardly have heaped more agonizing tortures on an enemy than were heaped on the flesh and bones of our beloved Master. Never let it be forgotten that he had a real human body, a body exactly like our own, just as sensitive, just as vulnerable, just as capable of feeling intense pain. And then let us see what that body endured.

Our Lord, we must remember, had already passed a night without sleep, and endured excessive fatigue. He had been taken from Gethsemane to the Sanhedrin, and from the Sanhedrin to Pilate's judgment hall. He had been put on trial twice, and unjustly condemned twice. He had been already flogged and beaten cruelly with sticks. And now, after all this suffering, he was handed over to the Roman soldiers, a body of men no doubt expert in cruelty, and, of all people, least likely to behave with delicacy or compassion. These hard men at once proceeded to work their will. They "gathered the whole compny of soldiers round him" (verse 27); they stripped our Lord and put on him, in mockery, a scarlet robe (verse 28); they "twisted together a crown of thorns," and in derision placed it on his head (verse 29). They then knelt in front of him in mockery, as nothing better than a pretend king; they "spat on him" (verse 30); they "struck him on the head again and again"; and finally, having put his own clothes on him, they led him out of the city to a place called Golgotha (verse 33), and there crucified him between two thieves.

But what was a crucifixion? Let us try to realize it and understand its misery. The person crucified was laid on his back on a piece of timber, with a cross-piece nailed to it near one end – or on the trunk of a tree with branching arms, which answered the same purpose: his hands were spread out on the cross-piece, and nails driven through each of them, fastening them to the wood; his feet in like manner were nailed to the upright part of the cross. Then, the body having been securely fastened, the cross was raised up and fixed firmly in the ground. And there hung the unhappy sufferer, till pain and exhaustion brought him to his end – not dying suddenly, for no vital part of him was injured; but enduring the most excruciating agony from his hands and feet, and unable to move. Such was the death of the cross. Such was the death that Jesus died for us! For six long hours he hung there before a gazing crowd, naked, and bleeding from head to foot – his head pierced with thorns, his back lacerated with flogging, his hands and feet torn with nails, and mocked and reviled by his cruel enemies to the very last.

Let us meditate frequently on these things: let us often read over the story of Christ's cross and passion. Let us remember, not least, that all these horrible sufferings were borne without a murmur: no word of impatience crossed our Lord's lips. In his death, no less than in his life, he was perfect. To the very last Satan had no hold on him (John 14:30).

2. Christ's sufferings were vicarious

Second, let us observe that all our Lord Jesus Christ's sufferings were vicarious. He suffered not for his own sins, but for ours. He was eminently our substitute in all his passion.

This is a truth of the deepest importance. Without it the story of our Lord's sufferings, with all its minute details, must always seem mysterious and inexplicable. It is a truth, however, of which the Scriptures speak frequently, and that too with no uncertain sound. We are told that Christ "bore our sins in his body on the tree" (1 Peter 2:24); that he "died for sins once for all, the righteous for the unrighteous" (1 Peter 3:18); that "God made him who had no sin to be sin for us, so that in him we might become the righteousness of God" (2 Corinthians 5:21); that he "became a curse for us" (Galatians 3:13); that "Christ was sacrificed once to take away the sins of many people" (Hebrews 9:28); that "he was pierced for our transgressions, he was crushed for our iniquities" (Isaiah 53:5); and that "the LORD has laid on him the iniquity of us all" (Isaiah 53:6). May we all remember these texts. They are among the foundation-stones of the Gospel.

But we must not be content with a vague general belief that Christ's sufferings on the cross were vicarious. We are intended to see this truth in every part of his passion. We may follow him all through, from the bar of Pilate to the minute of his death, and see him at every step as our mighty substitute, our representative, our head, our surety, our proxy – the divine friend who undertook to stand in our place, and by the priceless merit of his sufferings, to purchase our redemption. Was he flogged? It was done so that "by his wounds we are healed" (Isaiah 53:5). Was he condemned, though innocent? It was done so that we might be acquitted, though guilty. Did he wear a crown of thorns? It was done so that we might wear the crown of glory. Was he stripped of his clothes? It was done so that we might be clothed in everlasting righteousness. Was he mocked and reviled? It was done so that we might be honored and blessed. Was he reckoned a criminal, and counted among those who have done wrong? It was done so that we might be reckoned innocent, and declared free from all sin. Was he declared unable to save himself? It was so that he might be able to save others to the uttermost. Did he die at last, and that the most painful and disgraceful of deaths? It was done so that we might live forevermore, and be exalted to the highest glory.

Let us ponder these things well: they are worth remembering. The very key to peace is a right apprehension of the vicarious sufferings of Christ.

Let us leave the story of our Lord's passion with feelings of deep thankfulness. Our sins are many and great, but a great atonement has been made for them. There was an infinite merit in all Christ's sufferings: they were the sufferings of one who was God as well as man. Surely it is right and proper to praise God daily because Christ has died.

Last, but not least, let us learn from the story of the passion always to hate sin with a great hatred. Sin was the cause of all our Saviour's suffering. Our sins twisted the crown of thorns; our sins drove the nails into his hands and feet; on account of our sins his blood was shed. Surely the thought of Christ crucified should make us loathe all sin. As the Church of England Homily of Passion says so well: "Let this image of Christ crucified be always printed in our hearts. Let it stir us up to the hatred of sin, and provoke our minds to the earnest love of Almighty God."

Christ's death, and the signs accompanying it *(27:45–56)*

In these verses we read the conclusion of our Lord Jesus Christ's passion. After six hours of agonizing suffering, he became obedient to death, even death on a cross, and "gave up his spirit" (verse 50). Three points in the narrative demand a special notice: let us confine our attention to them.

1. Jesus' words, "My God, why have you forsaken me?"

First, let us observe the remarkable words which Jesus uttered shortly before his death: "My God, my God, why have you forsaken me?" (verse 46).

There is a deep mystery in these words, which no mortal can fathom. No doubt they were not wrung from our Lord by mere bodily pain: such an explanation is utterly unsatisfactory, and dishonorable to our blessed Saviour. They were meant to express the real pressure on his soul of the enormous burden of a world's sins; they were meant to show how truly and literally he was our substitute – was made sin, and a curse for us, and endured God's righteous anger against a world's sin in his own person. At that awful moment the iniquity of us all was laid on him entirely. The Lord chose to crush him and cause him to suffer (Isaiah 53:10). He bore our sins: he carried our transgressions. That burden must have been heavy; our Lord's substitution for us must have been real and literal when he, the eternal Son of God, could speak of himself as for a time "forsaken."

Let the expression sink down into our hearts, and not be forgotten. We can have no stronger proof of the sinfulness of sin, or of the vicarious nature of Christ's sufferings, than his cry, "My God, my God, why have you forsaken me?" It is a cry that should stir us up to hate sin, and encourage us to trust in Christ.

[The following quotations deserve notice, and throw light on this particularly solemn part of Scripture.

Our Lord said this under a deep sense of his Father's wrath unto mankind, in whose stead he now underwent that which was due for the sins of the whole world. When he said "Why hast thou forsaken me?" he implied that God had for the time withdrawn from him the sense and vision of his comfortable presence. When he said, "My God," he implied the strength of his faith whereby he did firmly apprehend the sure and gracious aid of his eternal Father. – Bishop Hall.

All the wailings and howlings of the damned to all eternity, will fall infinitely short of expressing the evil and bitterness of sin with such emphasis as these few words, "My God, my God, why hast thou forsaken me?" – Jamieson.

2. The words describing our Lord's end

Second, let us observe how much is contained in the words which describe our Lord's end. We are simply told, "he gave up his spirit" (verse 50).

There never was a last breath drawn of such deep significance as this. There never was an event on which so much depended. The Roman soldiers, and the gaping crowd around the cross, saw nothing remarkable. They only saw a person dying as others die, with all the usual agony and suffering which attend a crucifixion. But they knew nothing of the eternal interests which were involved in the whole transaction.

That death discharged in full the mighty debt which sinners owe to God, and threw open the door of life to every believer; that death satisfied the righteous claims of God's holy law, and enabled God to be "just and the one who justifies" the ungodly (Romans 3:26). That death was no mere example of self-sacrifice, but a complete atonement and propitiation for man's sin, affecting the condition and prospects of all mankind. That death solved the hard problem of how God could be perfectly holy, and yet perfectly merciful. It opened to the world a fountain for all sin and uncleanness; it was a complete victory over Satan, and spoiled him openly; it "put an end to sin, to atone for wickedness, to bring in everlasting righteousness" (Daniel 9:24). It proved the sinfulness of sin, when it needed such a sacrifice to atone for it; it proved the love of God to sinners, when he sent his own Son to make the atonement. Never, in fact, was there, or could there be again, such a death. No wonder the earth quaked when Jesus died in our place as he made "a guilt offering" (Isaiah 53:10).

3. The miracle in the temple

Third, let us observe what a remarkable miracle occurred at the hour of our Lord's death, in the very middle of the Jewish temple. We are told that "the curtain of the temple was torn in two" (verse 51). The curtain which separated the holy of holies from the rest of the temple, and through which the high priest alone might pass, was suddenly torn "from top to bottom."

Of all the wonderful signs which accompanied our Lord's death, none was more significant than this. The midday darkness, for three hours, must have been a startling event; the earthquake, which split the rocks, must have been a tremendous shock. But there was a meaning in the sudden tearing of the curtain from top to bottom which must have pricked the heart of any intelligent Jew. The conscience of Caiaphas, the high priest, must have been hard indeed if the news of that torn curtain did not fill him with dismay.

The tearing of the curtain proclaimed the termination and passing away of the ceremonial law. It was a sign that the old dispensation of sacrifices and ordinances was no longer needed: its work was done, its business finished from the moment that Christ died. There was no more need of an earthly high priest, a mercy-seat, a sprinkling of blood, an offering of incense and a day of atonement. The true High Priest had at length appeared; the true Lamb of God had been slain; the true mercy-seat was at length revealed. The symbols and shadows were no longer wanted. May we all remember this! To set up an altar, a sacrifice and a priesthood now is to light a candle at noon-day.

The tearing of the curtain proclaimed the opening of the way of salvation to all mankind. The way into the presence of God was unknown to the Gentile, and only seen dimly by the Jew, until Christ died; but Christ having now offered up a perfect sacrifice, and having obtained eternal redemption, the darkness and mystery were to pass away. Everyone was now to be invited to draw near to God with boldness, and approach him with confidence, by faith in Jesus. A door was thrown open, and a way of life set before the whole world. May we all remember this! From the time that Jesus died, the way of peace was never meant to be shrouded in mystery: there was to be no reserve. The Gospel was the revelation of a mystery which had been hidden from ages and generations. To clothe religion *now* with mystery is to mistake the grand characteristic of Christianity.

Let us turn from the story of the crucifixion, every time we read it, with hearts full of praise. Let us praise God for the confidence it gives us as to the ground of our hope of pardon. Our sins may be many and great but the payment made by our great Substitute far outweighs them all. Let us praise God for the view it gives us of the love of our Father in heaven. "He who did not spare his own Son, but gave him up for us all—how will he not also, along with him, graciously give us all things?" (Romans 8:32). Not least, let us praise God for the view it gives us of the sympathy of Jesus with all his believing people. He can sympathize with our weaknesses; he knows what suffering is. He is just the Saviour that a weak body, with a weak heart, in an evil world, requires.

Christ's burial *(27:57–66)*

These verses contain the story of our Lord Jesus Christ's burial. One more thing was needed to make it certain that our Redeemer accomplished that great work of redemption which he undertook. That holy body, in which he bore our sins on the cross, must actually be laid in the grave, and rise again. His resurrection was to be the seal and headstone of all the work.

The infinite wisdom of God foresaw the objections of unbelievers and provided against them. Did the Son of God really die? Did he really rise again? Might there not have been some delusion as to the reality of his death? Might there not have been imposition or deception, as to the reality of his resurrection? All these and many more objections would doubtless have been raised if opportunity had been given. But he who knows the end from the beginning prevented the possibility of such objections being made. By his overruling providence he ordered things so that the death and burial of Jesus were placed beyond a doubt. Pilate gives consent to his burial; a loving disciple wraps the body in linen and lays it in a new tomb cut out of a rock, "in which no one had yet been laid" (Luke 23:53); the chief priests themselves set a guard over the place where his body was deposited. Jews and Gentiles, friends and enemies, all alike testify to the great fact that Christ did really and actually die and was laid in a grave. It is a fact that can never be questioned. He was really "crushed"; he really "suffered"; he really "died"; he was really "buried." Let us mark this well: it deserves recollection.

1. Christ has friends of whom little is known

First, let us learn from these verses that our Lord Jesus Christ has friends of whom little is known.

We cannot have a more striking example of this truth than we see in the passage now before us. A man named Joseph, of Arimathea, comes forward when our Lord is dead and asks permission to bury him. We have never heard of this man at any former period of our Lord's earthly ministry: we never hear of him again. We know only that he was a disciple who loved Christ and did him honor. At a time when the apostles had deserted our Lord – at a time when it was a dangerous thing to profess regard for him – at a time when there seemed to be no earthly advantage to be gained by confessing his discipleship – at such a time as this, Joseph comes forward boldly, and begs the body of Jesus, and lays it in his own new tomb.

This fact is full of comfort and encouragement. It shows us that there are some quiet, retiring souls on earth, who know the Lord, and the Lord knows them, and yet they are little known by the church. It shows us that there are "different kinds of gifts" among Christ's people: there are some who glorify Christ passively, and some who glorify him actively; there are some whose vocation it is to build the church, and fill a public place, and there are some who only come forward, like Joseph, in times of special need. But each and all are led by one Spirit, and each and all glorify God in their different ways.

Let these things teach us to be more hopeful. Let us believe that "many will come from the east and the west, and will take their places at the feast with Abraham, Isaac and Jacob in the kingdom of heaven" (Matthew 8:11). There may be in some dark corners of Christendom many who, like Simeon, Anna and Joseph of Arimathea, are at present little known, but who will shine brightly among the Lord's jewels on the day he appears.

2. God can make wicked people's actions work to his own glory

Second, let us learn from these verses that God can make the devices of wicked men work round to his own glory.

We are taught that lesson in a striking manner by the conduct of the priests and Pharisees after our Lord was buried. The restless enmity of these unhappy men could not sleep, even when the body of Jesus was in the grave. They recalled the words which they remembered he had spoken about "rising again": they resolved, as they thought, to make his rising again impossible. They went to Pilate and obtained from him a guard of Roman soldiers; they set a watch over the tomb of our Lord; they placed a seal upon the stone. In short they did all they could to make the tomb secure (verse 64).

They little thought what they were doing; they little thought that unwittingly they were providing the most complete evidence of the truth of Christ's coming resurrection. They were actually making it impossible to prove that there was any deception or imposition. Their seal, their guard, their precautions, were all to become witnesses, in a few hours, that Christ had risen. They might as well have tried to stop the tides of the sea, or to prevent the sun rising, as to prevent Jesus coming out of the tomb. They were caught in their own craftiness (1 Corinthians 3:19): their own devices became instruments to display God's glory.

The history of the church of Christ is full of examples of a similar kind. The very things that have seemed most unfavorable to God's people have often turned out to be for their good. What harm did the persecution do to the church of Christ after Stephen's death? Those who were scattered "preached the word wherever they went" (Acts 8:4). What harm did imprisonment do St. Paul? It gave him time to write many of those letters which are now read all over the world. What real harm did the persecution of bloody Mary do to the cause of the English Reformation? The blood of the martyrs became the seed of the church. What harm does persecution do the people of God at this very day? It only drives them nearer to Christ: it only makes them cling more closely to the throne of grace, the Bible, and prayer.

Let all true Christians lay these things to heart, and take courage. We live in a world where all things are ordered by a hand of perfect wisdom, and where in all things God works for the good of those who love him (Romans 8:28). The powers of this world are only tools in the hand of God: he is always using them for his own purposes, however little they may be aware of it. They are the instruments by which he is forever cutting and polishing the living stones of his spiritual temple, and all their schemes and plans will only turn to his praise. Let us be patient in days of trouble and darkness, and look forward. The very things which now seem against us are all working together for God's glory. We only see half now: a little while longer, we shall see all; and we shall then discover that all the persecution we now endure was, like "the seal" and "the guard" (verse 66), tending to God's glory. God can make the "wrath of man praise him" (Psalm 77:10, KJV).

Matthew
Chapter 28

Christ's resurrection *(28:1–10)*

The principal subject of these verses is the resurrection of our Lord Jesus Christ from the dead. It is one of those truths which lie at the very foundation of Christianity, and has therefore received special attention in the four Gospels. All four Evangelists describe minutely how our Lord was crucified: all four relate, with no less clearness, that he rose again.

We need not wonder that so much importance is attached to our Lord's resurrection: it is the seal and headstone of the great work of redemption which he came to do. It is the crowning proof that he has paid the debt which he undertook to pay on our behalf, won the battle which he fought to deliver us from hell, and is accepted as our surety and our substitute by our Father in heaven. Had he never come out of the prison of the grave, how could we ever have been sure that our ransom had been fully paid (1 Corinthians 15:17)? Had he never risen from his conflict with the last enemy, how could we have felt confident that he has overcome death? Or that he has overcome him who holds the power of death – that is, the devil (Hebrews 2:14)? But thanks be to God, we are not left in doubt: the Lord Jesus was really "raised to life for our justification" (Romans 4:25). True Christians have been given "new birth into a living hope through the resurrection of Jesus Christ from the dead" (1 Peter 1:3). They may boldly say with Paul, "Who is he that condemns? Christ Jesus, who died – more than that, who was raised to life" (Romans 8:34).

We have reason to be very thankful that this wonderful truth of our religion is so clearly and fully proved. It is striking that of all the facts of our Lord's earthly ministry, none are so incontrovertibly established as the fact that he rose again. The wisdom of God, who knows the unbelief of human nature, has provided a great crowd of witnesses on the subject. Never was there a fact which the friends of God were so slow to believe as the resurrection of Christ; never was there a fact which the enemies of God were so anxious to disprove. Yet, in spite of the unbelief of friends and the enmity of foes, the fact was thoroughly established. Its evidences will always appear to a fair and impartial mind unanswerable. It would be impossible to prove anything in the world if we refuse to believe that Jesus rose again.

1. The glory and majesty with which Christ rose

First, let us notice in these verses the glory and majesty with which Christ rose from the dead. We are told that "there was a violent earthquake" (verse 2). We are told that "an angel of the Lord came down from heaven and, going to the tomb, rolled back the stone and sat on it" (verse 2). We need not suppose that our blessed Lord needed the help of any angel when he came out of the grave; we need not for a moment doubt that he rose again by his own power; but it pleased God that his resurrection should be accompanied and followed by signs and wonders. It seemed good that the earth should shake, and a glorious angel appear, when the Son of God arose from the dead as a conqueror.

Let us not fail to see in the manner of our Lord's resurrection a type and pledge of the resurrection of his believing people. The grave could not hold him beyond the set time, and it will not be able to hold them. A glorious angel was a witness of his rising, and glorious angels will be the messengers who gather believers when they rise again. He rose with a renewed body, and yet a body, real, true and material. And so also shall his people have a glorious body, and be like their head. "We shall be like him, for we shall see him as he is" (1 John 3:2).

Let us take comfort in this thought. Trial, sorrow and persecution are often the lot of God's people; sickness, weakness and pain often hurt and wear away their poor earthly tabernacle; but their good time is yet to come. Let them wait patiently, and they will have a glorious resurrection. When we die, where we are buried and what kind of a funeral we have matters little: the great question to be asked is this, "How shall we rise again?"

2. The terror of Christ's enemies at his resurrection

Second, let us notice the terror which Christ's enemies felt at the time of his resurrection. We are told that, at the sight of the angel, "the guards were so afraid of him that they shook and became like dead men" (verse 4). Those hardy Roman soldiers, though used to dreadful sights, saw a sight which made them quail. Their courage melted at once at the appearance of one angel of God.

Let us again see in this fact a type and symbol of things yet to come. What will the ungodly and the wicked do on the last day, when the trumpet sounds and Christ comes in glory to judge the world? What will they do when they see *all* the dead, both small and great, coming out of their graves, and *all* the angels of God assembled round the great white throne? What fears and terrors will possess their souls when they find they can no longer avoid God's presence, and must at length meet him face to face? Oh, that men were wise, and would consider their end! Oh, that they would remember that there is a resurrection and a judgment, and that there is such a thing as "the wrath of the Lamb" (Revelation 6:16)!

3. The angel's words of comfort

Third, let us notice the words of comfort which the angel addressed to the friends of Christ. We read that he said, "Do not be afraid, for I know that you are looking for Jesus, who was crucified" (verse 5).

These words were spoken with a deep meaning. They were meant to cheer the hearts of believers in every age, at the prospect of the resurrection; they were intended to remind us that true Christians have no cause for alarm in the last day whatever may happen to the world. The Lord will appear in the clouds of heaven and the earth will be burned up; the graves will give up the dead, and the sea will give up the dead that are in it; the judgment will be set, and the books will be opened; the angels will sift the wheat from the chaff, and divide between the good fish and the bad. But in all this there is nothing that need make believers afraid. Clothed in the righteousness of Christ, they will be found spotless and blameless; safe in the one true ark, they will not be hurt when the flood of God's wrath breaks on the earth. Then the words of the Lord will receive their complete fulfilment: "When these things begin to take place, stand up and lift up your heads, because your redemption is drawing near" (Luke 21:28). Then the wicked and unbelieving will see how true was that word: "Blessed is the nation whose God is the LORD" (Psalm 33:12).

4. Christ's message to his disciples

Fourth, let us notice the gracious message which the Lord sent to the disciples after his resurrection. He appeared in person to the women who had come to do honor to his body. Last at the cross and first at the tomb, they were the first privileged to see him after he rose. He commissions them to carry news to his disciples. His first thought is for his little scattered flock: "Go and tell my brothers" (verse 10).

There is something deeply touching in those simple words, "my brothers": they deserve a thousand thoughts. Weak, frail, erring as the disciples were, Jesus still calls them his "brothers." He comforts them, as Joseph did his brothers who had sold him, saying, "I am your brother Joseph" (Genesis 45:4). Much as they had come short of their profession, sadly as they had yielded to the fear of man, they are still his "brothers." Glorious as he was in himself – a conqueror over death and hell, and the grave – the Son of God is still "gentle and humble of heart." He calls his disciples "brothers."

Let us turn from the passage with comfortable thoughts if we know anything of true religion. Let us see in these words of Christ an encouragement to trust and not be afraid. Our Saviour is one who never forgets his people; he pities their weaknesses: he does not despise them. He knows their weakness, and yet does not cast them away. Our great High Priest is also our elder brother.

Christ's parting commission to his disciples (28:11–20)

These verses form the conclusion of the Gospel of St. Matthew. They begin by showing us what absurdities blind prejudice will believe, rather than believe the truth; they go on to show us what weakness there is in the hearts of some disciples, and how slow they are to believe; they finish by telling us some of the last words spoken by our Lord upon earth – words so remarkable that they demand and deserve all our attention.

1. The honor God has given Christ

First, let us observe the honor which God has put on our Lord Jesus Christ. Our Lord says, "All authority in heaven and on earth has been given to me" (verse 18).

This is a truth which is declared by St. Paul to the Philippians: "God exalted him to the highest place and gave him the name that is above every name" (Philippians 2:9). It is a truth which in no way takes away from the true notion of Christ's divinity, as some have ignorantly supposed. It is simply a declaration that, in the counsels of the eternal Trinity, Jesus, as Son of Man, is appointed heir of all things; that he is the Mediator between God and mankind; that the salvation of all who are saved is given to him, and that he is the great fountain of mercy, grace, life and peace. It was for "the joy set before him" that he "endured the cross" (Hebrews 12:2).

Let us embrace this truth reverently and cling to it firmly. Christ is the one who has the keys of death and hell; Christ is the anointed priest, who alone can absolve sinners; Christ is the fountain of living waters, in whom alone we can be cleansed; Christ is the Prince and Saviour, who alone can give repentance and forgiveness of sins. In him all fullness dwells. He is the way, the door, the light, the life, the shepherd, the altar of refuge. "He who has the Son has life; he who does not have the Son of God does not have life" (1 John 5:12). May we all strive to understand this! No doubt people may easily think too little of God the Father and God the Spirit; but no one ever thought too much of Christ.

2. The duty which Jesus gives his disciples

Second, let us observe the duty which Jesus entrusts his disciples with. He tells them to "go and make disciples of all nations" (verse 19). They were not to confine their knowledge to themselves, but to communicate it to others; they were not to suppose that salvation was revealed only to the Jews, but to make disciples of all nations, and to tell the whole earth that Christ had died for sinners.

Let us never forget that this solemn injunction is still in full force. It is still the duty of every disciple of Christ to do all he can in person, and by prayer, to make others acquainted with Jesus. Where is our faith if we neglect this duty? Where is our love? It may well be questioned whether people know the value of the Gospel themselves if they do not desire to make it known to all the world.

3. The public profession Jesus requires

Third, let us observe the public profession which Jesus requires of those who believe his Gospel. He tells his apostles to "baptize" those whom they received as disciples (verse 19).

It is very difficult to conceive, when we read this last command of our Lord's, how people can avoid the conclusion that baptism is necessary, when it may be had. It seems impossible to define the word here except as an external observance, to be administered to all who join his church. External baptism is not absolutely necessary to salvation, as the case of the penitent thief plainly shows: he went to paradise unbaptized. External baptism alone often confers no benefit, as the case of Simon Magus plainly shows: although baptized he remained "full of bitterness and captive to sin" (Acts 8:23). But it seems at variance with our Lord's words in this place to assert that baptism is a matter of entire indifference, and need not be used at all.

[I purposely abstain from saying anything on the subject of infant baptism. There is nothing in this text which can be fairly used either way in settling this much-vexed controversy. It is certain that the missionaries of the Church of England carry out the meaning of this text as fully and thoroughly as the missionaries of Baptist churches. The point settled by the text is not so much what ought to be done with the *children* of Christians as what ought to be done with heathens when converted.]

The plain practical lesson of the words is the necessity of a public confession of faith in Christ. It is not enough to be a secret disciple: we must not be ashamed to let men see whose we are, and whom we serve. We must not behave as if we did not like to be thought Christians; but take up our cross, and confess our Master before the world. His words are very solemn: "If anyone is ashamed of me, . . . the Son of Man will be ashamed of him when he comes in his Father's glory with the holy angels" (Mark 8:38).

4. The obedience Jesus requires

Fourth, let us observe the obedience which Jesus requires of all who claim to be his disciples. He tells the apostles to teach them to obey everything he has commanded them (verse 20).

This is a searching expression. It shows the uselessness of a mere name and form of Christianity; it shows that the only people who are to be counted true Christians are those who live in practical obedience to his word, and strive to do the things that he has commanded. The water of baptism and the bread and wine of the Lord's Supper alone will save no one's soul. It does not help at all if we go to a place of worship and hear Christ's ministers, and approve of the Gospel, but our religion goes no further than this. What are our lives? What is our daily conduct at home and abroad? Is the Sermon on the Mount our rule and standard? Do we strive to copy Christ's example? Do we seek to do the things that he commanded? These are questions that must be answered in the affirmative if we want to prove ourselves born again, and children of God. Obedience is the only proof of reality. "Faith by itself, if it is not accompanied by action, is dead" (James 2:17, 20, 26). "You are my friends," says Jesus, "if you do what I command" (John 15:14).

5. The solemn mention of the Trinity

Fifth, let us observe the solemn mention of the blessed Trinity which our Lord makes in these verses. He tells the apostles to baptize "in the name of the Father and of the Son and of the Holy Spirit" (verse 19).

This is one of those great plain texts which directly teach the mighty doctrine of the Trinity. It speaks of Father, Son and Holy Spirit as three distinct persons, and speaks of all three as co-equal. What the Father is, that the Son is too, and the Holy Spirit. And yet these three are one.

This truth is a great mystery. Let it be enough to receive and believe it, and let us always abstain from any attempt at explanation. It is childish folly to refuse assent to things that we do not understand. We are poor crawling worms of a day, and know little at our best about God and eternity: suffice it for us to receive the doctrine of the Trinity in unity, with humility and reverence, and to ask no pointless questions. Let us believe that no sinful soul can be saved without the work of all three Persons in the blessed Trinity, and let us rejoice that Father, Son and Holy Spirit, who cooperated to make mankind, also cooperate to save mankind. Here let us pause: we may receive practically what we cannot explain theoretically.

6. Jesus' gracious promise

Sixth, let us observe in these verses the gracious promise with which Jesus closes his words. He says to his disciples, "I am with you always, to the very end of the age" (verse 20).

It is impossible to conceive words more comforting, strengthening, cheering and sanctifying than these. Though left alone like orphan children in a cold unkind world, the disciples were not to think they were deserted: their Master would always be "with them." Though commissioned to do a work as hard as that of Moses when sent to Pharaoh, they were not to be discouraged: their Master would certainly be "with them." No words could be more suited to the position of those to whom they were first spoken; no words could be imagined that would be more consoling to believers in every age of the world.

Let all true Christians lay hold on these words and keep them in mind. Christ is "with us" always: Christ is "with us" wherever we go. He came to be "Emmanuel, God with us" when he first came into the world: he declares that he is always Emmanuel, "with us," when he comes to the end of his earthly ministry and is about to leave the world. He is with us daily to pardon and forgive, with us daily to sanctify and strengthen, with us daily to defend and keep, with us daily to lead and to guide: with us in sorrow and with us in joy, with us in sickness and with us in health, with us in life and with us in death, with us in time and with us in eternity.

What stronger consolation could believers desire than this? Whatever happens, they at least are never completely friendless and alone: Christ is always with them. They may look into the grave and say with David, "Even though I walk through the valley of the shadow of death, I will fear no evil, for you are with me" (Psalm 23:4). They may look forward beyond the grave, and say with Paul, "we will be with the Lord for ever" (1 Thessalonians 4:17). He has said it, and he will stand to it: "I am with you always, to the very end of the age." "Never will I leave you; never will I forsake you" (Hebrews 13:5). We could ask nothing more. Let us go on believing, and not be afraid. It is everything to be a real Christian. No one has such a King, such a Priest, such a constant Companion and such an unfailing Friend as the true servant of Christ.